Running Gîtes and B&Bs
in
France

A Survival Handbook

by
Jo Taylor

SURVIVAL BOOKS • LONDON • ENGLAND

First Edition 2007

Survival Books Limited
26 York Street, London W1U 6PZ, United Kingdom
☎ +44 (0)20-7788 7644, 🖨 +44 (0)870-762 3212
✉ info@survivalbooks.net
💻 www.survivalbooks.net

British Library Cataloguing in Publication Data.
A CIP record for this book is available
from the British Library.
ISBN-10: 1-905303-30-0
ISBN-13: 978-1-905303-30-4

Printed and bound in India by Ajanta Offset.

ACKNOWLEDGEMENTS

I would like to thank all those who contributed to the successful publication of this book, in particular the staff at the head offices of Gîtes de France and Clévacances, UK holiday agencies too numerous to mention individually, my own guests (some of whom have become close friends over the years), friends and family, and everyone else who provided information or contributed in any way. I would also like to thank Joe Laredo (editing and proofreading), Kerry Laredo (layout) and, last but not least, Jim Watson for his great cover design and maps.

TITLES BY SURVIVAL BOOKS

The Best Places To Buy A Home
France; Spain

Buying a Home
Australia & New Zealand; Bulgaria,
Cyprus; France; Greece; Italy;
Portugal; South Africa; Spain;
Buying, Selling & Letting Property (UK)

Buying and Renting a Home
London; New York

Culture Wise
Australia; Canada; England; France;
New Zealand; Spain

**Foreigners Abroad: Triumphs
& Disasters**
France; Spain

Living and Working
America; Australia; Britain
Canada; France; Germany

The Gulf States & Saudi Arabia;
Ireland; Italy;
London; New Zealand;
Spain; Switzerland

Earning Money from Your Home
France; Spain

Making a Living
France; Spain

Retiring Abroad
France; Spain

Other Titles
Investing in Property Abroad;
Renovating & Maintaining
Your French Home;
Running Gîtes and B&Bs in France;
Rural Living in France;
Shooting Caterpillars in Spain;
Wild Thyme in Ibiza

WHAT READERS & REVIEWERS

'If you need to find out how France works then this book is indispensable. Native French people probably have a less thorough understanding of how their country functions.'

LIVING FRANCE MAGAZINE

'The ultimate reference book. Every subject imaginable is exhaustively explained in simple terms. An excellent introduction to fully enjoy all that this fine country has to offer and save time and money in the process.'

AMERICAN CLUB OF ZURICH

'Let's say it at once. David Hampshire's Living and Working in France is the best handbook ever produced for visitors and foreign residents in this country. It is Hampshire's meticulous detail which lifts his work way beyond the range of other books with similar titles. This book is absolutely indispensable.'

RIVIERA REPORTER MAGAZINE

'A must for all future expats. I invested in several books but this is the only one you need. Every issue and concern is covered, every daft question you have but are frightened to ask is answered honestly without pulling any punches. Highly recommended.'

READER

'In answer to the desert island question about the one how-to book on France, this book would be it.'

THE RECORDER NEWSPAPER

'It's everything you always wanted to ask but didn't for fear of the contemptuous put down. Its pages are stuffed with practical information on everyday subjects.'

SWISS NEWS MAGAZINE

'A must for all future ex-pats. Deals with every aspect of moving to Spain. I invested in several books but this is the only one you need. Every issue and concern is covered, every daft question you have on Spain but are frightened to ask is answered honestly without pulling any punches. Highly recommended!'

READER

'If I were to move to France, I would like David Hampshire to be with me, holding my hand every step of the way. This being impractical, I would have to settle for second best and take his books with me instead!

LIVING FRANCE MAGAZINE

HAVE SAID ABOUT SURVIVAL BOOKS

'The amount of information covered is not short of incredible. I thought I knew enough about my birth country. This book has proved me wrong. Don't go to France without it. Big mistake if you do. Absolutely priceless!'

READER

'A mine of information. I might have avoided some embarrassments and frights if I had read it prior to my first Swiss encounters. Deserves an honoured place on any newcomer's bookshelf.'

ENGLISH TEACHERS ASSOCIATION, SWITZERLAND

'A thoroughly interesting and useful read, it crams in almost every conceivable bit of information that a newly-arrived immigrant could need. A great book to read and have close at hand when you arrive in Canada to begin your new life. The best all-round handbook on Canada.'

READER

'A concise, thorough account of the DO's and DON'Ts for a foreigner in Switzerland. Crammed with useful information and lightened with humorous quips which make the facts more readable.'

AMERICAN CITIZENS ABROAD

'Covers every conceivable question that might be asked concerning everyday life — I know of no other book that could take the place of this one.'

FRANCE IN PRINT

'I found this a wonderful book crammed with facts and figures, with a straightforward approach to the problems and pitfalls you are likely to encounter. The whole laced with humour and a thorough understanding of what's involved. Gets my vote!'

READER

'We would like to congratulate you on this work: it is really super! We hand it out to our expatriates and they read it with great interest and pleasure.'

ICI SWITZERLAND, AG

'If you are thinking of moving to New Zealand this is the book for you. Of all the books about New Zealand I've bought, this is the only one I still refer to.'

READER

'A vital tool in the war against real estate sharks; don't even think of buying without reading this book first!'

EVERYTHING SPAIN MAGAZINE

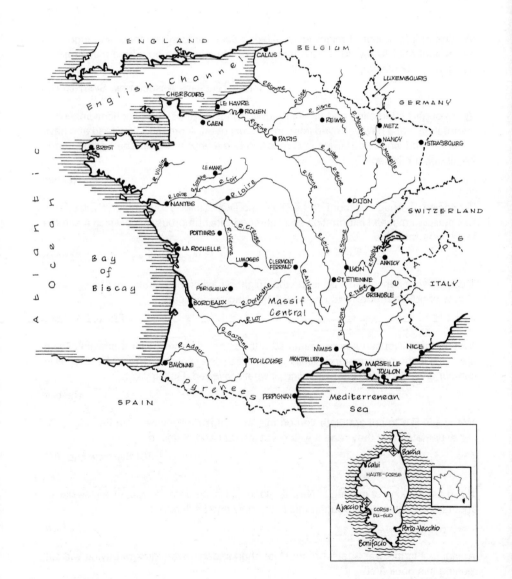

CONTENTS

1. WHY RUN GITES & B&BS IN FRANCE? 17

2. GITES 47

3. BED & BREAKFAST 121

THE AUTHOR

Jo Taylor is originally from Devon, England, where she attended art college, subsequently working in graphic design and advertising. She has lived in Normandy, France, since 1993, running a B&B and *gîte* business in addition to being a freelance designer and illustrator. This is her second book, the first being *Earning Money from Your French Home*. She has also illustrated several titles for Survival Books (🖳 www.blue-moon-design.co.uk).

AUTHOR'S NOTES

- Times are shown using the 24-hour clock; for example, two o'clock in the afternoon is written as 14.00.

- His/he/him/man/men (etc.) also mean her/she/her/woman/women (no offence ladies!). This is done simply to make life easier for both the reader and, in particular, the author, and isn't intended to be sexist.

- British English is used throughout, but American English equivalents are given where appropriate.

- Warnings and important points are shown in **bold type**.

- French words and phrases are given in brackets in italics (usually in the singular).

- The following symbols are used in this book: ☎ (telephone), ▤ (fax), 💻 (internet) and ✉ (email).

- Lists of sources of further information, further reading and useful websites are contained in **Appendices A, B** and **C** respectively.

- Maps of France showing the departments and regions and transport networks are in **Appendix D**.

- Official organisations and their requirements are detailed in **Appendix E**.

Important Note

France is a large country with myriad faces and many ethnic groups, religions and customs. Although ostensibly the same throughout the country, many laws, rules and regulations, especially those associated with doing business, are open to local interpretation. Many of the French organisations responsible for the regulation of holiday accommodation operate on an autonomous basis, and the rules set by one department can be quite different from those set by the next. The costs and prices mentioned in this book were correct at the time of writing but should be regarded as examples only, as these may vary from one region or department to another.

I therefore cannot recommend too strongly that you check with an official and reliable source (not always the same) before making any major decisions or undertaking an irreversible course of action. However, don't believe everything you're told or have read, even – dare I say it? – in this book! Always check and double check things yourself.

To help you obtain further information and verify data with official sources, useful addresses and references to other sources of information have been included in all chapters and in **Appendices A to C**. Important points have been emphasised throughout the book **in bold print**, some of which it would be expensive or foolish to disregard. **Ignore them at your peril or cost.** Unless specifically stated, the reference to any company, organisation, product or publication in this book doesn't constitute an endorsement or recommendation.

BIENVENUE   Jo Taylor

INTRODUCTION

France's beautiful and varied landscape and relaxed lifestyle have wide appeal, and over the last few decades thousands of foreigners have purchased property there. Buying a home in France continues to be at the top of many people's wish-list, but, increasingly, property owners want to make the most of their investment and supplement their income or pension. One of the best ways to do this is by running *gîtes* or providing bed and breakfast accommodation.

The purpose of *Running Gîtes & B&Bs in France* is to provide you with a step-by-step guide to establishing and running a successful *gîte* or bed and breakfast business in France. Whether you plan to do this from abroad, using a French agent or manager, or full- or part-time while resident in France, this book is essential reading. It describes in detail everything you need to know, including what type of property to buy and where; whether to buy an existing business or start from scratch; how to go about conversion and renovation; obtaining grants, loans and mortgages; legal considerations; record-keeping and taxation; equipment and provisions; advertising, marketing and publicity; handling enquiries and bookings; providing extra services; employing an agent and hiring staff; and much, much more.

Information is derived from a variety of sources, official and unofficial, not least my own experiences and those of other foreigners who have already bought property in France and run *gîtes* and bed and breakfast businesses. *Running Gîtes & B&Bs in France* is designed to make your investment in a French home less stressful and more profitable, and will save you valuable time, trouble and money, repaying its modest cost many times over. (For complimentary information see this book's sister publications: *The Best Places to Buy a Home in France*, *Buying a Home in France*, *Living and Working in France*, *Making a Living in France* and *Renovating & Maintaining Your French Home*).

France is one of the world's most popular holiday destinations and a wonderful place to invest in a home – few countries can compete with its stunning scenery, charming villages, delicious cuisine and fine wines – not to mention the seductive French lifestyle, with its emphasis on relaxation and enjoying yourself. I trust *Running Gîtes & B&Bs in France* will help you find the right property investment and enjoy it to the full.

Bon courage !

Jo Taylor
July 2007

Jo Taylor

1

WHY RUN GITES & B&BS IN FRANCE?

1

Buying property abroad has never been as popular as it is today. There are endless magazine articles and television (TV) programmes about buying a home in the sun, whether for permanent living or as a holiday home, which are fuelling an already smouldering desire among many northern Europeans, in particular, for a change of climate and lifestyle. Property exhibitions, magazines and websites advertising an overwhelming choice of properties – from small stone ruins to substantial farmhouses and magnificent *châteaux* – have proliferated in recent years. More than a million properties in France are owned by foreigners, half of them British, and an increasing number of people are jumping on the bandwagon: the total is rising by around 30 per cent per year. Buying an overseas property is a popular choice for older people, who often buy a holiday home with a view to later making it a permanent residence for a peaceful retirement. There are also an increasing number of buyers under 40 who are investing in property in France, with the aim of revitalising their lives and starting a business or generating an income from the property itself.

Whether you're just dreaming, planning a purchase abroad with a view to investment, already the owner of a holiday home in France, from which you wish to earn money, or planning a permanent move, this book will help you assess the potential of such an investment and, should you decide to take the plunge, make the most of it.

Long-term letting is not covered in detail in this book, though if you have a holiday cottage or second home you might be considering renting it out on a longer contract outside the holiday season (see **Longer Lets** on page 112).

DREAMS & REALITY

What could be better, in addition to realising your dream of buying property in France, than to earn income from it? One of the most popular ways of doing this is to run a bed and breakfast (B&B) or self-catering holiday cottage (*gîte*) business. Many foreigners dream of moving to France and living the 'good life', growing vegetables, keeping goats and chickens, and living on the income from a converted ruin or barn. Reality, unfortunately, can be a little less rosy, but applying some careful planning and thought could help you achieve your dream.

To begin with, you must be absolutely clear as to your aims in buying a property in France and utterly realistic in assessing the likely income from it. Your aims may be any of the following:

● **Holiday home** – If you want a holiday home in France, but cannot afford it simply to be left empty when you aren't using it (i.e. for most of the year), you could let it as self-catering accommodation to earn income to pay the mortgage or, if you're fortunate enough to have been able to buy it outright, to cover the running costs and/or provide 'pocket money'.

- **Capital growth** – You may purchase a property as an investment, as you believe that you'll make more money by tying up capital in a property and re-selling it in a number of years than by saving or investing it elsewhere. In recent years, many people have invested in property to provide an income in their retirement. Until that day comes you might want to augment your income by making the property available for holiday letting.

- **Earning money from an existing property** – You might already own a property in France, either with more bedrooms than you need or with outbuildings that could be converted for self-catering holiday letting, and wish to generate income from it.

- **Business** – If you want to live permanently in France but cannot or don't want to get a job there and must therefore make money from your principal home, you may be planning to buy an up-and-running *gîte* or B&B (*chambres d'hôte*) business, or a property with potential to convert bedrooms or buildings into accommodation as a business venture.

It's all too easy to see France as a 'theme park' when on holiday and imagine that living there is all sunshine, wine and croissants and that because the people are so laid-back making money is far easier than in your home country. In fact, the opposite is often true, and the disadvantages – including overwhelming bureaucracy, crippling social charges, language difficulties, cultural differences, lack of support (emotional as well as physical) from family and friends – often seem to outweigh the benefits. Life in France isn't necessarily better or worse than in any other country, just different – and it can take time to adjust.

Many people see life in France as an idyllic rural dream, but you must consider the realities. If you're used to living in a town, will you be able to cope with rural isolation? Will you be able to learn the language and make friends? If you have children, will they be able to adjust? Ask yourself whether you would still move to France if you could buy the same type of property in your home country for the same price. If the answer is no, then you should seriously consider whether you wish to take on the complications and problems of living a foreign country merely in order to save money on a property.

Running a *gîte* or a B&B is hard work and not suitable for those looking for an activity compatible with semi-retirement.

Market Forces

France is the top holiday destination in Europe and one of the world's most popular countries, with over 70m tourists every year (see **Tourism Figures** on page 29), so it might seem that the market for holiday accommodation is so vast that there will always be room for one more B&B or *gîte*. In many areas, this isn't the case, and the market is already saturated, with an increasing number of owners chasing a constant or even dwindling number of potential clients.

> **⚠ CAUTION**
> **It's difficult to make a living providing holiday accommodation in most areas, as the season is too short and there's too much competition (the market is saturated in many regions).**

If you're planning to let to holidaymakers, you should also bear in mind (although you shouldn't need reminding) that tourism is a fragile industry, being affected by a host of factors outside the control of property owners, travel agents, tour operators, airlines and other 'service providers'.

One of the most influential factors is the economic climate of both the host country and those parts of the world from which its clientele is attracted. People's spending power (and habits) change in line with their wealth and their sense of financial security. A downturn in the economy of, say, the US or the UK, not to mention a currency devaluation or stock market crash, can cut your clientele in half virtually overnight. On the other hand, of course, you may find new markets in countries where the economy is booming, such as China.

Needless to say, people's propensity to travel – especially by air – is affected by political unrest and, particularly, global terrorism. Even a bad air or rail crash can dissuade holidaymakers from travelling abroad.

The holiday industry is also affected by the weather – one summer's reported floods, heat wave or hurricanes can have a serious adverse effect on the number of bookings received the following year.

To these one can add such factors as changes in school holiday dates, transport price rises, outbreaks of disease or mere anti-French feeling... the list of things that can make your dream turn sour is long!

Income

If you're planning to let a property, it's important not to overestimate the earnings, particularly if you're relying on letting income to help pay the mortgage and running costs. Buyers who over-stretch their financial resources often find themselves on the rental treadmill, constantly struggling to find sufficient income to cover their running costs and mortgage payments – **you're highly unlikely to meet your mortgage payments and running costs from rental income alone**. When buying to let, you must ensure that the rental income will cover the mortgage (if applicable), outgoings and vacant (void) periods.

SURVIVAL TIP
Most experts recommend that you don't purchase a home in France if you must rely on rental income to pay for it.

Bear in mind also that you must pay French income tax on earnings from a letting business, even if you're a non-resident. If you're a French resident, you must also make social security and social charge contributions, which are higher than in many other countries and considerably higher than in the UK, for example (see **Chapter 4**).

RESEARCH

If you haven't yet bought a property, you're in the best position to turn your purchase into a viable business proposition. You can choose the region, the area and the property with your specific requirements in mind. You can choose to buy an existing business or a property suitable for conversion.

You might have visited a region that you think will make an ideal location for a holiday accommodation business, but before rushing into buying a property, you must carry out detailed research – leaving behind the rose-tinted spectacles. It's a good idea to take a few holidays in the area you've chosen; once you've been a B&B or *gîte* customer, you're more likely to appreciate what is needed to satisfy the holidaymaker. Visit at times outside the holiday season – that delightful sunny country hideaway might not be as welcoming in the cold, windy, wet, muddy winter. Some areas with the highest summer temperatures suffer from sleet, hail, show and bitingly cold winds in winter.

Once you've chosen an area, consider renting for a while before buying, so that your capital isn't tied up while you're researching and finding properties for sale.

Don't believe all you see and hear in TV programmes or magazine articles – many were made some years ago, and prices and availability may be seriously out of date; articles may be biased to encourage you to buy in an area, and TV programmes may paint an artificially rosy picture. Earning

1

money from a property in France isn't as easy as it looks, and an article or programme seldom points out the pitfalls, hardly touches upon the legal processes involved and never explains the (often fundamental) differences between the French legal system and culture and those of other countries.

Regulations

Owning and operating a *gîte* or B&B isn't usually considered a professional activity by the French authorities (except for taxation), provided you don't operate on a scale that necessitates setting up a trading company or registering as a business. Operating as an individual rather than trading through a company usually means lower taxes and social security payments. However, a property with five (in some areas six) or more rooms to let for B&B, or accommodating more than 15 people, is classed as a professional business, as is a *gîte* complex with more than three or four units (depending on the area), and is consequently more expensive to establish and operate.

As with so many aspects of French legislation, regulations vary from one department to another – in some cases even the law of the land is interpreted in different ways – so you must check specifics with the local authority before embarking upon a project.

Income

Yields vary considerably with the region or city and the type of property. The yield is your annual profit on your investment, usually expressed as a percentage of its cost or of its current value, and can be used to compare the effectiveness of your property as an investment with that of other investments, such as savings and shares. You must take into account all outgoings – purchase price, purchase fees and taxes, mortgage payments, local taxes, income tax, maintenance and repairs, utility bills, marketing, etc. – and balance these against your projected rental income in order to estimate your potential profit (see **Viability** on page 75).

The main causes of failure of B&B and *gîte* businesses include the following:

- paying too much for a property (e.g. taking on too large a mortgage);

- purchasing a property in an unsuitable location;

- underestimating the cost of refurbishment or modernisation required to bring a property up to the required standard;

- underestimating the time required for renovation, restoration and decoration required to bring the property up to the required standard;

- underestimating other expenses, such as taxes, advertising, running costs and insurance;

- overestimating the rent you can charge;

- overestimating occupancy (i.e. the number of weeks or days the property will be let) or the amount of time it will take to achieve the desired level;

- failing to allow for problems, such as tenants who cause damage or demand refunds.

> **SURVIVAL TIP**
> **Whatever the state of the property market, the best way to make money when selling property is to not pay too much in the first place!**

When buying solely for investment (or as a second home), you must also take into account that capital gains tax will be payable if you sell the property, as it won't be your principal residence and, if you let it, that you must pay income tax on your earnings (see **Chapter 4**).

> **SURVIVAL TIP**
> **Before buying for investment, think how easy a property will be to sell – if it will be easy to sell, it will also be a good investment.**

BUYING A PROPERTY

Investing in property is attractive as long as property values rise faster than inflation. Not long ago, buying property in France (and in most other countries) wasn't perceived as a good investment compared with the return on income that could be achieved by investing elsewhere. The property slump of the '90s caused many overseas buyers to lose money – and even to lose their French homes. In recent years, however, many investors have lost money on the stock market and lost confidence in pension funds and companies, while property has become a more attractive investment proposition.

The Current Market

In the last five years or so, in particular, French property has been an excellent investment, prices having performed well in many parts of France. Some properties in parts of Paris and the Côte d'Azur have doubled in value, far out-performing the stock market and all forms of savings.

As a rule of thumb, property values in France double every seven years, although in recent years in some areas a similar increase has occurred in as little as three or four years (i.e. annual price rises of over 20 per cent), even without the owners making any improvements. Even in rural areas, where in past years prices didn't rise substantially, a price increase of 10 to 20 per cent per year isn't uncommon. This is partly due to the increase in the number of foreigners buying – in one area of the department of Manche (Normandy), 19 per cent of **all** property sales in 2004 were to British buyers. (On average house prices in France are around 40 per cent less than the UK.)

Nevertheless, property values are affected by a myriad of factors and can plummet almost overnight, so a property investment should be considered over the medium to long term: a minimum of five and preferably at least 10 or 15 years. Investments can be risky over the short to medium term – unless you get an absolute bargain or add value without spending more than you could hope to recoup when selling.

The price of new builds and apartments has since started to slow down, but that of rural and character properties continues to rise. The year 2006 saw a significant downturn – prices even fell in some areas – which was good news for buyers, who had time to do their homework and not be tempted to buy the first property that took their fancy.

Speak to a number of people, including estate agents, and assess the current market before committing yourself to a property.

Major Considerations

Good investment properties generally include the following:

- a property that's under-priced because the owner needs to sell rather than because it has defects;

- a property with a large garden, part of which can be built on or sold as a separate building plot;

- a property with the potential to add value such as a loft conversion, extension or swimming pool (but check that you will be able to obtain permission);

- a property in an up-and-coming area;
- a property with good transport links (road/rail) or planned links;
- a property close to good amenities (shops, leisure facilities, parks, etc.);
- a property near a good school (e.g. an international school);
- a property with well proportioned rooms;
- a period or character property;
- a large property that can be converted into apartments or split into two or more semi-detached homes or terraced homes;
- a reasonably priced apartment in the centre of a major town or city;
- a property with off-road parking or a garage (particularly in a city);
- a waterside property, particularly in a popular resort;
- a property in a historic or tourist town.

SURVIVAL TIP
If you plan to live in a property for a long time, it's best to buy a home, not simply a 'good investment'. Nevertheless, it pays to have one eye on the investment potential of a home, as you never know when you may need to sell!

Poor or indifferent investments generally include the following:

- a property that's over-priced on account of supposedly 'special' features;
- a property in a rundown area or an area with high unemployment (however attractive the property itself may be);
- an unusual, poorly designed or 'individual' house, which will inevitably have limited appeal;
- a house near to any source of noise such as a busy motorway, airport or factory (or the future site of any of these);
- a property susceptible to flooding;
- a property in a town without private parking and no nearby on-road parking;
- a nondescript 'modern' home.

Location

1

When buying with the intention to provide holiday accommodation, you should obviously choose an area popular for tourism. Location is your number one priority, but for a B&B or *gîte* particular considerations need to be made, including the following.

In many popular holiday areas, the rental market is now saturated, and owners are unable to find enough customers to generate sufficient income.

Accessibility

The journey to your property should be easy – both the long haul (ferry trips or flights) and the drive from the port or airport. For holidaymakers from overseas it's a great advantage for a property to be situated within easy travelling distance of a channel ferry port, major airport or *TGV* station. If you want to attract British families, ferry port proximity is important, as they tend to travel by car (having more luggage than couples). Many holidaymakers prefer not to travel more than 45 minutes to their destination after arriving in France. This isn't as important for B&B as it is for *gîtes*, but it's desirable if you're targeting long-stay clients. Some may choose a combination of air transport, train and hire car. Make sure you choose an airport with frequent flights from the UK, if that's where you intend to advertise. Many visitors from the US and other parts of the world travel via the UK; others come via Paris. Properties close to a major airport generally have good letting potential, but airlines (especially budget operators) change routes frequently, or even go out of business, and you shouldn't rely on a particular airline service for your clientele. **It isn't wise to rely on an airport served only by budget airlines, as they may alter or cancel routes at short notice.**

You may dream of owning a country hideaway, far from the madd(en)ing crowd, and it's true that there's a growth market in 'green tourism' (*le tourisme vert*), as urban residents seek peace and quiet in the countryside. But make sure you aren't **too** hidden away. Your guests won't return (or recommend you) if they spend hours finding the place or must drive miles along unmade roads or halfway up a mountain to reach you – and every time they want to go out for the day.

If it's in a rural area where signposts are all but non-existent, not only must you provide a detailed map with plenty of landmarks, but you may also need to erect signs, for which permission might be necessary (see **Chapter 5**). However detailed your diagrams may be, a surprisingly large number of people cannot read maps so it's essential to give detailed instructions too. The use of global positioning system (GPS) navigation has contributed greatly to the number of lost holidaymakers, some of whom may arrive at their destinations merrily singing '*Lost in France*' whereas others will be very tired and very frustrated. Do your utmost to ensure that this doesn't happen; customers who spend hours driving around trying to find your home are unlikely to return or recommend it!

Flying isn't for everyone: families with small children and/or a lot of luggage will find flying expensive or inconvenient, or both, so it's an advantage if a property is served by public transport (e.g. local buses) or is situated in a town where a car is unnecessary. If a property is located in a town or development with a maze of streets, you should provide a detailed map. Maps are also helpful for taxi drivers, who may be unfamiliar with the area. If you're in a rural area that's poorly served by public transport (buses may run only on Wednesdays), be sure to advise your potential guests that their own car (or a hired car) is necessary. If you won't be living in or near the property, it should be easily accessible to you so that you can carry out necessary repairs and maintenance.

Attractions

People who choose *gîte* holidays usually want a week or fortnight's holiday in one location. Some may have two weeks' holiday, spending the first in one place and the second in another. This makes the type of location rather different from that needed for a hotel or B&B, where a lot of the clients are passing through for one or two nights.

If you want to attract *gîte* clients and longer-stay B&B guests, the property should be as close as possible to a major attraction (or more than one), e.g. a beach, theme park, area of scenic beauty or tourist town. If you want to let to families, a property should be within easy distance of leisure activities such as theme parks, water parks, sports facilities (e.g. tennis, golf, horse riding or boating) and nightlife. If you're planning to run a B&B or *gîte* in a rural area, it could be somewhere with good hiking possibilities, preferably near one of France's many natural parks. Proximity to one or more golf courses is also an advantage to many holidaymakers and is an added attraction outside the high season, particularly in northern France, where there may otherwise be little to attract visitors in the winter.

Properties in coastal regions (or departments within those regions) will always let well (subject to competition).

1

Climate

Properties in an area with a pleasant year-round climate, such as the Mediterranean coast and Corsica, have a greater letting potential, particularly outside the high season (subject, of course, to the level of competition). If it's to be a holiday home also for you, it's important that you let it during the summer months, when rental rates are at their highest, and use it yourself in May or October and still enjoy fine weather.

This doesn't eliminate other areas which let well for other reasons – people looking for a walking or sight-seeing holiday will prefer a more temperate climate and many people find the south of France far too hot in high summer; even those who live there often travel north to escape the heat!

Letting Season

The letting season is longest in Paris, where you can let year-round either as holiday accommodation or for longer lets and may achieve 35 weeks' rental. Southern France, particularly the Côte d'Azur, is the next most popular for letting and you may be able to let an apartment for 30 weeks or a villa for 25 during the spring, summer and early autumn. In Normandy and Brittany, if you're within 30 minutes of the coast (and within an hour of a Channel port) and your marketing is efficient, you can also achieve 30-plus weeks. In other coastal areas, the summer season may be limited to around 20 weeks. Inland properties are generally restricted to a maximum of 16 weeks and in some areas the letting season can be as short as ten weeks. **However, you're unlikely to achieve this many weeks' occupancy and you should budget for around half these figures, even when letting full time.** The Alps are a special case, as there are two letting seasons, summer and winter; however, properties in ski resorts are astronomically expensive.

TOURIST BOARD STRUCTURE

Tourism is the responsibility of various government structures, as outlined below.

The State

Central government regulates, agrees to and classifies tourist organisations and activities; it promotes French tourism abroad and helps local authorities in the development of tourism. The Direction de Tourisme is the central administration, which works out and puts into effect general tourism policies that have been defined by the Minister of Tourism. It defines regulations and classifications used by tourism organisations, activities and businesses, which it then regulates. It standardises and gathers data and forecasts on tourism activity and contributes to the output of general tourist information. It also prepares and implements social policy on holidays and leisure and prepares and evaluates employment and vocational training in the leisure sector. Lastly, it oversees associated organisations which have varied responsibilities falling under the umbrella of tourism e.g. the Conseil National des Villes et Villages Fleuris, Maison de la France (which promotes French tourism abroad), and the Agence Nationale pour les Chèques-Vacances.

The Region

Medium-term objectives in terms of tourism and leisure development are worked out at regional level – the Conseil Régional can create a Comité Régional du Tourisme (CRT) to co-ordinate the region's public and private initiatives in the field of tourism development, promotion and information. Within the framework of the state's and region's obligations, Observatoires Régionaux du Tourisme (ORT) were set up to study economic figures and to prepare studies of tourism in their regions.

The Department

Each department (*département*) can create a Comité Départemental du Tourisme (CDT), which carries out its activities in harmony with the local authorities and in partnership with organisations interested in the development of tourism in the department, whilst taking into account the objectives of the regional scheme.

The Commune

A commune (*commune*) can create an Office du Tourisme (the term Syndicat d'Initiative is being phased out) to promote local tourism and supply information.

TOURISM FIGURES

According to figures published by the Banque de France, tourism represents the highest surplus in the country's balance of payments. Tourism was at a record level in 2002 and, though it has dropped slightly since then, continues

1

to perform well, exceeding even the car industry, whose balance fell in 2005. In the figures for 2005 foreign tourism shows a surplus balance of €8.9bn, the car industry €8.5bn and the agricultural and food industry €6.3bn. (The energy industry shows a negative balance of €37.4m!)

Details of French tourism statistics and further information can be found on the Ministry of Tourism website (🖥 www.tourisme.gouv.fr). This book's sister publication, *The Best Places to Buy a Home in France* (Survival Books – see page 314) provides details of each of France's 22 regions, including a guide to property prices.

Nationality & Spend

France is the most popular tourist destination in the world, with 76m foreign visitors in 2005 (the most recent year for which statistics are available) and even more predicted for 2007. This figure is for tourists who spend at least one night in the country; a further 107m visit without staying overnight – mostly shoppers from the UK and business people.

The table below shows how France compares with the world's other top tourist destinations (2005 figures).

Country	Visitors (millions)	Spend (US$bn)
France	76.0	42.3
Spain	55.6	47.9
United States	49.4	81.7
China	46.8	29.3
Italy	36.5	35.4
United Kingdom	30.0	30.4
Mexico	21.9	(unavailable)
Germany	21.5	29.2
Turkey	20.3	18.2
Austria	20.0	15.5

The number of British visitors to France is greater than that from any other country. Of the above-mentioned 76m holidaymakers, the breakdown by nationality is shown in the table below.

Country	Visitors	Spend
UK & Ireland	19.7%	15.5%
Germany	17.4%	11.2%
Netherlands	15.3%	5.4%
Belgium & Luxembourg	11.8%	9.9%
Italy	9.5%	7.4%
Spain	4.2%	4.8%
Switzerland	4.0%	9.0%
US	3.6%	13.4%
Japan	0.9%	2.5%
Other	13.6%	20.9%

It's interesting to note that Dutch visitors, in spite of their numbers, spend very little money. They prefer camping holidays – witness the queues of Dutch camper vans in the summer season! On the other hand, Americans, Swiss, Japanese and visitors from Africa and the Middle East spend a lot of money per head (see table below) but they prefer to stay in luxury hotels and so are unlikely to be included in your target market. Most international visitors stay for four to six nights on average.

Non-Europeans, despite the strength of the euro, continue to spend more per head per night. They represent around 10 per cent of visitors and generate 30 per cent of national income from foreign tourism, but it must be remembered that these figures are greatly skewed by the number of day and short-stay visitors to Paris as part of a whistle-stop European tour.

The table below shows the average spend per night by visitors of each nationality.

Country	Average Spend per Night
Japan	€204.80
Middle East	€169.00
US	€162.30
Switzerland	€158.00

Africa	€121.40
Italy & Greece	€51.70
Belgium & Luxembourg	€51.20
UK	€49.50
Central & South America	€42.90
Germany & Austria	€39.60
Canada	€36.30
Spain & Portugal	€34.80
Netherlands	€25.30
Other European Countries	€53.20
Other Asian and Pacific Countries	€44.60

The table below shows the total spend by visitors of each nationality.

Country	Total Spend
UK	€5,030m
US	€4,544m
Germany	€3,801m
Belgium & Luxembourg	€3,373m
Switzerland	€3,059m
Italy	€2,502m
Africa	€1,852m
Netherlands	€1,851m
Spain	€1,648m
Japan	€847m
Sweden	€537m
Middle East	€477m

Central & South America	€469m
Austria	€309m
Denmark	€331m
Greece	€302m
Portugal	€239m
Ireland	€228m
Canada	€39m
Other European Countries	€768m
Other Asian Countries	€809m

Regions

Statistics relating to where in France people spend their holidays are gathered by the Institut National de la Statistique et des Études Économiques (INSEE) and the French Ministry of Tourism, which use different ways of presenting the results (see below). Unfortunately, these figures include French nationals holidaying within their own country, at an average ratio of 64 per cent French to 36 per cent foreigners – thought the actual ration varies from region to region. Ile-de-France (the Paris region) is the only region with a greater number of foreign visitors than French, though most of the former stay for only one or two nights.

When visitor numbers are broken down into a percentage share by region, the highest scoring region is Provence-Alpes-Côte d'Azur followed closely by Rhône-Alpes (both of which attract winter sports visitors in addition to summer holidaymakers), then Ile-de-France. Next is Languedoc-Roussillon with its Mediterranean beach resorts, followed by the Atlantic coastal resorts of Aquitaine. Brittany (with 25 per cent of France's coastline) comes next, then Pays-de-la-Loire (which includes the Atlantic coast departments of Loire-Atlantique and Vendée as well as the *châteaux* of the Loire valley). Next is Midi-Pyrénées – again with a share of the skiing market – followed by Poitou-Charentes (Atlantic coast) and Lower Normandy, the remaining regions having low figures.

When the number of overnight stays is expressed as a ratio of the number of inhabitants of each region, Corsica becomes the most popular region, with 95 overnight stays per inhabitant, then come Lower Normandy, Brittany and the two Mediterranean coastal regions – Languedoc-Roussillon and Provence-Alpes-Côte d'Azur – all having a ratio in excess of 40:1. Aquitaine and Poitou-Charentes have between 30 and 40, followed by Pays-de-la-Loire, Midi-Pyrénées, Rhône-Alpes, Auvergne, Limousin, Burgundy and Franche-Comté with between 20 and 30. The remaining nine regions (in central and north-east France) score less than 20, Nord-Pas-de-Calais having the lowest ratio of all at just 9:1. Although Paris is the most popular tourist destination in the world, the Paris region is among the bottom nine regions. This is partly because of Paris's huge population, partly because most visitors to Paris stay for only one or two nights and partly because most French people go to the south (and Corsica) for their summer holidays, though those who live in the south of the country may go north for cooler weather, or to visit relatives or friends.

The size of the region is obviously a significant factor in both methods of expressing visitor numbers, Aquitaine, for example, being over four times the size of Alsace.

In terms of tourist consumption (e.g. how much money visitors spend), urban areas come out on top at 38.2 per cent of the market – again skewed by the number of short-term visitors to Paris. Next comes the seaside with 26.4 per cent, followed by the countryside (19.3 per cent) and the mountains (16.1 per cent).

In terms of overnight stays the seaside is most popular with 34.8 per cent of the market, with urban areas next at 29.3 per cent., followed by countryside locations at 28 per cent and mountain areas with 7.9 per cent.

Bear in mind that these statistics include hotel accommodation as well as registered *gîtes* and B&Bs. **They don't take account of the many thousands of *gîtes* and *chambres d'hôtes* which aren't registered with Gîtes de France or the tourist board**. In some regions, the number of unregistered B&Bs may exceed that of registered establishments. This is probably true to an even greater extent of *gîtes*. It's easy for non-residents to let out their second homes without this ever coming to the notice of the French tourism authorities; even if they do it 'by the book' there's no requirement to register (the income, of course, must be declared).

Attractions

Properties offering holiday accommodation that are near or within a day trip of major tourist attractions will attract booking, although inevitably the more popular the attraction, the more competition for customers there will be.

The figures below are the annual visitor numbers (in 2004) of France's top 20 cultural attractions (museums, historical sites, etc.) and top ten non-cultural attractions (theme parks, etc.). All these sites charge an entrance and therefore the lists don't include locations such as the D-Day landing beaches, the World War I battlefields and monuments, or other attractions that are free to visit.

1

Attraction	Location	Visitor Numbers
Louvre Museum	Paris	6.6m
Eiffel Tower	Paris	6.2m
Pompidou Centre	Paris	5.4m
Château de Versailles	west of Paris	3.3m
Cité des Sciences de la Villette	Paris	2.8m
Musée d'Orsay	Paris	2.6m
Arc de Triomphe	Paris	1.2m
Mont-Saint-Michel	Lower Normandy	1.1m
Musée de l'Armée	Paris	1m
Musée d'Histoire Naturelle	Paris	739,000
Musée Grévin (waxworks)	Paris	705,000
Sainte-Chapelle	Paris	689,000
Château de Chambord	Centre	658,000
Mémorial de la Paix, Caen	Lower Normandy	557,000
Palais des Papes, Avignon	Provence-Alpes-Côte d'Azur	532,000
Musée Rodin	Paris	529,000
Château du Haut-Konigsbourg	Alsace	521,000
Tour Montparnasse	Paris	500,000
Musée Picasso	Paris	480,000
Bayeux Tapestry	Lower Normandy	410,000

As will be seen, the Paris region has 14 of the country's top 20 cultural attractions; the next most 'attractive' region is Lower Normandy, with three sites. The top ten non-cultural sites are as follows:

1

Attraction	Location	Visitor Numbers
Disneyland	east of Paris	12.4m
Parc Astérix	north of Paris	1.8m
Parc Futuroscope	Poitou-Charentes	1.3m
Parc Zoologique de Lille	Pas-de-Calais	1.2m
Le Puy-du-Fou (theme park)	Pays de la Loire	1.1m
Chemin de Fer de la Mer de Glace	Rhône-Alpes	932,000
Aquaboulevard (aquatic park)	Paris	834,000
Aquarium de La Rochelle	Poitou-Charentes	830,000
Parc Zoologique de la Palmyre	Poitou-Charentes	750,000
Boat trips around Strasbourg	Alsace	672,000

In the non-cultural stakes, Disneyland Paris is way ahead of the competition, being the biggest tourist attraction in Europe, followed by four other leisure parks. France has 100 such parks with over 100,00 visitors per annum, many of which are seasonal – the total number of visitors per year is estimated at around 65m. Of these, 24 per cent go to amusement parks, 23 per cent to zoos and animal parks, 16 per cent to aquariums, 12 per cent to theme parks and 11 per cent to aquatic parks. The amusement parks and zoos have the most recurring visits due to their popularity with families with children, who number 61 per cent of their clientele. As can be seen, the Poitou-Charentes region in western France boasts several of the country's top non-cultural attractions.

Second Homes

Many foreigners and French nationals buy second homes in France, for their own holidays, as an investment for retirement, or to let out as holiday accommodation (or a combination of all three). Second homes are mainly located in coastal areas and in the mountain regions, the top ten regions being Provence-Alpes-Côte d'Azur, Rhône-Alpes, Languedoc-Roussillon, Brittany, Pays-de-la-Loire, Aquitaine, Midi-Pyrénées, Lower Normandy, Poitou-Charentes and Auvergne.

In excess of 220,000 owners of second homes in France are non-residents. Almost a quarter (53,200) of these are British. In 2002 the British represented 45.2 per cent of all foreign house-buyers, 60 per cent of those purchases being in rural locations and many being let out when their owners aren't in residence. Since, then these figures have fallen somewhat, but there's still a high proportion of British owners letting property in France – and therefore competing with you. (The next three highest groups were the Swiss, Italians and Germans who generally buy just over their own borders.)

WHAT TO BUY

Once you've decided on the best area to buy in, you must make sure that you purchase the right type of property for your chosen purpose. If you're planning a holiday letting business, you will need an attractive property that people want to come and stay in – this may seem like stating the obvious, but many people buy cowsheds which, after conversion, still look like cowsheds! They may be beautifully renovated and equipped, but the point at which you sell a holiday is when the client sees the advertisement. Saunas, luxury kitchens, wi-fi connections and video games machines don't sell holidays – photographs do. A pretty house with stunning views and a swimming pool (which **does** make a difference), even if fairly basically equipped, will let well in both the *gîte* and B&B markets. A luxuriously appointed property that looks like a barn or a concrete toilet block won't, unless you spend an exorbitant amount of time and money in marketing.

Find out what type of property is in demand in your chosen area by asking holiday letting agencies which properties sell best.

If you aren't intending to live in France, don't buy a huge property that requires a lot of maintenance – paying a caretaker or property manager will eat up your profits. Even if you're planning to become a French resident, don't be tempted to take on too much or you may regret it later. Maintaining a large property is like painting the Eiffel Tower: as soon as you reach the top, it's time to start again at the bottom.

> **SURVIVAL TIP**
> **If you're combining a desire for a more relaxed lifestyle with a plan to run a letting business to help finance it, don't forget the lifestyle side of the equation – you want to sell accommodation, not your happiness and well-being!**

1

Community Properties

Many French properties are community properties (*copropriétés*), i.e. an apartment or house in a development where there are shared facilities. The properties themselves are owned outright, but ownership of communal areas (staircases, lifts, gardens, etc.) is shared. Check before buying an apartment that letting is permitted and what restrictions apply (you may be required to notify the community 'manager', for example). You must also inform your insurance company if a property is to be let.

Land

Most people's dream French property is a picturesque country cottage with extensive land and gardens, and it's often tempting to acquire a vast amount of land. But too much land is usually a liability, **not** an asset. Bear in mind the costs, time and hard work involved in maintaining such a property. If you don't live there all the time, who will do this work? If you want a tidy garden, the lawn will have to be mown twice a week at some times of the year (everything grows **much** faster in France than in the UK, for example) and you will spend all your holidays hacking away the undergrowth. Allowing a farmer to use the land might seem a good idea, but this often has legal implications, in some circumstances leading to his having rights of tenancy and even first refusal on the land should you decide to sell. If you plan to live in the property, dreams of self-sufficiency are all very well, but you don't need ten hectares (or even one hectare) of fields to keep hens and grow a few vegetables!

Buildings

Another frequent mistake made by foreign buyers, in whose home country such properties are either scarce or unaffordable, is to purchase a property with several outbuildings, which are often in a poor state of repair. What will you do with them? Do you have the money, skills, energy and motivation (and can you obtain the planning permission) to convert them into holiday accommodation units? If not, they will need constant maintenance just to keep them from falling down, which costs time and money. If you're no longer young, consider whether you're prepared to take on the burden of never-ending property maintenance – will you still be able to cope with it in ten years' time?

Old or New?

The 'perfect' French property for holiday letting may be a traditional house or cottage at least 100 years old, made of stone, brick or wood. But new properties can be an excellent alternative as an investment, often working out cheaper than an older home, particularly when the cost of renovation is taken into account (see below). There are other advantages to buying new: new buildings must be sold with a ten-year guarantee, with a further two-year warranty on equipment, and must comply with modern building regulations; modern buildings have modern facilities, such as central heating and plenty of sockets. On the other hand, most modern properties lack character and are therefore less attractive to holidaymakers.

Renovation

Many owners will tell you that they never foresaw the amount of work and money that's absorbed by a restoration or renovation project and advise others against it. Complete renovation of tumbledown buildings often exceeds the cost of buying a more modern property, or even that of building from scratch – and it can take far longer.

The average person's experience of do-it-yourself won't be sufficient to undertake a major restoration project. You may be handy at putting up shelves and decorating but rebuilding, plumbing and wiring – to unfamiliar regulations in a foreign language – is another challenge altogether. It's far better, from the outset, to include in your budget the employment of specialist artisans and builders. They can do most jobs more quickly, more efficiently and ultimately more cost-effectively than the amateur (however enthusiastic!). And their work is insured for ten years.

When looking for a property that needs refurbishing or modernisation or one where you can add value with a loft conversion, annexe or extension, it's essential not to pay too much for it. **One of the most common mistakes that people make is to pay too much for a restoration property and to underestimate the cost of the work required.** If you buy a ruin for restoration, you must be prepared to spend a lot of money, probably a lot more than you bargained for, as a major restoration almost never comes in on budget! It will also take you much longer than planned.

It isn't always easy to get a loan on a property requiring complete restoration.

CAUTION

1

Before committing yourself to a purchase, you must check that you will be allowed to make the alterations you have in mind, as planning regulations can be restrictive, especially in historic or scenic villages or towns.

If you're planning to buy a property that needs renovation or restoration, you should arrange for a builder to inspect it and provide a quotation (add **at least** 25 per cent for unforeseen problems). You must know **exactly** what you plan to do before starting work and to have architect's drawings for all structural alterations. This can add at least a further €2,000 to €3,000, even for a simple barn conversion. You must also know how much each job will add to the value of a property – so that you don't waste money doing non-essential work that adds little or no value – and obtain an accurate valuation of what the restored property will be worth. **Spending too much money on renovation is a common mistake.** A property must be well renovated, but there's little point in spending a fortune on a designer kitchen, fancy bathrooms, double glazing, conservatories and power showers if they're out of character with the property, or if the sort of tenant or buyer you can expect to attract won't be interested in paying for such things.

When you've calculated the likely cost of renovation, work out not only whether you'll be able to recoup the cost in lettings but whether the property will be worth what you've spent on it if you need or choose to sell it. **Note that it's no longer possible to offset DIY renovation work against capital gains tax even if you have receipts to account for it.** In order for you to be entitled to offset expenditure against capital gains tax when selling, work must be carried out by registered, not 'on the black' by people working illegally nor even by yourself.

Somewhere between the estimated value after restoration and the cost of renovation is the amount you should pay for a property. For example, if the restored value is estimated at €300,000 and the cost of restoration will be €100,000 (allowing for contingencies), you should pay no more than €200,000 – much less if you want to make a reasonable profit. You must allow for budget over-runs and the fees associated with buying and selling, if you eventually plan to sell. **You must also bear in mind that the property market could fall by the time that you're ready to sell.**

For detailed information on this subject, refer to *Renovating & Maintaining Your French Home* (Survival Books – see page 314).

CASE STUDY 1

Living in Buckinghamshire, near London, we had always enjoyed holidaying in France because of the variety of beautiful regions, food and wine and the humane lifestyle. In 1995, we were inspired by a holiday in a B&B in the Beaujolais area, where we realised that this was a way we could work together to earn a living: Bob was an architect/interior designer who had worked in the fashion business and had renovated several homes before (as well as being a wonderful cook) and I, Celia, enjoy meeting people and interior design.

Although we loved the Beaujolais area, which had the most beautiful scenery (and not bad wine), it had a continental climate and we knew that to run a holiday business we needed a warmer, Mediterranean climate. This, we discovered, started below the town of Valence, in the Drôme region. We holidayed there, to check it out, as it was then fairly unknown; most people careered down to the Luberon and the south coast. We found it beautiful, with affordable property and well situated in relation to motorways, airports and the towns of Lyon, Valence and Avignon. We loved it and felt that we'd discovered a new holiday destination.

We had a detailed brief to follow in searching for a house or farm:

- It should be in a semi-rural area.

- It should have a potential habitable space (including renovated lofts and agricultural buildings) of 500m².

- It should be built of stone (and the stonework should be exposed).

- It should have a lovely view.

- It shouldn't be too far from basic amenities and services.

- It should have not more than 1ha (2.5 acres) of land.

We saw around 50 properties in the space of two years (using all our holidays to search) and were happy to find a farm that needed total rebuilding, which meant that we could plan exactly how to use the space available. It had two habitable rooms and a collection of filthy, semi-ruined agricultural buildings. We bought it in 1997.

It was a good choice, and Bob redesigned the space to suit our business needs and give us the income we needed: five chambres d'hôte and two gîtes.

We marketed mainly through the Chez Nous homeowners' catalogue published in the UK and a Canadian website called 'En France'. Chez Nous, which cost around GB£700 per year, has provided 80 per cent of our clientele, and En France, costing around £100, a further 10 per cent. The

1

remaining 10 per cent consists of friends and acquaintances. We have an 80 per cent return rate but must always keep new people coming, so we continue to advertise with these two companies.

Several cheap or free internet sites haven't been worthwhile — we've had maybe five bookings from them in total. We may consider one of the leading (and more expensive) sites if Chez Nous, which also has a website, should ever slow down.

In general, we've had delightful customers, but we're absolutely dedicated to making sure that their holiday is really good. This involves being always available — virtually 24 hours a day between April and October — to give advice, suggest trips, organise wine tastings, walks, pony rides and visits to artists' studios, etc., as well as preparing and serving breakfasts and evening meals. We steal around one-and-a-half hours to rest in the afternoons, but otherwise we're committed to the business and have no social life at all (one of us manages to go to church on Sundays).

Our worst experience was a Swiss couple who appeared trustworthy (Range Rover, cashmere sweaters, etc.) and stayed for six weeks in one of our gîtes and left without paying. Screaming children can be painful for other guests, so we normally suggest that families with small children stay in one of the gîtes.

We were reasonably pleased to have a good number of bookings in our first year, and those people who returned plus new visitors gave us a healthy second year. The only glitch was that, having stated our prices in sterling, we lost a substantial amount in 2002/3 on account of the poor exchange rate to euros. We quote all prices in euros now.

We think the fact that we cook evening meals, everyone eating en famille, is one of our greatest attractions, which people return for — but which makes life exhausting! Often, couples want to have interesting company to interact with over a home-cooked evening meal (including vegetables from the garden) in the courtyard, with plenty of good Côtes du Rhône wine.

We encountered some mystifying rules relating to planning permission, which proved painful when we were trying to build extensions to ex-farm buildings — inflexible, unreasonable old rules which don't apply today but **are** applied, as that's how it has always been done!

Our biggest problem initially was trying to get advice on how to run a business within the French system. Talking to as many people as possible is important. Had we not needed to have the VAT on all the building work refunded, which necessitated setting up a formal business, we would certainly not have become an *entreprise*, but remained private individuals, paying normal income tax. The very high social charges we must pay for widows', orphans' and unemployment benefits, as well as for healthcare, eat into our profits – on an escalating scale, the more we earn. It makes us want to reinvest our money to reduce our profit, on which the charges are calculated.

Employing staff is complicated and expensive: it necessitates the completion of umpteen forms for various bodies, and you pay out virtually double the employees' wages to cover their social charges. The system encourages employers to pay people cash in hand, which doesn't seem right.

With hindsight, we're glad to have calculated accurately the income we expected to generate from the size of property we had (ten weeks' letting is a good initial projection). It's easy to romanticise about growing one's own vegetables, living from the land and getting by on next to nothing, but life isn't much cheaper in France than in the UK (electricity is madly expensive), and it's important to be realistic about how much you must earn.

Couples with children must really enter the French social security system, but an older couple can take out private medical insurance, have a private income without registering with the Chamber of Commerce, and be liable just for income tax. This would have been our ideal scenario but, once committed, it's difficult to withdraw unless you move or close your business.

We require the extra income from B&B and meals, as we have a mortgage. But when it's paid off, our aim is to have self-catering accommodation only, which is generally filled in high season. Offering B&B and meals can extend the season at both ends (May and September) and is worth the enormous commitment and relentless effort while you're fit enough to manage it.

We started with dinner seven evenings a week, now it's five and next year perhaps it will be four. However, many customers come especially for the camaraderie and fun at dinner time, so there's a fine balance to be made.

Also, we try not to be too upmarket, as attracting a five-star-hotel-type person, who's picky and demanding, can give you lots of headaches. Our prices are reasonable and we attract a wide variety of people, including window-cleaners, lawyers, chip shop owners and teachers, all of

1

whom mix unexpectedly well. And they're all on holiday to enjoy themselves, which makes our job easier!

We offer the following advice to others contemplating a similar business:

- Make sure the location and climate are right to attract visitors throughout your planned season – and to suit your planned lifestyle. Bear in mind that there's never much business to be had in winter, when France can be cold, so it isn't worth opening.

- Make sure you have enough money to create the accommodation from which you intend to earn a living; we worked on renovation for 20 months with no income.

- Add 20 per cent to all projected costs; there are many unexpected expenses.

- Be prepared, if you do B&B with meals, to have no other life during the season and to be working relentlessly. You can look forward to a tranquil winter!

- Stay out of the formal business system as far as possible, but do have an accountant to fill in all the forms for you.

- Create a private space for yourselves.

- Make sure, above all, that your own accommodation gives you what you've dreamed about when living in France. You have to live there 12 months a year; your visitors are there only for very short periods.

Bob & Celia Christmas, La Roche Colombe, route de Manas, 26450 Charols (☎ 04 75 90 48 22, 🖳 www.larochecolombe.com)

TOP TEN TIPS FOR RUNNING GITES & B&BS

- Do your research and choose the area carefully according to your needs and expectations.

- Ascertain the letting potential in the area you've chosen by talking to agents and local people and by searching internet holiday sites.

- By the same means, get an idea of the rental you can charge.

- Don't buy a property that's unsuitable for the purpose you have in mind, however attractive it might appear. Viewing houses for sale is one of the later stages in the process – not to be done whilst on a sunny holiday!

- Do your sums carefully, then reduce your expected income and increase your anticipated costs by 25 per cent and do them again.

- Ensure that you have enough information to make a dispassionate decision.

- Ensure that you're aware of all the risks involved and that you're comfortable taking those risks.

- Ensure that you can afford to tie up your capital for as long as it takes to show a profit.

- Research your market and give yourself the best possible chance of attracting clients, but don't overestimate occupancy levels, particularly in the first few years.

- Be prepared to work hard!

For further information on buying property, refer to *Buying a Home in France* (Survival Books – see page 314).

Jo Taylor

2

GITES

2

*G*îte is a French word meaning, literally, resting-place, shelter or lodging. It has become the generic term for what is known in the UK and elsewhere as a holiday cottage or, more generally, self-catering accommodation, and may be anything from a converted outhouse to a large luxury property with a number of self-contained apartments or cottages. In this chapter we deal mainly with the popular conception of a *gîte* – a rural self-catering cottage.

The word *gîte* came into use in the '50s when the government organisation Gîtes de France (see page 69) introduced a scheme for farmers to convert and let out their spare buildings in the holiday season so that they could make some extra money to augment their waning agricultural income. Since then, other French people and, particularly, foreigners have established *gîtes* to supplement their income or even as a primary business.

Running one or more *gîtes* is a popular choice for those relocating abroad because the legal implications of setting up an accommodation business aren't as restrictive as those for other types of enterprise in France. In general, setting up as self-employed involves a huge amount of bureaucracy and paperwork, which is difficult enough for French people to wade through – even more so if you aren't fluent in French and are unfamiliar with the process. However, the grindingly slow French bureaucratic system is taking some time to catch up with the idea that letting holiday accommodation can be a viable concept, which is fortunate for anyone wanting to run a *gîte* or B&B business as a supplementary activity. It isn't considered a professional activity unless the revenue exceeds €23,000 or 50 per cent of your income so it isn't necessary to register as a business if you're operating on a small scale (see **Registering as a Business** on page 63). It makes sense to have a number of units, thus reducing the running cost per unit and spreading the cost of installing amenities such as a swimming pool, but bear in mind that you may then have to register. In any case, you do, of course, have to pay tax on the income earned (see **Chapter 4**).

> **SURVIVAL TIP**
> **You won't earn enough to live on unless you have a**
> **number of luxury *gîtes* with a pool.**

ADVANTAGES & DISADVANTAGES

Running a *gîte*, compared with running any other business in France, and particularly bed and breakfast accommodation (see **Chapter 3**), has a number of advantages and disadvantages. These depend to a certain extent on the type of business you're running. *Gîte* owners generally fall into three categories:

- those who buy expressly with the purpose of running a business, as an investment – in which case profit is the prime consideration;

- second home owners (whose principal residence is in France or in another country) who let their holiday home when they aren't using the property themselves – in which case any income is welcome but probably not essential;

- those who live in France, or are planning to, and have spare buildings on the site of their principal residence to convert in order to supplement their income (a popular choice among UK residents) – in which case the major consideration may be balancing the need to make money with the desire to have a relaxing lifestyle.

Running a *gîte* business can be rewarding and pleasurable, as well as helping to contribute towards the running costs of a property. It's less intensive than running a bed and breakfast (B&B); with a little consideration and care in setting up, you can preserve your privacy and enjoy your own home.
Advantages include the following:

- tax breaks (legislation in France favours anything to do with the tourist industry and in particular *gîtes*);

- no formal qualifications or experience required (see page 50);

- no permission/licence required (unless your business is large enough to need to be registered – see **Registering as a Business** on page 63);

- no need to be on site to cater to guests (unlike B&B) – you can even run your business 'remotely' (e.g. from another country), although you'll need a caretaker and other maintenance staff;

- guests largely look after themselves (unlike B&B guests);

Possible disadvantages include the following (some apply only to a property you use yourself as a holiday home):

- the cost of purchase – a property suitable for use as a *gîte* can cost €80,000 or more, in addition to the cost of your home (see also **Buying a Business** on page 60);

- the cost of maintaining the property to a high standard;

- not enough income to live on unless you have a number of *gîtes* or a complex;

- having to decorate and furnish your property to appeal to others rather than yourself;

- having to remove your belongings when letting;

- the possibility of having your property damaged;

- not being able to use the property in peak season, when most of your income is generated, or for as many weeks/at the time of year you want;

- having to take all your holidays in the same place;

- having to spend the majority of your time in your holiday home doing repairs and maintenance, gardening and decorating.

QUALIFICATIONS & EXPERIENCE

Although no formal qualifications or particular experience are required to run *gîtes*, certain attributes are desirable if not essential if you're to make a success of your enterprise.

Language

Unless you have a reasonable grasp of French – including reading and writing – you'll find it very difficult to navigate the rules and regulations, cope with tax forms and deal with the never-ending bureaucracy for which France is famous, and you'll be severely limited in the number of French clients you can attract. It's therefore virtually essential that you learn the language or improve your skills **before** starting a *gîte* business. Even if you're using an agency and dealing mainly with English-speakers, you still have to deal with paying your property and income taxes, and negotiate with builders, suppliers, architects, etc. If you're intending to let to French people, speaking their language is a must.

Maintenance

Tasks you must be able to do efficiently and professionally include cleaning, building maintenance, gardening, and laundry. You can of course employ others to do these jobs but, if you choose to do so, bear in mind the costs when putting together your business plan.

People Skills

You must be able to smile and be nice to strangers – even if you don't like them! This may seem obvious, but you must be realistic about the prospect of sharing your idyllic home and/or pool with other people. You may enjoy socialising, but it's an entirely different thing to have people staying with you who aren't your friends – they may have little in common with you (apart from liking France). Ask yourself how you'll cope with a people-carrier driving onto your lovingly maintained lawn, disgorging a quantity of disgruntled teenagers or tired but overactive toddlers who then run amok in your flowerbeds and start wrenching branches off your beautifully pruned shrubs (having arrived three hours later than expected, when you'd planned a much-needed evening out), or with the reluctant partner who moans from the moment of arrival – he or she would much rather be in a modern apartment on the Costa del Sol than facing two weeks in a 300-year-old cottage in rainy Brittany… Your job will be to smile, welcome them, sympathise, and enable them to make the most of their stay so that, if they don't return (heaven forbid!), at least they put in a good word for you among their friends and relatives back home.

You must be prepared to deal diplomatically with any badly behaved children, broken appliances, leaking roofs and any other problems, both real and imagined. Whether problems are within your control or not, they're ultimately your responsibility to resolve, as you're providing a service for which your guests are paying. In short, you must be able to put yourself in the place of your clients and act as you would expect your host to act. Note, however, that some people will attempt to obtain a refund by complaining about almost everything, including the size of the pool or fridge and a lack of air-conditioning equipment or tennis court. You must decide (in advance) whether you'll budget for 'goodwill' refunds in such cases or whether you'll refuse a refund and accept that these clients will give you a bad reference (they probably will anyway!).

THE MARKET

It's impossible to state accurately the number of *gîte* and related self-catering properties in France, as many are independently run and not subject to any central registration. The following list of figures, therefore, applies **only** to those properties registered with Gîtes de France (see page 69), the majority (80 per cent) of whose clients are French.

- There are currently 43,000 owners and 56,000 properties (43,800 *Gîtes Ruraux*); on average, a further 2,500 are created each year.

- 35m days' holiday are taken in *Gîtes Ruraux* each year, which means that the total market for *Gîtes Ruraux* is around 3.5m people.

- The average rental period is 16 weeks per year, with guests staying 1.5 weeks on each visit (in other words, roughly half of guests stay for one week and half for two), and the average annual occupancy rate (the number of weeks' rental as a percentage of the number of weeks the *gîte* is open) is 43.4 per cent.

- The average cost of creating a *Gîte Rural* is €58,400, including building work and interior furnishing and decoration.

- Overseas visitors represent one fifth of Gîtes de France's clientele – mainly English and Belgian, but also Dutch and German.

- The average weekly rent is €408 during the high season and €267 during the low season; the average weekend rate is €163.

- *Gîtes* are extremely popular with families, mainly couples aged between 25 and 44 with two children under 15, who live in cities and own their own homes. 50 per cent of customers are middle managers, senior executives or professional people; 18 per cent work in offices. Although customers remain loyal, only 15 per cent go back to the same *gîte* on a regular basis, whereas 72 per cent choose a different location within the Gîtes de France (GdF) network every year.

Recent reports state that the *gîte* market is reaching (or in some areas has already reached) saturation point, with more accommodation available than there are clients – in some areas there are as many as five *gîtes* for every potential booking. Moreover, interest in buying French property has never been higher, and a lot of prospective buyers will be considering converting one or more buildings to accommodation use. It's therefore more important than ever to research the market – you need to know what makes a successful letting business, why some *gîtes* are let for over 30 weeks per year while other owners are struggling to achieve five or six weeks' occupation.

As demand has increased, so too have the expectations of clients. Whereas in the past a *gîte* was perceived as a fairly basic form of holiday accommodation, nowadays a higher level of comfort is expected and many holidaymakers expect a 'home from home' with all the amenities that implies – and of a much higher quality than in the past.

If you intend to register your *gîte* with Gîtes de France or Clévacances (see page 72), they will send a representative to inspect the property and advise you on facilities required and planning application procedures and costs, as well as providing an estimate of the income you can expect to earn. It might be possible to use this service even if you don't plan to register with these organisations in order to help you with your planning, although you may consider this unethical.

You stand a better chance of success if you:

- identify your target market and keep it as wide as possible, always looking for ways to expand and extend your season;

- do some research into how people choose their holiday destinations (weather, culture, facilities, easy travel, etc.) and promote the relevant features of your property;

- anticipate clients' requirements;

- exceed clients' expectations;

- adapt with a changing market – e.g. improve facilities, add a pool, etc.

- maintain contact with clients;

- foster word-of-mouth promotion;

- give your business the personal touch.

French or Foreigners?

It makes sense to target as many potential clients as possible. However, spreading your marketing too thinly can reduce its efficiency. One of the prime considerations is to decide whether to specifically target French guests, in which case registering with Gîtes de France, Clévacances and/or your regional or departmental tourist board is recommended, if not essential – 80 per cent of their customers are from within France. Most French people are quite traditional in their holidaying habits, the greatest demand being for the last week of July and the first two weeks of August, and the Easter and Whitsun (*Pentecôte*) holidays. If you have French clients, you must of course be able to read, write and speak French (including answering the telephone!). If you aren't fluent in French (which is increasingly being made a requirement of registration with tourist boards, etc.), it's better to concentrate on attracting clients who speak your language, which may in any case allow you to sell a larger number of weeks.

French clients are notorious for trying to squash a family of ten into a *gîte* intended for four!

Disabled People

If your property has disabled access, including wide doors, and no steps to at least one bedroom and bathroom, this can be a good selling point. Most agencies will have provision for emphasising this in their advertisements (GdF has a category for properties suitable for the disabled – see page 69), and there are some that specialise in this area, e.g. Access Travel (UK ☎ 01942-888844, 🖳 www.access-travel.co.uk).

Children

The largest group of clients who book *gîte* holidays is families, and not allowing children drastically reduces your letting potential, although children can cause more damage than adults or pets! There's likely to be more wear and tear and a greater number of breakages, however well meaning the parents; some toddlers leave sticky marks everywhere, older children may use furniture as trampolines... Some people don't let to families with children under five because of the risk of bed-wetting.

If you decide to welcome children, you should do your best to make your property child-friendly and can even apply for GdF's *Bienvenue Bébé* accolade (see page 69). You must supply cots, a highchair, changing facilities, toys, stair gates (the portable type are best, as they can be used to block access to any rooms), and a screen for open fireplaces. A securely fenced play area with swings and other play equipment will also be popular, and the garden should be enclosed. You must ensure that any equipment provided bears the CE mark, showing that it conforms to EU standards.

Let enquirers know in advance whether or not the property is enclosed and if there are steep stairs. Supply details of pushchair-friendly walks, and attractions in the area that are suited to younger children. If you have any animals (e.g. goats, sheep, donkeys) that don't mind being poked and prodded by children you could advertise these as an added attraction, but don't allow unsupervised access – children who aren't used to animals can be inadvertently cruel; on the other hand the most even-tempered animal has a limit to its tolerance, and might retaliate!

You should make such considerations **before** buying a property, as some are unsuitable for children. If you have a *bijou* little cottage that sleeps two, for example, you can target your advertising at couples wanting a peaceful getaway. (Brittany Ferries Owners in France have a section for 'Cottages for Grown-ups Only'; the publicity includes the phrase 'where the noise level is rarely higher than the clinking of wine glasses'.)

Groups

Problems can arise if you let to groups, particularly same-sex and younger people (e.g. a football team). If you don't wish to let to such groups, you can stipulate that they aren't permitted (or that the property isn't suitable) or simply say that you're fully booked.

Animals

Allowing animals should be seriously considered. Since the introduction of 'pet passports', it has become easy for travellers from the UK to take their dogs and cats on holiday with them. You could have a higher number of lets if you allow pets. Nevertheless, it's best to accept them only if your *gîte* is fenced; town dogs might regard your chickens as dinner or find the nearby field of sheep an irresistible temptation and be shot by the farmer. They might also run into the road. There are several other possible disadvantages, not least that pets might mess indoors, or leave hairs, causing allergy reactions in future guests. Check with your insurance company if you decide to allow pets.

WHERE TO BUY

If you haven't yet bought a property, you're in the best position to make your *gîte* business a viable proposition. You can choose the region, the area, the location and the specific property with your requirements in mind. You can choose to buy an existing business (see page 60), or to buy a property with one or more buildings to convert (see page 61).

Location is probably the most important factor in determining whether your business will succeed or fail. There are still some areas of France where you can buy a lovely old farm building that has barns ripe for conversion to *gîtes* at what might seem a reasonable cost. If you find one, ask yourself why someone hasn't already bought it with the same intention. Do people holiday in this area? Will the costs of renovation and/or conversion be too high? Will you even obtain permission to do so?

2

SURVIVAL TIP
If you're buying in France with a view to
setting up a business, you must buy where
other people want to go on holiday, not necessarily
where you want to live.

Although location is paramount, it's impossible to give details of the best locations in France to set up *gîtes* beyond a few more or less obvious generalisations. Coastal areas tend to be more popular than inland departments – with the exception of Dordogne. Anyone, anywhere can probably let the last two weeks of July and the month of August; you need to find something to attract holidaymakers outside these few weeks. It's therefore essential to carry out detailed research at regional, departmental and local levels.

For example, the Brittany and Normandy regions are particularly popular among British *gîte* clients – they're both well served by the Channel ferry ports and have plenty of attractions – and usually book up faster than properties in areas further south, coastal locations booking first of all. Brittany has over 25 per cent (3,000km) of the French coastline (nowhere in Brittany is more than an hour's drive from the sea). The main disadvantage of these two regions compared to the south is the variable weather, although for many British people this isn't a major concern.

The department of Mayenne is an example of a poor area for letting: although it borders both Normandy and Brittany, the number of holiday weeks per property let there is a fraction of the neighbouring departments. Holidaymakers have heard of Normandy and Brittany; there are few that know of Mayenne. Delightful though it is, it has none of the advantages mentioned above, neither does it enjoy the hot climate of places further south and the seaside is a long day trip.

Look for undiscovered potential – areas such as Dordogne, though popular, are saturated (some owners report that, although several years ago they could easily let 20 weeks, they're now struggling to fill six). For example, there's currently a shortage of holiday accommodation in Meuse and Ardennes, where properties suitable for conversion to *gîtes* are available from around €50,000 to €150,000 and properties for extensive renovation start at around €20,000. The First World War battlefields and monuments, the attractive countryside and the accessibility for British holidaymakers on short breaks all create a demand here.

If your preferred area is somewhere you've been on holiday, it's likely to be a popular spot – but how many *gîtes* are there already, and what about the low season? If you aren't familiar with the area or areas you're considering, find out what attractions it has to offer and when they're available (many are closed or have limited opening times out of season). When targeting off-season breaks there's little point in advertising your proximity to attractions if they aren't open until after Easter, or close at the end of September.

2

Most *gîte* bookings are for a week or two weeks as opposed to B&B bookings, which are usually for an average of three nights. *Gîte* letting is therefore more dependent on there being plenty of interest in the surrounding area, with day trips to major attractions being possible.

The majority of holidaymakers go to places they've heard of, for one reason or another. Even if wanting to 'get away from it all' and spend a week or two in an isolated rural idyll, they will choose an area that's close to a well known attraction – e.g. a famous historical town, good bathing beaches, spectacular scenery or sporting facilities. Of two equally pretty cottages in a brochure, it's the one near the sea or a tourist hotspot that gets more bookings.

If a property isn't within half an hour's drive of the coast, it's worth seriously considering installing a pool. Some of the better agencies won't even consider taking a property on unless it has a pool or is near the coast. Installing a pool can add €20,000 or more to your set-up costs and a great deal to your running costs, but a much higher rental can be charged and/or more weeks can be sold.

For further information on where to buy and a guide to the regions, refer to *The Best Places to Buy a Home in France* (Survival Books – see page 314).

WHAT TO BUY

Once you've chosen the area, consider renting for a while before buying, so that your capital isn't tied up while you're researching properties for sale and finding the most suitable one. It's wise to take one or more *gîte* holidays in the area before setting up your own business – once you've been a customer, you're more likely to appreciate what is needed to satisfy the holidaymaker!

Carry out some research by asking agencies that operate in that area (see list on page 96 and **Appendix A**) what their criteria are and what type of accommodation most of their clients are looking for. They will advise on the best type of property, the ideal number of bedrooms, whether or not you need a swimming pool to generate sufficient bookings, and the level of comfort required by their clients.

If you would like to register your property with the Tourist Board or an organisation such as Gîtes de France, ensure that the property will be able to meet its criteria (see page 69 and **Appendix E**). Consider also the following factors:

- **local access** – Rural locations are desirable, but remember that many people's idea of the countryside is idyllic rather than realistic. A great deal of the countryside is covered in mud – if your property has access by a private lane or drive, it must have a hard surface or gravel. Although your guests may arrive in a four-wheel drive vehicle, this doesn't necessarily mean they expect to be driving off-road!

- **noise** – What are the neighbours like? Neighbouring farms can be noisy and smelly places. Incessantly barking dogs, crowing cockerels and loud farm machinery don't make for a peaceful holiday retreat. Will the farmer be herding his Holsteins down your lane at 6am and 6pm for milking? Cows in neighbouring fields are pretty but can cause smells and flies. Cockerels are impressive but crow early in the morning, as soon as they see light, as well as on and off throughout the day; and in the lambing season they're often set off when the farmer is attending to the sheep in the middle of the night. If they're your own, you'll be used to it, but keep them shut in until a reasonable hour so that your guests aren't disturbed. If the property is adjoining another, whether your own home or another *gîte*, it must be sufficiently soundproof so that guests won't be disturbed by others' activities at any time of night or day (and so that they won't disturb you!). Finally, if you're thinking of buying in a village, find out when the local church bell rings and how loudly; some are set to chime as early as 6am, when they sound twice as loud as during the day.

- **garden** – In general, the type of person booking a *gîte* holiday is looking for peace and tranquillity. A typical *gîte* is a detached cottage with two to four bedrooms and its own enclosed garden or grounds. Avoid buying a property with too much land; your guests are unlikely to spend their time playing cricket or strolling around the grounds (although this could be an advantage if you use it as a selling point) – and they certainly won't help with the gardening! On the other hand, people staying in *gîtes* won't want to go out every day, so they must have a private outdoor area –

preferably a sunny garden – in which to relax, eat, play and generally enjoy their holiday. It's preferable that this space is enclosed, especially if you cater for families with young children.

If you do allow access to a larger part of your grounds, make sure there are no hazards (e.g. ponds, holes in the ground, old tractor parts hidden in long grass or animal mess) and that your insurance covers any accidents or damage (to clients as well as to your property). If you don't want to allow access, or don't have the appropriate insurance, you must make this clear (in writing as well as orally) that this is the case – 'entry at your own risk' won't do. Put up 'Private' signs and consider locking any barns or outbuildings if you don't want your garage or workshop treated as an adventure playground!

● **capacity** – Maintenance costs are proportional to a property's size; big isn't always better! On the other hand, there's demand for large properties sleeping 10 to 15 people. These are suitable for two or three families taking a holiday together or groups such as walking enthusiasts and other clubs and organisations. They book early for the high season, as groups have to co-ordinate their arrangements well in advance. Although you can obviously charge a lot more for a property of this size, you may not let as many weeks, as there's less demand outside school holidays for properties with more than two bedrooms. For maximum flexibility, you could consider two smaller adjoining units, which can be let individually or as one large property. There's also a good demand for one-bedroom cottages for couples wanting a quiet break or on a house-hunting trip, an additional advantage being that there's less wear and tear on properties that don't take children.

● **swimming pool** – Whether or not to install a swimming pool is one of the most important decisions to make, as this can double your income but greatly increases your costs and maintenance time. If you cannot afford, or have decided not to install a swimming pool, consider buying an above-ground pool. **In today's competitive market, many agencies won't consider promoting properties without pools unless they're very near the coast.**

An unsuitable property in an ideal location might work, provided it has the potential for renovation and conversion within your budget, but it's obviously preferable to find a property that's suitable for the purpose. For further information on buying property, refer to *Buying a Home in France* (Survival Books – see page 314).

BUYING A BUSINESS

Instead of setting up a *gîte* business from scratch, you can buy an existing business – there are plenty on the market. The major disadvantage of buying a business is the cost: an established *gîte* business with a good income will cost you at least €300,000 and possibly as much as €1m – depending on the size and quality of the property, how many units are in operation, the reputation of the business and the number of contacts and regular clients it has attracted. This cost is obviously in addition to the cost of your principal residence. You won't have the freedom to arrange and style the accommodation as much as you might wish, without spending an unnecessary amount of money.

On the other hand, there are several possible advantages to buying a business, including the following:

- You won't have to spend time and money renovating or adapting buildings for use as *gîtes*.

- You will (or should, if you buy a successful business) have guaranteed income from the outset, which reduces your marketing costs and lessens the risk.

- You won't be setting up in competition to existing *gîtes* and so further diluting the market, but will in effect be buying a slice of the market.

The various French property magazines (see **Appendix B**) carry advertisements for *gîte* businesses, which can also be found via the internet (see **Appendix C**). A website that specialises in *gîte* properties is 🖥 www.gitecomplexes.co.uk.

You should look for a business that has room for expansion and improvement – e.g. space for a pool, or a building that could be converted into a games room or an additional accommodation unit. Above all, check that the owners aren't exaggerating their profits or the potential of the site; ask for detailed accounts for the past few years. Do your own independent research, and ask the right questions, including the following:

- Why are they selling?
- Are there confirmed bookings for the coming season?
- How do they market the property?
- Do they keep a database of previous customers and their comments?
- Does the price include the fixtures and fittings?

- Does the price include any of the furniture? If it does, is it worth buying or would it need replacing?

If possible, buy a business in the autumn, to give yourself time to settle in, make any necessary alterations, do some marketing and (if necessary) improve your French before welcoming your first guests the following spring.

2

CONVERSION

Probably the most common conversions for *gîtes* are farm buildings, which can make ideal letting properties. On the other hand, such buildings may be in a poor state of repair, not having been used for decades, and lack basic services such as water and electricity. When buying, you must ensure that planning permission is obtainable, even making it a condition of purchase, and ensure there's sufficient land for drainage (e.g. a septic tank), a pool and other utilities. Planning permission is a complex subject and is beyond the scope of this book; for detailed information, refer to *Renovating & Maintaining Your French Home* (Survival Books – see page 314).

If you're converting a building or buildings that are part of a property where you live yourself, consider privacy – yours and that of your guests. Your guests are on holiday, you aren't, and some will waylay you at any time of day (or night) for a long chat when you want or need to be doing other things. If possible, plan your conversion so that you both have private outdoor space and you have an entrance away from that of the *gîte*. This way your guests won't feel that they're being scrutinised every time they leave or return (and nor will you!).

When considering a property for conversion, don't overestimate the number of bedrooms it will accommodate; bear in mind the space required for other areas. There's no point having sleeping space for eight people if you can only fit in a dining table that will seat six, or if half of your guests have to stand to watch television. If you aren't experienced at converting buildings and working out the potential accommodation layout, employ a surveyor or architect.

Note that large farmhouses with plenty of outbuildings in good repair are now few and far between in many parts of France. It may be preferable to buy a small village house, which is easier to maintain and service and can be sold at any time should the need arise.

If you already own a property and want to convert one or more buildings into *gîtes*, there are a number of points to consider:

- Are you able to obtain planning permission?

- Are you in a region and location where the number of weeks you can let makes it a viable proposition?

- If you aren't near the coast, are you prepared to install (and maintain) a pool – and are you able to?

2

- Do you have noisy neighbours or barking dogs nearby? Or seasonal nuisances such as farmers working combine harvesters all night in the harvest season?

- Is the building itself suitable and does it meet the relevant standards (see page 69 and **Appendix E**)?

- Will your existing *fosse septique* cope with the extra load? (If not, have you budgeted for installing a new one?)

- Will the building you're planning to convert photograph well or will it still look like a grain store or a pigsty? This is the first impression people have of a holiday property: they browse photographs, **then** read the price, **then** the details.

Above all, draw up a detailed budget for the project, and expect start-up costs to exceed your most pessimistic prognostications!

LETTING A SECOND HOME

If you have a second home in France, you may want to let it out as a *gîte* to gain some extra income or help pay the mortgage. All the previous points about location and suitability should obviously be borne in mind, but here are also other matters to consider. If you live in the property for part of the year it will suffer more wear and tear than a property maintained exclusively as a holiday let; conversely you'll have to put up with other people inflicting damage and wear on your precious 'bolt hole'. Make sure you're realistic about its suitability and that it's maintained to a high enough standard for people to pay good money to stay there. Whilst you might be prepared to put up with little quirks and minor irritations such as a sticking window or an underpowered shower, paying guests must not be expected to do the same.

SURVIVAL TIP
You must de-clutter before letting – clients have to feel that they're occupying their own space rather than camping out in someone else's home.

LEGAL CONSIDERATIONS

Before establishing a *gîte*, it's wise to obtain legal advice and contact your *mairie* regarding local regulations. Various rules and regulations apply to the letting of property in France and, if you're buying a property with the express intention of setting up *gîtes*, you should make sure that permission will be granted **before** you buy, or make obtaining permission a condition of purchase (though this may not be possible).

2

Registering a holiday let property as a business isn't necessarily obligatory (see below), and other types of registration (e.g. with Gîtes de France) are optional. If you're planning to buy a community property (e.g. an apartment), you must check whether there are any restrictions on letting. If you have a mortgage on the property, it's essential that you have written permission for the letting from the lender.

If you're considering letting your property long term (e.g. during the winter), you should be aware that lets of more than three months are subject to different rules and regulations (see **Longer Lets** on page 112).

Registering as a Business

Registering your *gîte* activity as a business is mandatory if the income is your only source **or** the main source **or** amounts to more than €23,000. If the income is less than this figure **and** less than 50 per cent of your total earnings, you're considered to be a non-professional landlord (*loueur en meublé non-professionnel/LMNP*). You may, in this case, choose to make a business registration if it suits your circumstances, but it isn't obligatory. If you're classed as an *LMNP*, there are two tax disadvantages: any capital gains on selling the property are taxed under private capital gains tax rules, and you cannot offset any losses against your main income, although they can be carried forward for five years against future rental income. The main advantage is that you can operate under the simplified *micro-BIC* tax regime (see page 172).

If you earn €23,000 or more per year **or** if the earnings represent more than 50 per cent of your total income, letting furnished property is considered a professional activity. You're deemed to be a *loueur en meublé professionel/LMP* and you **must** register with the local Chambre de Commerces. You'll pay higher social security contributions, but you can offset any losses against your total income (provided the losses don't result from depreciation) and you may be exempt from capital gains tax (your earnings must be under a certain limit and you must have been letting for at least five years).

Recent reports suggest that the French government and tax authorities are investigating foreign owners and internet property rental sites in order to clamp down on unregistered businesses and tax evasion.

2 Holiday Rental Law

In general, short-term furnished rentals are exempt from the *Loi Mermaz* (1989), which is designed to protect the rights of long-term tenants in unfurnished accommodation but a number of other laws apply. The main points of holiday rental law are explained below.

Contracts

A booking is made by signing a contract or by a simple exchange of letters. Two copies of the contract or letter must be signed when the booking deposit is paid (see below). One copy must be given to the client, who must agree to the clauses contained in it. A description of the accommodation must be included if it doesn't have an official grading. The contract or letter must also detail the following:

- the duration of the rental;
- the price (which must not vary with the number of occupants);
- the responsibilities of the owner and tenant, which can be anything you choose, e.g. that the owner should provide x, y and z and tenants should leave the accommodation as they found it, not invite friends and family who aren't listed as guests to stay, and should supervise their children in and near the pool;
- the deposits and guarantee, if applicable (see **Deposits** below);
- the cancellation conditions;
- details of the *taxe de séjour*, if applicable (see page 177).

Property Description

You (or your representative), on being asked, must give every client a signed description of the property in which they will be staying, containing:

- the address of the property;

- the grading category (if applicable);

- the nature and standard of the property;

- the arrangement of the interior and the furnishings;

- the terms and price of the rental and any supplements.

2

Deposits

There are two types of deposit to consider:

Booking deposit: The deposit paid when reserving a holiday is the booking deposit (*dépôt de réservation*); in French law there are two types: *arrhes* and *acompte*. If the client pays an *arrhes*, he loses it if he cancels at any time. If the owner cancels, he must pay the client twice the amount of the deposit. If the client pays an *acompte* and he cancels, he must pay the whole amount due; if the owner cancels, he can simply return the deposit, but the client may claim damages. If the type of deposit isn't specified, it's assumed to be an *arrhes*, so it may be to your advantage to specify that it's an *acompte*. If your contract is in English and simply uses the word 'deposit', you should stipulate the conditions under which it may be returned in full or in part.

If you, the owner, take the booking deposit, there are no restrictions: you may charge as much or as little and take it as far in advance as you wish. If an intermediary (e.g. an agent) is handling the transaction, the deposit cannot be more than 25 per cent of the total price or be taken more than six months in advance.

Security deposit: You should also take a security or guarantee deposit (*dépôt de garantie*), in case anything is damaged or broken. For a booking made without an intermediary (e.g. an agent), you should ask for the deposit to be paid on entering the property (and provide a receipt). You have the right to bank the deposit. For a booking made with an intermediary, the deposit is collected by the intermediary; it's a maximum of 25 per cent of the rental and cannot be taken more than six months in advance. The intermediary may charge you commission on the deposit. The security deposit is usually returned at the end of the stay, less an amount for breakages and other unusual costs incurred as a result of the tenancy. The contract must specify the time for the deposit to be returned. You may choose to send it back within, say, a week of the holiday's end if there's no opportunity to inspect the property until after the guests have departed but this condition **must** be made clear on the contract.

Cancellation

A booking may be cancelled, even if an advance payment has been made, but the consequences depend on whether the deposit was an *arrhes* or an *acompte* (see above).

2

Foreign Visitors

Since 1999, foreign visitors (including EU nationals) must fill in and sign a 'police card' (*fiche de police*) – obtainable from the *préfecture* – with the following information: their name and surname, date and place of birth, nationality, and the address of their normal residence. In theory, these cards must be handed in on the day of arrival to the local police or *gendarmerie*; in practice, you might be met with a look of bemusement! If this happens, ask if it's necessary to do this; you may be allowed simply to keep the cards on file.

Further Information

Further information about holiday rental law can be obtained from:

- your local (departmental or regional) Office du Tourisme or Syndicat d'Initiative – listed in yellow pages under *Offices de Tourisme* – and the national tourist board website (💻 www.tourisme.gouv.fr);

- your local Centre de Documentation et d'Information de l'Assurance (listed on 💻 www.ffsa.fr);

- the Fédération Nationale des Agents Immobiliers (FNAIM, 💻 www.fnaim.fr);

- the Syndicat National des Professionnels de l'Immobilier (SNPI, 💻 www.snpi.com).

REGISTRATION

There's no obligation to register with any of the recognised *gîte* organisations, but depending on your target clientele it may be to your advantage to do so.

The simplest form of registration is with your local Comité Départemental du Tourisme (CDT), which will then publicise your *gîte* for you. However, many tourist offices won't publicise your accommodation unless it's graded under their own system or registered with Gîtes de France or Clévacances. It may, in fact, be a Gîtes de France or Clévacances representative who performs the inspection, as they work closely together. This requirement is becoming increasingly frequent – ask your CDT for advice on whether it applies in your area. Some tourist boards charge for inspections, others don't, and the registration fee varies. Similarly, some charge for advertising (e.g. around €15), while others don't. Again, it's wise to check local regulations with your CDT.

The best known accommodation 'label' in France is the Federation Nationale des Gîtes de France et du Tourisme Vert (normally referred to simply as Gîtes de France – see page 69), a national organisation formed in the early '50s. Another government-approved organisation, Clévacances (see page 72), introduced in 1997, regulates *gîte* and B&B accommodation. Unlike those of Gîtes de France, Clévacances properties aren't exclusively rural. There are a few smaller organisations, including the following:

- **Accueil Paysan** – mainly for farmers with a subsidiary letting business (see page 282);

- **Bienvenue à la Ferme** – also mainly for farmers with a subsidiary letting business (see page 282);

- **Fleurs de Soleil** – deals with upmarket self-catering accommodation, but has only around 400 properties and is little known (see page 289).

Advantages & Disadvantages

There are advantages and disadvantages to registering with an officially recognised organisation. The advantages include the following:

- You're 'buying into' a recognised brand name, which appears on your publicity material and signs. According to a poll carried out (among French nationals) by the Institut Français d'Opinion Publique on the reputation of tourism businesses, the brand name Gîtes de France appeared third, below only Club Méditerranée and Nouvelles Frontières.

- You benefit from the organisation's promotional and publicity material (catalogues, internet site, etc.).

- Your accommodation will be known to meet certain recognised standards, which reassures clients.

2

- You'll attract a greater number of French visitors (who constitute 80 per cent of GdF's market).
- You may not be able to advertise your *gîte* with the local tourist board unless it's registered.
- You might not have to pay *taxe d'habitation* on the *gîte* (see page 176).
- You might be eligible for a grant (see **Grants** on page 189).
- You can use the organisation's booking system.
- You're supplied with documentation (e.g. contract forms).
- You can obtain free advice (e.g. on setting up your business).
- You have access to financial and legal assistance.

Disadvantages of registering with an officially recognised organisation may include the following:

- the cost of registration (see below);
- the cost of adapting your premises to meet their standards;
- adherence to their grading standards, some of which may seem odd to non-French people, e.g. you need provide only a two-ring hob (and no oven or kettle) for fewer than six people, but you must have a pressure cooker, an electric food mixer and a salad spinner! (see **Appendix E**);
- If you take advantage of a set-up grant from Gîtes de France (see **Grants** on page 189), you're tied to the organisation's booking system for a considerable time – up to ten years.
- Clientele are on average 80 per cent French, and the French are 'conservative' in their choice of holiday periods, which may limit the number of weeks you can sell; you would be able to fill the last week of July and the first two weeks of August ten times over, but bookings might be sparse for the rest of the year.
- Pricing is structured around French holidays, so that high season is limited to around six weeks in the summer.
- Marketing is mainly aimed at the French, although the major organisations have increased their overseas marketing in recent years. Gîtes de France, for example, has reciprocal advertising with some British agencies, but not all *gîtes* appear in the overseas advertising, making this somewhat of a lottery.

● Rents are often lower than can be obtained by direct marketing focused on British and other overseas clients.

 You may be asked to house people who have been evicted from social housing for several months in the low season. If they have no fixed abode, it may be difficult or impossible to get rid of them, so you should take legal advice before accepting tenants on this basis.

2

You can choose to take bookings directly, while benefiting from Gîtes de France accreditation; Gîtes de France grades your property and supplies contract forms and the familiar green signs, but you arrange your own publicity, including advertising at your local tourist office (many tourist offices won't advertise a *gîte* unless it's registered with one of the recognised organisations), and are responsible for bookings.

Gîtes de France

The original aim of Gîtes de France (GdF, La Maison des Gîtes de France et du Tourisme Vert, 59 rue Saint-Lazare, Paris 75439 Cedex 09, ☎ 01 49 70 75 75, 🖳 www.gites-de-france.fr) was to help struggling farmers earn a supplementary income and to encourage economic growth by revitalising dying rural areas; its properties are therefore mainly rural. As GdF is allied with the Ministry of Tourism, properties are graded in conformity with the national classification defined by a law of 1st April 1997 according to a rating system of *épis* (wheat ears) – from one to five – similar to the more familiar star ratings for hotels (see **Appendix E** for details).

GdF sends a representative to inspect the property and, if applicable, advises you on planning procedures and renovation costs, and provides an estimate of the expected rental income.

Gîtes de France has an office in each department capital and, as these are autonomously run, many of the regulations and standards are specific to a department (see Appendix E for addresses).

Categories

Your property is registered in one or more categories. *Gîtes Ruraux* (the plural of *rural*) is the main category of *gîtes* with GdF; there are also *Gîtes* d'Étape and Gîtes de Séjour, which are for large groups, and Gîtes d'Enfants, for children. Within the Gîtes Ruraux category are the sub-categories listed below. If your gîte qualifies as a Gîte Bienvenue Bébé, for example, it's 'flagged' as such in the GdF brochure, to attract those looking for baby-friendly accommodation.

2

- Gîtes Accessibles aux Personnes Handicapées – must have wheelchair access approved by the Association des Paralysés de France;

- Gîtes Bienvenue Bébé – offering all equipment necessary for the care and comfort of babies up to two years old, e.g. cot, highchair, potty, changing facilities, enclosed garden, protected electric sockets and stair gate;

- Gîtes de Caractère – in a building or buildings particular to the region, carefully restored and preserved;

- Gîtes de Charme – selected for their 'charm';

- Gîtes à la Ferme – as the name suggests, situated on a working farm belonging to the 'Bienvenue à la Ferme' network;

- Gîtes de Jardin – properties whose proprietors share their knowledge of gardening with their guests;

- Gîtes de Mer – must be within 2km (1.2mi) of the coast and within 10km (6mi) of a seaside resort, with equipment suitable for seaside holidays, including deckchairs, beach games and parasols;

- Gîtes de Neige – 'snow gîtes', which must be no more than 15km (11mi) from a ski resort;

- Gîtes Panda – situated in regional or national parks, offering nature trails and wildlife watching, under the jurisdiction of the World Wildlife Foundation;

- Gîtes de Pêche – with fishing facilities, information and equipment hire available on site or nearby.

Additional labels are available, including Séjours Équestres for gîtes offering riding holidays and Séjours en Vignoble for those on wine-growing estates, offering information about viticulture, tours of the winery and wine tasting. GdF also gives its label to campsites and to chambres d'hôte.

Fees & Conditions

There's an annual contract and fee, which varies by department; for example, in some departments the fee is €15 for each rental, in others it's 50 per cent of the cost of one week's rental in high season per year.

Conditions vary from one department to another and you should seek advice from the relevant departmental office (see **Appendix E** for addresses). For example, properties must usually be available for a minimum of three months of the year.

Grants & Services

If you choose to register with GdF, you can apply for a grant to convert your property (see **Grants** on page 189), which must be applied for before you start work. There are also tax concessions available, including possible exemption from *taxe d'habitation* on the *gîte* if it's part of your main residence (e.g. an outbuilding you've converted, on the same site as your main house). If you've accepted a grant, it's obligatory to be signed up with GdF's booking service, normally for eight to ten years (the duration varies by department). There's a clause in the agreement whereby you agree not to sign up with any other booking services, which can be very restrictive.

GdF publishes numerous guides, in which your accommodation is listed as appropriate:

- **national guides** – one for new *gîtes*; one for *Gîtes d'Etape and Gîtes de Séjour* and one for *Gîtes de Charme*;

- **themed guides** – one each for *Séjours à la Neige, Séjours Nature au Coeur des Parcs Naturels, Séjours Pêche*, and *Séjours à la Ferme* (including both *Gîtes Ruraux* and *chambres d'hôte*);

- **regional guides** – Corsica (*Gîtes Ruraux* and *chambres d'hôte* – 934 properties listed), Normandy (2,400 *gîtes*), Brittany (4,500 *gîtes*) and Midi-Pyrénées (4,500 *gîtes*). Other regions and departments have smaller guides; some are grouped, such as Ardèche-Drôme (2,000 *gîtes*) and Massif-Central (4,000 *gîtes* in Auvergne and Limousin). A full list is on the GdF website (🖳 www.gites-de-france.fr).

Once you're registered with GdF, you may use its booking service (*service de réservation*), whereby GdF in effect acts as your agent, handling all bookings and contracts between you and your clients, although you aren't obliged to (unless you've had a grant). It's possible to register with GdF if you live outside France, but you **must** in this case have an agent or caretaker nearby to deal with maintenance and to handle changeovers. Grants, concessions and services vary from one department to another and you should seek advice from your departmental office (see **Appendix E** for addresses).

2 Clévacances

The other official French organisation regulated by the Ministry of Tourism is Clévacances, which has two main categories of accommodation: *La Location Clévacances* for self-catering accommodation, and *La Chambre Clévacances* for B&B (see page 136). There are around 24,000 Clévacances *gîtes* registered in 80 departments. Unlike Gîtes de France, Clévacances handles urban as well as rural properties, including houses, flats and maisonettes.

Properties are graded with one to five *clés* or keys (the maximum for apartments and studio flats is four), a similar system to GdF's *épis* or tourist board stars. The standards for the various grades are detailed in **Appendix E**. You'll notice that French priorities can be different from those of the British or Americans, for example – even for the lowest grade, your property must have a pressure cooker, but it's permissible to have a two-ring burner rather than a proper cooker; and a salad spinner is considered more important than a kettle! Three main criteria are taken into account, as follows:

- the environment, i.e. the quality of the building, the site and its surroundings and absence of nuisances such as noise and smells;

- the quality of the interior, i.e. comfort, furnishings, decoration, facilities, and the arrangement and function of rooms;

- the welcome and assistance offered by the owner or caretaker.

For an inspection by a Clévacances representative (which can cost from €100) you must apply to the relevant Comité Départemental du Tourisme or the local tourist office. The inspection must be made in the presence of the owner or caretaker (and possibly an inspector from the CDT). The inspector prepares a report, which is submitted to the departmental *préfecture* for assessment and grading (according to the ministerial decree for standards in tourist accommodation). Subject to a satisfactory inspection, you receive accreditation from Clévacances and a grading of one to five *clés*. If your property isn't accepted, you must pay a forfeit fee of around €40. The annual registration fee, payable in October, is around €70. (Charges vary from one department to another; ask at your CDT). Further information is available from the Clévacances website (⌨ www.clevacances.com).

FINANCIAL CONSIDERATIONS

If you're a second home owner, you might just want to earn a little extra money from your property, which would otherwise be standing empty, when you aren't using it, and you may be tempted to let it for a nominal rent to be sure of attracting clients. Bear in mind, however, that there's little point in letting if you barely cover your costs (marketing, cleaning, etc.) and that you might as easily obtain the going rate. You must also take into account depreciation through wear and tear. Moreover, if you under charge, you won't make yourself popular with those in the area who are trying to make a living from *gîte* rental!

Conversely, if you're running your *gîte* as a business, bear in mind that you might be up against competition from second home owners who let at low rates, even in high season, which will obviously make it more difficult for you to charge a commercially viable rent.

In any case, one *gîte* won't generate enough income to live on and, however many you intend to run, you must budget carefully.

Letting Rates

In order to calculate what you should or can charge, research what other owners are charging – find similar properties sleeping the same number and with the same facilities as your accommodation and make a note of the prices, bearing in mind, of course, that they might not actually have any bookings! Some sites have availability calendars, which you can use to check which ones are letting well. Also, check with agencies – they know which type of property lets for what amount in which locations and can advise on what to charge. Take an average figure and see how this works in your calculations (see **Viability** below).

Letting rates vary considerably according to the time of year, the area, and the size and quality of a property. A house sleeping six in an average area can be let for around €750 to €1,000 per week in high season. A luxury property in a popular area with a pool and accommodation for 8 to 12 can be let for between €4,000 and €6,000 per week in high season. If you're letting to the non-French market, high season generally includes the months of July and August and possibly the first two weeks of September. The mid-season usually comprises June, September and October (and possibly

Easter, Christmas and New Year), when rents are usually around 25 per cent lower than in high season; the rest of the year is low season. Rates are much lower for winter lets, when you shouldn't expect to earn more than around €500 per week or €2,000 per month in most regions for a *gîte* sleeping six.

Before you can set your rates (unless, of course, you use an agency that sets them for you), you should take into account the following factors:

- **Supply & demand** – There's a fundamental relationship between price and quantity: consumers buy greater numbers of a product at a lower unit price than at a high price. For example, if the price of a week's rental is €200, you might sell 15 weeks; if it's €400, you might sell ten weeks; if it's €600, you might only sell five. Based on these assumptions, you would take most money by charging €400 (15 x €200 = €3,000, 10 x €400 = €4,000 and 5 x €600 = €3,000).

  The actual number of weeks you can sell at each rate largely depends on demand, which in turn is dependent on the competition. There might be other *gîtes* in the same area, similar properties in the same brochure or on the same website, properties that offer added value in terms of facilities (e.g. a pool) or have an established clientele. Identify what the competition is charging and take this into account when pricing your property.

- **Gross & net revenue** – Using the above example, if your costs were €50 per unit per week, your net revenue would also be highest at a letting rate of €400. (Gross revenue minus costs = net revenue.) At €200 per week your net revenue would be €3,000 – (15 x €50) = €2,250. At €600, your net revenue would be €3,000 – (5 x €50) = €2,750. At €400, it would be €4,000 – (10 x €50) = €3,500.

- **Break-even point** – The next step, based on a reasonable projection of fixed and variable costs, is to establish your break-even point, which is when takings are equal to costs. This is the minimum you'll need to charge **before** you start to make a profit. Experiment with differing prices and numbers of weeks using the equation $P \times N = F + (V \times N)$ where P is the price, N the number of weeks, F the fixed costs, and V the variable costs.

- **Yield** – The yield on a property is the profit on your investment (after the deduction of expenses, but before tax), which can be compared with the gain on other types of investment, such as shares. Generally, the cheaper the property, the higher the yield. For example, if you buy a property for €100,000 and the gross receipts for your letting in one year total €12,000, your gross yield is 12 per cent. If you buy a property for €200,000, you're unlikely to be able to let it for €24,000 to achieve the same yield; you might only take €16,000, in which case your gross yield will be 8 per cent.

Viability

To ascertain the viability of a *gîte* business, you must estimate your gross annual revenue, i.e. your earnings before expenses and taxes, which depends on the number of weeks you let and the rates you charge (see **Letting Rates** above).

2

Then you must establish the following:

- your initial capital outgoing, including the purchase price of the property you intend to buy and the cost of restoration or renovation, equipment and fittings;

- the fixed and variable expenses you expect to incur each year relating to the property and business.

Fixed costs include mortgage payments, most maintenance expenses, taxes and insurance, which decrease per unit the more units you have. Variable costs are those that change according to the number of weeks and/or units sold, e.g. agent's fees, cleaning and laundry costs, wages, consumables, marketing, repairs, maintenance and (re)decorating. Void periods (when the property is unoccupied, between lets) also count as expenses.

Expenses must be deducted from your gross income in order to calculate your net income and net yield. For example, if you buy a €200,000 property, earn €16,000 a year in rent and have annual expenses of €6,000, you have a net income of €10,000. Your net yield is therefore €10,000 divided by €200,000 = 0.05, multiplied by 100 = 5 per cent – but bear in mind that you still have to pay tax on your net income. Note that you should always use the current market value of a property to calculate the yield.

If your property is divided between your own accommodation and one or more *gîtes*, base your calculations proportionally – for instance if you paid €480,000 for the whole, and your own house is worth one third of that figure, your yield should be calculated on the remaining €320,000.

Charging for Extras

It's generally acceptable to charge extra for certain services, including the following:

- **heating** – You can charge a fixed figure at certain times of the year according to the climate in your area or, with electric heating, read the meter on arrival and departure. Many owners include an allowance (e.g.

8kwh per person per day) in the rental price that covers lighting and hot water, any surplus being charged for. This is fair – some guests leave all the radiators on all the time with the windows open while others are more conscious of the cost and of energy conservation. If the heating system is wood or coal-fired, combustibles may be included in the rental price or charged at cost, or you can supply an initial quantity and charge thereafter.

- **cleaning** – *Gîte* clients are normally expected to leave the property clean, but even if they're scrupulous you'll have to clean and tidy before the next guests arrive. Nevertheless, most contracts include a clause to the effect that a charge will be deducted from the security deposit if 'excessive' cleaning is required. You might want to include cleaning in the price of rental as an added selling point but this may be an invitation to clients to leave the place in a mess. Some agencies advertise that cleaning is included, but this doesn't mean the property can be left filthy. Beware of agencies that sub-contract through travel companies in other countries and don't send clients full booking conditions; if this is the case, make sure guests are aware of any requirement to clean before they leave.

> **SURVIVAL TIP**
> **Make sure any extra charges are clearly stipulated in the contract.**

Taxation

An important consideration for anyone running a *gîte* in France is taxation, which includes property tax, income tax and in some cases other local and special taxes (see **Chapter 4**).

 You must declare tax in France on all income from property letting, irrespective of where you live.

Before buying a property for letting, you should obtain expert advice regarding French taxes. This will (hopefully) ensure that you take maximum advantage of your current tax status and that you don't make any mistakes that you'll regret later.

FACILITIES

Clients expect certain facilities – particularly a swimming pool, telephone and television. There are many considerations to be made in respect of these, detailed below.

2

Swimming Pool

Having a swimming pool can significantly increase your letting potential and your income; it also significantly increases your costs, and you must weigh up the advantages and disadvantages before deciding whether to install a pool and what type of pool to install.

To maximise your letting, a pool is essential – and some letting agencies won't handle properties without a pool unless they're near a beach, lake or river where swimming is possible. It's usually necessary to have a private pool with a single-family home, but a shared pool is sufficient for an apartment or townhouse. You can ask higher rent for a property with a pool and can charge up to double for a property with a private (not shared) pool.

Cost

According to a report by the International Swimming Pool Exhibition, the cost of installing or building a private pool varies from €6,000 to €18,000, with an average of €12,500. The price depends mainly on whether the pool is prefabricated or custom built. The report also indicates that annual pool maintenance (including depreciation, e.g. of a cover and liner) costs €587 and chemical products (de-scaling, pH control, algaecides, chlorine and bactericides) €247. This means a total cost of around €20,000 over ten years, or €2,000 per year (without allowing for inflation) that must be recouped in **extra** net letting income just to break even. These figures exclude the cost of heating a pool, which can add thousands of euros per year.

The most economical option is a kit pool, which costs from €4,000 to €14,000 depending on size. They come with prefabricated sections for the vertical structure, a liner and filtering and purification equipment. The seller will be able to recommend installation companies. For a medium budget, you can buy a fibreglass shell, made in one piece, which must be installed by specialists. This costs between around €9,000 and €18,500. A more luxurious option is a cast concrete pool, costing from €15,000 upwards, which also requires professional installation.

Your budget must include excavation and installation, accessories, maintenance products and pool cleaning equipment, safety systems (see below), heating equipment if applicable, steps and terraces, landscaping and poolside furniture, electricity and water supply and, if applicable, fuel for heating the water.

Further information is available via the internet, and the following websites are particularly useful:

🖳 www.eauplaisir.com – This site has a lot of practical information, a readers' forum and a newsletter, as well as product descriptions.

🖳 www.irrijardin.com – Irrijardin offers a wide range of products and the site provides comprehensive information.

Regulations

Note that new safety regulations regarding pools used by the public, including pools at private homes that are let for holidays, came into force in 2004 (see below). Make sure you understand the regulations before installing a pool or letting a property.

Location: You aren't normally allowed to build a pool less than 3m from a boundary or within view of a road – the sight of half-naked bathers is believed to be the cause of many road accidents! Check with your town hall what local regulations apply.

Planning permission: Planning permission is required for any construction over 20m² (there's little point in installing a pool smaller than this).

Safety: A recent law requires that certain types of pool must be equipped with an approved safety system (*un dispositif de sécurité normalisé*).

Failure to comply with the regulations can lead to a fine of up to €45,000. If you haven't installed the required system and someone drowns in your pool, your third-party liability insurance could be invalid and you could be sued for millions of euros!

Pools inside a building and inflatable or demountable above-ground pools are exempt from the requirement. All other pools must have at least one of the following systems:

● **an alarm system** (*un système d'alarmes*) – conforming to national standard (*norme française* or *NF*) P90-307, costing around €900. An alarm must be no more than 7m from any point in the pool; this means that one alarm positioned in the middle of one of the long sides of a 10m x 5m pool is adequate, but two alarms are required for an 11m x 6m (or larger) pool. No more than two alarms may be used. Bear in mind also that you must remember to switch an alarm off before you swim and on again afterwards, and that , like a house or car alarm, it can easily be ignored!

● **an enclosure or roof** (*un abris*) – conforming to national standard P90-309. There are various types of enclosure, all of which are expensive and most of them unsightly. Fixed enclosures, costing around €7,500 for a 10m x 5m pool, are also difficult to remove when you want to swim or clean the pool; 'telescopic' enclosures are easy to slide back but cost around twice as much.

● **a barrier or fence** (*une barrière de protection*) – surrounding the pool no less than 0.5m from its edge and at least 1.1m high conforming to national standard P90-306. If you're letting a property, the fence must incorporate a self-closing (e.g. spring-loaded) gate. Fencing costs around €80 per linear metre (i.e. around €3,000 to fence a 10m x 5m pool). Although unsightly, fencing is generally recommended as the most practical system.

● **a safety cover** (*une couverture de sécurité*) – conforming to national standard P90-308. A safety cover, as opposed to an ordinary 'solar' cover, incorporates metal bars so that a child can walk on it without sinking into the pool; for this reason, it's heavy and difficult to roll up when you want to have a swim – for a 10m x 5m pool, two people are required! A safety cover costs around €1,800.

 Some letting agencies and even French insurers won't accept an alarm, enclosure or safety cover as the only safety system, as any of them can – inadvertently or otherwise – be left 'off'. Check before installing any of these systems.

Standards are set by the national standards agency, the Association Française de Normalisation (AFNOR, ☎ 01 41 62 76 44, 🖳 www.afnor.fr), but only general information (in French) is available from them; the standards themselves cost around €67 each and are incomprehensible to anyone but an engineer! However, a reputable pool installation company should have details of the latest requirements.

Sanitation: If you wish to install a pool which will be shared by two or more dwellings, its sanitation system must meet more stringent regulations, as the pool will be classed as 'semi-commercial' (*demi-commercial*).

Extending the Season

2

Even in southern France, the swimming season is normally limited to little more than half the year (e.g. April to October). In northern parts, you may be lucky to have five months of swimming. There are several ways you can extend the swimming season, which may help you to let your property outside the summer, including the following:

- **heating** – There are a number of ways to heat a pool to make it useable for a longer period or even all year round. However, not only is heating extremely costly, it's unlikely that your clients will want to swim (even in a heated pool) when it's pouring with rain or in the depths of winter.

- **indoor pool** – An indoor pool heats up slightly more quickly and retains its heat for slightly longer (a difference of maybe two or three weeks per year). There's the added advantage that you can swim on days when you wouldn't want to swim outdoors, e.g. when it's raining or there's a high wind. A covered pool also needs less cleaning, and safety systems (see above) aren't required, provided the pool room can be (and is) locked when the pool isn't in use. Disadvantages include the extra cost of walls and a roof, possible unsightliness of the construction, and the fact that in summer the air temperature can reach 50C or more.

- **covered pool** – It's possible to install a low removable roof, which doesn't require walls and provides some of the benefits of an indoor installation, but which obviously needs removing and replacing each time you want to use the pool.

- **cover** – A 'solar' cover helps not only to keep a pool clean but also to prevent heat gained during the day from being lost overnight.

For further information on installing, heating and maintaining a swimming pool, refer to *Renovating & Maintaining Your French Home* (Survival Books – see page 314).

Telephone

Most holidaymakers have mobile phones, but it's worth considering having a telephone installed in your property, especially if it's your own holiday home and you need it when you're there. Particularly if the French mobile networks don't have good coverage in your area or if there's no nearby payphone, a fixed line telephone can be a useful facility for guests – and a boon to your privacy if they receive calls from home with news of sick relatives or failed exams; if you live on site and have only one telephone (your own), your guests may give the number to all their friends and family, despite your pleas for it to be used for emergencies only! If you have a separate line installed for clients, you can ask France Télécom for a *service restreint* (FT calls it '*Téléséjour*'), which blocks usage apart from local, emergency and incoming calls. Details are available on France Télécom's website (💻 www.agence. francetelecom.com). Alternatively, guests can purchase a *Ticket Téléphone International* to make long-distance calls (to 75 countries) using a code number. These cards are available from France Télécom outlets, *tabacs* and newsagents', in denominations of €7.50 and €15.

Note that the installation of a telephone can be prohibitively expensive if there's no existing line.

Television

It's recommended to provide a television (TV) – either French terrestrial TV or an English-language satellite system depending on your clientele. Having the latter will increase bookings, especially during major European sporting events, while cartoons to keep the kids quiet seem to work in any language! **You must have a TV licence for each *gîte* that has a TV set.** If you live on site, your licence covers only sets in your home. A French television licence (*redevance audiovisuelle*) is charged as part of your *taxe d'habitation* (see page 176). Your annual tax return has a box to tick if you **don't** have a TV. The licence fee is €116.

A video/DVD player is increasingly becoming a 'must' in holiday accommodation. Most TV sets nowadays are multi-standard and should therefore be suitable for viewing both French and UK videos.

French Television

The six main French TV channels (TF1, France2, France3, Arté, France 5 and M6) can be received with a UHF roof aerial or with an analogue satellite receiver and dish, which is better in areas with poor reception. For Canal+ you need a subscription, a decoder and a VHF aerial. There are two digital satellite systems available in France: Canal Satellite and TPS. Canal Satellite carries the main terrestrial broadcasters except TF1, some films in

English, Sky News and BBC World programmes. TPS has all the French terrestrial broadcasters, some films in English, and BBC Prime and BBC World programmes. A French digital decoder (*terminal numérique*) and dish (*parabole*) cost around €80 to €100. You then pay a subscription for the service, which varies according to the package you choose. Details are available on the relevant websites (🖥 www.tps.fr, 🖥 www.canalsat.fr).

If you have French TV, give your guests a TV listings magazine for the week – most will be grateful for it and even those who don't watch TV may find the weather forecasts useful!

British Television

Any digital satellite receiver can receive the BBC, ITV and other 'free-to-air' (FTA) channels. (This shouldn't be confused with Freeview, a terrestrial service in the UK which uses set-top boxes.). The Astra 2D satellite, which provides the BBC FTA channels, covers most of France, though reception may be patchy in the south, where you might need a larger dish. You can find coverage maps for the Astra satellite on the Satcure site: 🖥 www.satcure.co.uk/2d/ and on the Astra2D website: 🖥 www.astra2d.com/astra 2d-france.htm.

Channels 4 and 5 are 'free to view' (FTV) – not the same as Freeview or free-to-air! To receive these you need a Sky digibox and a Sky card, obtainable only if you have a British address. You don't need a subscription. A new Sky digibox costs £200 to £300, second-hand ones much less, and a Sky card is currently £20. Although you can receive the Sky subscription channels outside the UK and Republic of Ireland, this contravenes the company's terms and conditions (yet there are countless expats who take their Sky systems abroad and it's difficult to see how this prohibition could ever be enforced).

A useful website, providing information about receiving British digital TV in France, is 🖥 www.bigdishsat.com.

Other Facilities

If you wish to attract guests outside the summer season, when a swimming pool is less of a draw, you should consider offering extra facilities, such as a table tennis or pool table, sports equipment, bicycles, table football and other indoor games, or a sauna, steam room and exercise equipment. Don't forget the potential appeal to business clients; you might convert a building into conference and meeting rooms, and offer (free) internet access (including wi-fi connection and webcam/video conferencing, perhaps), for example.

FURNISHINGS, FITTINGS & DECORATION

Furnishing a *gîte* is a compromise between style and durability. If you fill it with precious family heirlooms, some clients will think it wonderful – 'just like a magazine!' – whereas others will complain that the place is full of second-hand furniture and want their money back; others will break things or, in very rare cases, steal them. Furnishings must be durable and in excellent condition. If you install antiques, make sure they're robust enough for use by people who possibly won't appreciate their value, e.g. brass beds but not intricately carved wooden beds (little Johnny might decide he could improve the carving with his penknife or colour in the designs with permanent markers). A holiday cottage isn't a place to dump all the furniture that you don't want in your own house; on the other hand, it isn't worth spending a fortune on bespoke furnishings. A luxury or high-priced property must be furnished with quality fittings and equipment; a low-cost one must nevertheless be well equipped with good quality basics.

Furnishings and fittings should be easy to clean and maintain. In the peak season (and hopefully at other times of the year) you'll have only a few hours between departing guests and new arrivals to restore the property to pristine condition. Although most contracts include a clause to the effect that clients should leave the property clean, there's always plenty of work to be done and too little time in which to do it.

Those who let to non-French holidaymakers should be warned that, although their clients have booked a French country cottage, which traditionally has stone, tiled or wooden floors, many of them will expect to find fitted carpets throughout (their concept of a rural idyll, or indeed a French house, often bears little relation to reality!).

Ensuite bathrooms are desirable but not necessary (unless yours is a top-of-the-range property), but cottages sleeping more than six people should have more than one lavatory. Your guests will expect a good-sized fridge/freezer, washing machine and microwave oven, and, depending on the price, quality and capacity of the accommodation, possibly a dishwasher.

If you use the property yourself, have a lockable area where you can store your possessions when it's let.

Heating

Central heating is necessary if a property is to be let all year round. (Gîtes de France stipulates a minimum temperature of 19C if you let outside the summer season.) Otherwise, convection heaters that can be individually regulated are usually adequate. An open fire or a wood-burning stove is an added attraction, especially in winter, but you should bear in mind that it will add to your cleaning time between lets, and it shouldn't be the main heating method as some people won't want to fiddle about with laying and cleaning out fireplaces (though some love it!).

Decoration

Decoration should be light and bright, with fresh colours, not gaudy or too individualistic. Some people like frills and flounces, others prefer clean modern lines, so keep a happy medium. It's best to keep walls white or a standard off-white (*blanc cassé*), as it's then easier to redecorate. Use a brand of paint that you're likely to be able to buy again if (or rather when!) you need to touch up or repaint a wall.

Add colour with soft furnishings (throws, cushions, table covers, etc.) and rugs, plenty of pictures and a selection of bits and pieces to make the property welcoming. Chains such as Gifi and Casa and larger supermarkets sell inexpensive and attractive home décor.

Keep all appliances well maintained, door and window fastenings working, tile grouting whitened, light fittings working, and above all everything **clean**!

Sitting Room

You must provide sufficient comfortable seating for the maximum number of people for which your cottage caters. This might seem obvious, but it's often tempting to squeeze in extra bedrooms to increase the capacity (and consequently revenue) whilst not giving adequate consideration to the living space.

Sofas and armchairs must be matching and have stain-resistant, washable covers. One spare set is essential, two is advisable. Add throws, which are easier to clean than loose covers. Three-piece suites are generally far cheaper and better designed in the UK than in France, so consider buying there or get them from IKEA (🖳 www.ikea.com or 🖳 www.ikea.fr). Provide plenty of cushions – particularly if you have typical French furniture with wooden arms. Many French sofas are *canapé-lits* or *clic-clacs* (sofa-beds, usually rather unsightly!), which can be an advantage if you want to increase occupancy; most agencies, however, won't consider them as providing extra capacity and in any case they aren't usually comfortable and some are also very heavy to move when cleaning.

If you let to British clients and the floors are tiled, as is usual in most parts of France, consider laying a large carpet covering the main part of the floor, or plenty of rugs. Have a bookshelf with a good selection of paperbacks in good condition and some toys, board games and jigsaws. French versions of well known games such as Cluedo and Monopoly are always popular – everyone knows the rules so it's fun to play in another language. (Scrabble and Trivial Pursuit are also available for those whose French is up to it!)

Dining Area

Provide a large enough table with sufficient 'elbow-room' and with the appropriate number of sturdy dining chairs for the capacity of your *gîte*. Don't use a precious polished table. Varnished, easily cleanable surfaces are essential; you can buy excellent PVC tablecloths in France for everyday use and provide a fabric tablecloth for those who prefer to use one. Have a high chair available for small children (make sure it has the CE mark indicating conformation to EU standards).

Kitchen

The kitchen should be well equipped with utensils, crockery, appliances, glasses and cutlery. Make sure these are sufficient for the maximum number of people the property accommodates and that you have spares to hand. Some agencies and organisations require you to provide the exact quantity, others two of each (more if you have a dishwasher, especially teaspoons). All should be checked between visits and replaced or replenished as necessary. Make a careful compromise between quality and cost – choose crockery and cutlery that you can buy individually rather than in sets (teaspoons, for example, always go missing). Apply the same logic to cooking pans; it takes just one heavy-handed family to destroy the non-stick surfaces on a whole set of expensive pans. Alternatively, most supermarkets sell cheap and cheerful sets of crockery and pans which, if necessary, can be replaced each year – or more frequently if you have clumsy guests (but don't buy shoddy, cheap, bendy cutlery)!

If you're in a rural area, it's likely that you'll have bottled gas for cooking. Ensure that there are instructions for lighting the oven and for changing the gas bottle (if you're on site, it's best to do this yourself; better still to check between lets that there's enough gas left for the period of rental). Be aware that the connecting tube has a 'use-by' date – check that it hasn't passed.

2

French cookers often don't have separate grills, so you might like to provide one, and a microwave oven is normally expected, along with other electrical equipment such as a kettle and toaster (often lacking in French-owned properties!). If you're with a French organisation (e.g. GdF), its representative will insist on certain items you may not have thought of, such as a pressure cooker and salad spinner, and not even mention an electric kettle!

Other essential equipment and supplies include an iron and ironing board, a clothes line and pegs (if there's no room, a tumble drier must be provided – preferably both), a dustbin, mop and bucket, broom, dustpan and brush, vacuum cleaner, spare light bulbs, a torch, candles, matches, scissors, dishwasher tablets if necessary, and plenty of cleaning products, cloths and dusters.

Provide plenty of (mouse-proof) cupboard space for guests to store food and a large refrigerator with a freezer compartment. Check between lets that all food is removed.

Bedrooms

The number one requirement is solid beds with good mattresses. Give careful consideration to the number and type of beds in each room. Too many double beds limits the permutations of guests – if you have two large rooms, put a double bed in one and two singles in the other or, if there's space, a double and a single in each. If you have three bedrooms, make one a double and the other two twin-bedded. If there are three or more rooms, you could put bunk beds in one of them for children. (Bunk beds should be used **only** by children.)

If you want to install antique beds from a *brocante*, measure the length before buying, as some older beds are too short for modern mattresses. The mattresses must not, under any circumstances, be of a similar vintage! While comfort is subjective and you cannot please all tastes (some like their beds hard, some soft, some in-between), if the mattresses are new there's little that can be complained about. There's no shortage of good mattresses in France; every town has frequent visits from mattress-sellers – it's a national obsession.

Use waterproof mattress and pillow protectors, as people dribble in their sleep (not to mention other accidents that can occur). Keep a spare set and clean them between lettings.

Supply a cot for young children, ideally the 'umbrella' type (*un lit parapluie*) which folds down and can be stored in an unobtrusive place (make sure it has the CE mark, conforming to EU standards). It's normal for parents to bring their own cot linen, but keep a set just in case. A changing mat is also advisable – again, most parents bring their own, but it's cheaper to buy one than pay for extra cleaning of duvets and bedspreads.

Provide plenty of hanging space or a wardrobe, with shelves or a separate chest of drawers (or a dressing table with drawers), a mirror, a wastebasket and somewhere for guests to store empty suitcases. Other furniture might include a small table and a couple of chairs, and perhaps a bookshelf. Have a bedside table and lamp for each person and non-slip rugs beside each bed.

Bed Linen & Towels

In the past, it was normal practice for guests to take their own bed linen and kitchen towels (i.e. sheets, pillowcases, towels and tea towels) on self-catering holidays. Nowadays, there are three options regarding the provision of linen: you can ask clients to bring their own; you can hire (rent) it to them; or you can supply it, included in the rental price. Bear in mind that customers travelling by air won't be able to bring their own linen; if you're targeting this category of clients, it's therefore preferable to provide linen.

If you choose to hire linen, charge a set rate per person (between €12 and €15 per person per week is acceptable), which gives guests the choice of bringing their own. If you aren't on site or your caretaker isn't prepared to cope with laundry, you may decide to ask guests to bring their own, although this isn't recommended – it's a negative factor for many people and will affect the number of bookings you attract; you'll also get the occasional clients who don't bring any, thus soiling the mattress, duvet and pillows.

If you don't provide linen, or guests choose to bring their own, check on their arrival that they've brought enough for the number of beds they're going to use. Be subtle: say that if they've left anything at home, you're happy to lend it to them (and make sure you have spare linen available). You should also ask them not to use duvets and pillows without covers.

Generally, including linen in the rental price is the best option – guests' first impression of a bedroom will be far better if the beds are made up, and the last thing they want to do after a tiring journey is to start wrestling with duvets! Providing linen also ensures that beds and bedding are protected, and duvet covers and pillowcases fit properly – if you provide square pillows, British visitors' standard pillowcases won't fit, and duvets come in a variety of sizes.

Buy good quality bed linen; cheap sheets and pillowcases soon become thin and tired-looking. Consider sticking to white rather than colours and patterns – it's easier and cheaper to replace one item than to buy a whole new matching set. Cotton is best, but you may prefer polycotton for easier laundering. Pillows should have synthetic filling, as many people have allergies; you could keep some feather pillows in case guests request them. If you let out of season, have some winter-weight duvets. (Remember that *'duvet'* isn't the French word for duvet; although it's a French word, it refers to feather or down filling – the correct word is *couette*.)

2

Supply **at least** one bath towel and a hand towel for each person, plus bath mats, tea towels and a kitchen hand towel. Beach towels aren't normally included, but have a few available in case guests haven't brought their own.

Bathroom & WC

If the capacity of the *gîte* is more than six people, you should have more than one bathroom and WC. Ease of cleaning is the number one priority. Bathrooms and WCs need plenty of efficient ventilation. Shower cubicles with rigid sides are more expensive than those with curtains but far easier to clean. Tile as much as you can. France is well provided with shops offering a huge choice of tiling to suit all budgets and tastes; tiles are far easier to clean than painted walls and will cope far better with the moisture caused by a family of six each having two showers a day.

Provide plenty of shelving, a cabinet, and a mirror, clothes hooks and towel rails, a lidded waste bin and non-slip bath mats. Provide plenty of cleaning materials – it's to be encouraged!

If you have a septic tank, supply the appropriate toilet paper and disposal bags for sanitary products. (The latter aren't easily found in France but are sold in the major supermarkets in the UK so you might wish to stock up there – though you might attract some funny looks at the checkout!) Make sure there's a clearly displayed notice that warns of the horrendous consequences of anything unsuitable being flushed down the lavatory.

GARDEN & GROUNDS

The garden should have a lawn where children can play, which must be kept mown (sometimes twice a week in the wet, warm areas of France). Shrubs, trees and flowers should be fairly robust – children and teenagers aren't always careful with plants, so keep fragile and rare specimens in your own area of garden, where you can tend and enjoy them. Avoid plants with poisonous leaves and berries such as foxgloves, laburnum and yew. If you choose not to let to families with children, your adult guests will appreciate some well laid out flowerbeds.

If you have space, families appreciate an area for ball games, and a play area with a swing, small slide, etc. is a valuable addition. If space is limited and you provide any other outdoor equipment, limit the potential for damage and injury – badminton rackets and shuttlecocks are better than footballs, for example.

Supply a good quality set of garden furniture – a big enough table and sufficient chairs for the capacity of your *gîte*. Cheap plastic ones are a false economy; they will need replacing each year (or more often), as they scratch easily and can even be blown away and broken in sudden summer storms. Guests appreciate a few loungers or deckchairs, a parasol and some outdoor lighting so that they can sit outside in the evening. You can also supply mosquito-repellent candles in pots or jars for outdoor use.

A barbecue is a must for the summer season, either a built-in one or the smaller portable type that can be wheeled undercover for storage out-of-season.

Gravel must be weed-free – use a long-term systemic herbicide such as Herbatak that doesn't leach into flowerbeds and lawns. Patios and terraces, etc. must be equally well maintained with moss and algae removal products.

PRESENTATION

When you show visitors their *gîte*, their first impressions are all-important. Beds should be made, soft furnishings and cushions neatly arranged and towels folded. Everything must be spotlessly clean and should smell pleasant – make sure the property is thoroughly aired between lets. Put vases of fresh flowers in some of the rooms. Use house plants and ornaments to decorate, soften and add colour. If it's after dusk, turn on lights and draw the curtains; close the shutters if it's cold and wet outside and light a fire or turn on the heating (your visitors will be coming in from a warm car). You should be dressed neatly – don't welcome your guests in an apron and gardening boots! Making an effort and paying attention to detail creates an overall ambience enabling your guests to feel at home, and gives them a positive impression from the start of their holiday.

SERVICING & MAINTENANCE

It's essential to have someone to handle changeovers. It's unacceptable to rely upon outgoing guests to leave the property clean and ready for the subsequent clients. One person or a couple living on site or nearby might efficiently handle one or two *gîtes*, but if you have a greater number to run you must consider employing a cleaner and/or gardener if you're to maintain the properties to an acceptable standard.

The obvious advantages of handling your own changeovers are that it saves you money and you can 'keep your eye on the ball'. The personal touch also means a great deal to your guests. On the other hand, it means that you must be there every changeover day – and it's hard work!

The amount of laundry can be overwhelming, so look into the cost of sending a weekly load to your local *blanchisserie* – but beware: these vary in quality as well as price, and some iron more creases in than they remove!

Between lets you (or your caretaker) must carry out some, or all, of the following tasks. It helps to write a checklist tailored to the specific requirements of your own property.

- **bathroom & WC** – Clean, disinfect, remove old soap and toiletries, check bins, replenish cleaning products and toilet paper, check ventilator filter, wash floors, wash and polish tiles, taps and mirrors.

- **bedrooms** – Remove all used linen and towels, check that mattresses, pillows and protectors are clean and there aren't any socks or other unmentionables tucked under them, air and remake beds. Turn mattresses frequently. Vacuum (including under the beds), clean and polish. Check all drawers and hidden corners for lost property, then dust and polish them.

- **bins** – Check that they're all empty, wash and disinfect them and replace bags and liners.

- ceilings & beams – Dust, vacuum and remove cobwebs.

- **electrics** – Check that all appliances and switches are working, and change any blown light bulbs. Dust bulbs and lampshades.

- **floors** – Clean, bleach, vacuum or polish as appropriate, check under furniture and beds for stray items, dirt and dust.

- **furniture** – Clean, polish and check for damage. Check that drawers and cupboards are empty.

- **kitchen** – Clean surfaces, check the fridge and icebox (defrost if necessary), clean the oven and hob, replenish cleaning materials, remove leftover food, check that cutlery, glasses, dishes, pans and utensils are all present and spotless. De-scale kettle. (Kettle de-scaler is another product you may need to import, as only vinegar-based products are sold in France, which are almost useless.)

- **living room** – Clean. Check that loose covers, throws and cushions are clean; replace and launder as necessary.

- **outside** – Clean garden furniture and barbecue. Check lawn and drives for animal mess. Mow grass, weed borders and rake gravel. Carry out pool maintenance.

- **safety equipment** – Check that pool and fire alarms, smoke alarms, fire blankets and fire extinguishers are functioning and in date. Check safety stickers on glass doors. Check that the gas bottle has enough gas in it for the next let and that its hose is in date.

- **visitors' book & information** – Check that all is in place for the next visitors.

- **washing machine & dishwasher** – Check filters and run a load to test.

- **windows** – Check fastenings and clean panes.

SURVIVAL TIP
Keep the property well aired in winter and leave minimum heating on even if there are no bookings.

Employing a Caretaker

If you aren't on site or cannot or don't want to carry out the above tasks, you must ensure that you have someone reliable to do so on your behalf, as well as carry out routine maintenance – gardening, pool maintenance, repairs, etc. – and to welcome guests to the property. At the very least, you may need someone from whom guests can collect a key.

There are many and varied companies offering caretaking services, including large property management companies, estate agents who handle (usually longer-term) lettings and sometimes perform management tasks or employ people on your behalf, and other 'management companies' that are no more than self-employed caretakers.

A property management company should be located in the same area as the property and provide all necessary services. These may include letting the property, as well as caretaking, welcoming clients and being on call for emergencies, although such businesses are normally outside the budget of *gîte* owners and are more appropriate for the letting of luxury villas.

At the other end of the scale is the 'lady down the road' who will do your changeovers (see **Employing Others** on page 182). Whatever choice you make, be sure to maintain contact with your caretaker – ultimately any problems that arise are your responsibility. If the property is your second home, you might be prepared to put up with broken appliances or pest problems when you stay there, but paying guests won't; problems must be dealt with as soon as they arise.

 As the majority of routine tasks must be done on changeover day and the usual day is a Saturday, it can be extremely difficult to find a caretaker in popular areas. Don't take on bookings unless you're sure you have this aspect covered.

You should be realistic (even pessimistic) about your caretaking costs and bear in mind that a caretaker might need to be retained during the months when you have few or no lets. The amount you pay is obviously related to the extent of the services offered. If you have a luxury five-bedroom villa on the Côte d'Azur with gardens and swimming pool, it could cost at least €6,000 for an annual contract for a weekly caretaking visit. For a small rural *gîte* a weekly changeover should cost €50 to €70 (maintenance and grass cutting is extra). Generally, you should allow up to €15 per hour for each employee.

Welcoming Guests

It's an advantage if you can arrange for someone to be on hand to welcome your guests when they arrive, explain how things work, and deal with any questions, requests and minor problems. **It's essential to make your guests feel welcome.** You (or your caretaker) should obviously be at the property to greet them. If their arrival time is inconvenient, you can leave the keys in a concealed place or arrange for them to be collected from a third party, but this isn't recommended (unless they've made a prior arrangement to arrive outside of your normal time frame).

First impressions are important; a smiling, helpful owner is the best start to your guests' holiday, reassuring them you'll be on hand to deal with enquiries and problems if required. Show them around the property as if you're selling it. Point out any important details such as how to regulate radiators, how the bathroom basin and bath plug operate and how window fastenings and door locks work (often different from those in the UK or other countries), give severe (but humorous) warnings about the misuse of septic tank drainage, etc.. This avoids having to put notices everywhere. Tell guests how to contact you if there's anything they need to know, ask if they need anything (such as teabags, coffee and milk), point out the welcome pack, information folder and tourist brochures, then leave them in peace to settle in. Call on them a day later to make sure that everything is satisfactory.

If you really want to impress your guests, you may wish to arrange for fresh flowers, fruit, a bottle of wine and a grocery pack to greet them on their arrival (see **Extras** on page 116). It's little personal touches such as this that ensure repeat business and recommendations. If you 'go the extra mile', it will pay. Many people return to the same property each year or recommend it to their friends and you should do an annual mail-shot to previous clients and send them some brochures. **Word-of-mouth advertising is the cheapest and always the best.**

You should provide a visitor's book, in which guests can write their comments and recommendations regarding local restaurants and attractions, etc. Some owners (and agencies) also send out questionnaires.

CASE STUDY 2

We moved to France from the busy, overcrowded south-east of England in 1992 to find a quiet, low-stress lifestyle and better weather. Financing this lifestyle meant providing accommodation in which others could enjoy the same benefits, albeit only for a holiday. We decided to offer self-catering accommodation, as it seemed to involve less day-to-day work than bed and breakfast, although 12 years on I'm not sure that's how it has worked out.

House-hunting was fun, at first, but looking around endless decaying, smelly houses with crumbling barns did get a bit depressing even though the estate agents pointed out the potential at every turn. We decided to live in a part of France we wanted to live in and in a house we liked rather than research the market and buy something that was ideal for self-catering holidays. So, although there had to be potential for holiday accommodation and a swimming pool, our own needs were top of the list. With very little research and no business plan we chose Dordogne and a house on the edge of a village. We've since come to appreciate the many advantages and conveniences of being part of a thriving community, and a lot of our visitors have come to us having spent their previous holiday isolated and miles from anywhere – literally up a goat track in some cases.

When we lived in England we had a house, garden and garage on the edge of a reasonable-size town, full-time jobs, no children and were in our mid-30s. We're now in our late 40s and during those 12 years we've gained a larger house, a larger garden, a swimming pool, two self-catering cottages and a large workshop/garage (all on the edge of a small village), have become self-employed and are raising two children. Sadly, two gîtes (or even the three we had for many years) didn't provide an income we could live on, and Charles has to work full-time, as well as helping with changeover chores during the summer months.

As soon as we arrived in France, we immediately started to renovate one half of the house (which had at some point been a separate house), as the plan was to start letting, and earning money, as soon as possible. We moved into the house in July, having already decided to advertise with Chez Nous and contacted them to get an idea of deadlines and costs. When we were house-hunting, we'd chatted to one of the agents, whose wife ran gîtes and a B&B, and over a cup of coffee she had said that she 'swore by Chez Nous', who were well established and very helpful and seemed professional. We decided to book space in their 1993 brochure and had to commit to this, and pay the money, in September 1992, which was quite scary. We got our first deposit cheque in early January 1993 when I was in hospital having our son and in our first season we were full from the end of May until early September. We were obviously novices: the place was only just ready and I'm sure our naiveté showed, but we were happy. We've advertised with Chez Nous ever since.

The money we grandly call our 'annual advertising budget' is around £1,000 and most of this goes to Chez Nous, but we have, over the years, sometimes used the Sunday papers to fill odd weeks and have used France One Call's late availability service for about five years. We've never been particularly impressed with the plethora of French lifestyle magazines, whose advertising sales staff pester us, nor the small companies offering 'deal direct' advertising, and we avoid the host of website and internet services offered to us (almost weekly). We've built our own website, but most people find us through Chez Nous or France

One Call and we're happy with the level of bookings. The season here seems to be limited to June, July and August, with only a few people interested in May or September.

We had three gîtes for several years, but have now shrunk to two, as the original has been incorporated back into our house to meet our changed domestic needs (growing children!) and because I'd become fed up with having guests so close. This year we've bought a part share in a rental property nearby, which should increase our income without impacting, further, on our privacy.

Privacy is a big issue. Basically, there's precious little. Most guests are pleasant and we enjoy a drink or a chat with them. And most of them are considerate; some want their privacy as much as we do and we respect each other's space. However, some guests are simply a pain in the neck and we cannot wait to see them leave. I console myself with the knowledge that I've got their money and I get to stay while they have to drive home!

As a sweeping generalisation, most visitors on a self-catering holiday want hot water, clean, practical accommodation, comfortable beds and sunshine – lots of it. If there's a pool, it must be clean, all the time. There are, of course, exceptions to every rule: one of our clients complained that it was too hot and that she wouldn't have come if she had known. At the time, in August, the temperatures were around the mid-20s rather than the usual low 30s (let alone the high 30s and more that we experienced in 2003). Running holiday accommodation is stressful, and taking responsibility for everything (including the weather) goes with the territory and means providing the same welcome and service to 'all sorts'.

Self-catering is probably easier than B&B (we do B&B occasionally if bookings are down), but still hard work. We do all the work ourselves, although when the children were very small I got a babysitter for changeover Saturdays and last year I was really spoilt and employed a friend to do the largest gîte while I did the second and the smallest. I also use a laundry service now for the large bath towels and double-bed linen – I still do the rest. I'm not sure that either of us trusts anyone enough to delegate the maintenance and cleaning completely, and it's difficult – in fact, impossible – to take even a few days away in the summer, which, I feel, is becoming a nuisance.

Audrey & Charles Fleming, Route de Boisseuilh, 24390 Cherveix Cubas (☎ 05 53 50 12 39, ✉ Audrey@LesFlamands.com)

USING AN AGENCY

A major decision you must take is whether to let your property yourself or use an agency. If you don't have much spare time, you're better off using an agency, which takes care of your marketing and saves you the time and expense of advertising and finding clients

Apart from organisations such as Gîtes de France and Clévacances, a number of companies operate as property letting agents, including some French estate agents.

Agencies, wherever they're based, must nowadays operate under French law. If they're based abroad, they should have a subsidiary French company and their contract with you must be in French.

If you use an agency or tour operator, the agency may specify certain conditions. For example, you may not be permitted to make certain supplementary charges (e.g. for electricity). If you offer longer lets, e.g. more than three months (see **Longer Lets** on page 112) outside the high season, you need to ensure that you or your agent uses the appropriate contract, which is different from a holiday letting contract.

Agencies normally set the rental prices for your property, although some (e.g. Gites Direct) advertise your property and deal with the initial booking and deposit, thereafter passing the rest of the transaction on to you – they're neither an 'all-in' agency nor a simple advertising site and you're free to set your own rates.

If you want your property to appear in an agent's catalogue, you must contact the agency the summer before the year in which you wish to let it (the deadline is usually August or even earlier). If your property renovation isn't yet completed, this can be a problem – concentrating on finishing the roof and facade and strategically positioning container plants to get an attractive photograph might be a solution! (Interior photographs can always be added to the related website at a later date, when you actually have an interior...)

Advantages & Disadvantages

The advantages of using an agency may include the following:

● no advertising expenses;

● a large customer base;

● 'brand' loyalty – customers return to the same company year after year;

- clients have the assurance of knowing that the property exists, that it conforms to the standards of a (hopefully) reputable agent and that they have back-up should any problems arise, rather than handing over hundreds of euros to a stranger in a foreign country, with the risk of arriving to find a building site or a non-existent property!

- many holidaymakers prefer to book their holidays through an agency, making a one-step purchase rather than having to arrange accommodation, ferry crossings and insurance separately; it's simpler and often cheaper;

- time saving – you don't have to wait by the telephone or keep checking your email for enquiries;

- support services (e.g. meeting and greeting clients, caretaking);

- no paperwork except when filling in your tax return and banking cheques;

- a good agency will find you far more bookings than you can hope to find yourself.

Disadvantages can include:

- you cannot vet your clients;

- exclusivity at certain times of year (including peak season), restricting your own use and any private bookings (e.g. family and friends);

- fixed pricing structure;

- third-party intervention in disputes, although that can also be an advantage (see **Dealing with Problems** on page 110); for example, you might have to refund or compensate a client for reasons with which you don't agree.

The question of whether you'll earn more or less by using an agency has no simple answer. Most agencies don't charge a fee as such; they agree a rate to pay you, then sell a complete holiday to the customer. Of course, agencies take a commission; otherwise, they would soon cease trading! Some owners believe that agencies are simply taking profits that should rightly be theirs, while others appreciate the fact that agencies pay for expensive advertising and deal with all the paperwork, contracts and payments, thus saving them an enormous amount of time and effort. You might earn €75 less per week than you would for a private let in high season, but you have no advertising costs (which can run to several hundreds of euros to be effective) and the time you would spend on administration can be put to more profitable use.

Clients are often willing to pay more (sometimes considerably more) if they're booking through a reputable agency, as the product is better presented and they have the safeguard of being able to complain (and perhaps get money back) if the accommodation is unsatisfactory. The premium paid by the client may or may not, however, be passed on to you, the owner. Agencies can sometimes offer owners a higher rate than they would be able to charge privately owing to the reductions the agency can negotiate with ferry and insurance companies, which subsidise the packages they offer; it can even be cheaper for clients to book with an agency, particularly when ferry prices are high, because their package price includes discounted ferry fares, in which case everyone wins (except perhaps the ferry companies!): the client gets a better combined deal, and you earn more money than you would at private rates. Finally, you'll probably let a greater number of weeks due to the agency's scope for advertising, even if the weekly rate is lower than you'd charge privately – see **Viability** on page 75 to work out whether this will be to your advantage

---

SURVIVAL TIP
Regard any shortfall between your private letting rate and that which you receive from an agent as your advertising budget.

Choosing an Agency

At least initially, it may be less a question of choosing an agency than of finding one that will take your property on.

 Although self-catering holiday companies may fall over themselves to take on a luxury property on the Côte d'Azur, the top letting agents turn down as many as 90 per cent of the properties they're offered.

Each agency has its particular requirements, but as a rule your accommodation must be available throughout the high season (July and August), although you may be able to block one or two weeks for your own use. Most agencies send a representative to inspect the property (some

charge a fee for this – understandable, as you might just be wanting free advice) and will do so each year to ensure that it continues to meet standards.

It's absolutely essential to employ an efficient, reliable and honest company, preferably long-established. Make sure that your income is kept in an escrow account and paid regularly, or even better, choose an agent with a bonding scheme who pays you the rent **before** the arrival of guests (the better ones do). Ask for the names of satisfied owners and check with them. In particular, ask agents the following:

2

- who they let to;
- where they advertise;
- what information they send to potential clients;
- whether they have contracts with holiday and travel companies;
- what the payment arrangements are;
- what cancellation clauses are in their contracts with clients;
- what the restrictions are on your own use of the property;
- if they're based in another country, whether they're correctly registered with a French subsidiary and thus operating legally.

You should also check the type of contract you'll have with the agency: whether, for example, you will receive a detailed analysis of income and expenditure and what notice you're required to give if you decide to terminate the agreement.

The larger companies market homes via newspapers, magazines and other printed media, holiday companies and the internet, and have representatives in many countries. A good agency will do the following:

- advertise in the national press;
- produce a colour brochure;
- have quality standards;
- have an owners' helpline;
- have regional representatives in France;
- be registered in France, even if based elsewhere;

- provide a level of publicity and marketing that a private owner cannot compete with;

- provide checklists for owners;

- **have an online booking service where clients can book easily and pay using a credit or debit card** (although it's possible for you to set up a PayPal account – see **Online Payment** on page 192);

- obtain far more bookings than you could manage privately.

CASE STUDY 3

We arrived in France in 1992, from Sheffield, with a map of Normandy, a well thumbed copy of the magazine *Living France* and dreams of owning one of the ruins to renovate advertised therein. As it happens, we'd been unable to find any self-catering accommodation in the Suisse-Normande region, where we were hoping to buy, and this later influenced our decision to provide such facilities.

A friendly estate agent, in the pretty town of Thury-Harcourt, provided us with a gîte to stay in and showed us lots of properties within our budget of £10,000, but they were all in need of far too much work. The last one we saw, a large L-shaped barn near the town and the beautiful River Orne, had been up for sale for eight years because it lacked access to its small garden. However, this was amply compensated for by the fact that it was in excellent condition, had lovely views over the surrounding Calvados countryside and, most importantly, was less than an hour's drive from the port of Caen. We therefore decided to purchase it, and subsequently solved the access problem by making a wooden balcony and staircase so you could get to the garden from upstairs – and we heaved the septic tank round and over the farmer's fences!

By 1996, the conversion of one half of the barn into a spacious four-bedroom apartment (which we called 'Le Grenier') was completed. We enlisted a graphic designer to give our brochure and booking form a professional look, and started distributing copies among our family, friends and acquaintances.

We contacted Brittany Ferries Holiday Homes, whose brochure we'd seen many times whilst crossing the Channel, and agreed to let them publicise and handle the administration for Le Grenier in return for priority over all its peak season bookings of 1997. However, we were disappointed by the picture they had taken and the description of our property in the brochure and began researching alternatives.

We were introduced to Inghams, who were able to offer us a higher weekly rent for our 1998 season and whose contract had more flexible terms. By this time we were also filling our empty weeks through a basic advertisement in the Brittany Ferries Owners in France 'deal direct' brochure, costing us about £150 a year for a small advert. The substantial ferry discounts we qualified for subsidised this cost, but we soon realised that a photograph was essential to attract enquiries and upgraded the advert for the following year. We also became members of France One Call, who had initiated a telephone and internet service for clients seeking availability at the last minute.

In 1999, we heard about the sale of a small farmstead in the nearby Vire-Bocage region, which had been for sale for a couple of years. The owner, living in England, was desperate to sell the farmstead of five houses, two of which had been recently converted into living accommodation. He had already accepted a ridiculous offer, but the sale had fallen through; we immediately matched the previous offer (not thinking how we were going to finance it) and it was accepted. Luckily, the bank saw its potential too and agreed to give us a mortgage.

The farmhouse and cottage at the new site, Les Moueux, were updated and refurbished into gîtes ('La Valette' and 'Le Courty'), and were ready to let in 2000. We then discovered another agency, VFB, who put 'La Valette' on their books immediately, guaranteeing us a minimum fixed income, but disallowing any private bookings. However, we were again disappointed with their representation of our property in their brochure, and it stood empty for most of that year.

At this point, we had also finished converting our own home ('Le Poirier'), next door to 'Le Grenier' in Thury-Harcourt, and decided to let that too, so that we could move to Les Moueux. We had heard excellent reports, from holiday homeowners and clients alike, about French Country Cottages, and signed up 'Le Grenier' and 'Le Poirier' with them. We employed a local couple to clean and maintain the gîtes and to meet and greet our guests while we ran and developed Les Moueux.

However, running the two sites at the same time as bringing up a family required lots more help and much more expense, and in 2001 we sold 'Le Grenier' as a going concern, to concentrate on Les Moueux.

2

We still live in Les Moueux, having renovated two of the three ruins and converted them into three gîtes. However, over the past few years, with the ever increasing number of gîtes available, it has become a lot harder to fill even the August weeks.

Another factor contributing to this decline is that people have changed the way they book their holidays, booking direct with owners via the internet. We've therefore cancelled all our contracts with booking agencies for next year and arranged to let two of the gîtes long term to locals, which will save us the expense of providing for the ever more demanding expectations of clients, i.e. dishwashers, hi-fi, DVD, computer, pool. This also guarantees us a regular income with fewer running costs and less stress.

Hayley Shaw and Douglas Beal (☎ 02 31 66 00 17, 🖥 www.les moueux.com)

Leading Agencies

Most of the agencies listed below sell a complete holiday package to the customer, including travel and accommodation and sometimes holiday insurance, and handle everything up to the point of the visitors' arrival – advertising, enquiries, contracts and payment. Some may even be able to assist in locating caretaking services. Many of these agencies also produce a printed brochure or catalogue.

The main agencies include the following:

- **Allez France** (🖥 www.allezfrance.com) – offers over 3,000 properties, now in conjunction with Cottages4you (see below); no brochure, online booking only;

- **Bowhills** (UK ☎ 0870-235 2727, 🖥 www.bowhills.co.uk – part of the Hoseasons Holidays Group) – 300 properties in France; colour brochure and press advertising; strongest in Dordogne, Provence and Atlantic coastal regions; UK-based bilingual representatives, dedicated owners' telephone helpline; looking for properties with pools or within 20 minutes of a beach;

- **Brittany Ferries Holiday Homes** (UK ☎ 0870-900 0259, 🖥 www. brittany-ferries.co.uk) – the official UK representative of Gîtes de France;

offers reduced rates on Brittany Ferries ships for owners; 6,000 properties in its 'French Collection' brochure, which is distributed through travel agents and by direct mail; deadline for inclusion in the brochure 1st August;

2

- **Cottages4you** (UK ☎ 0870-078 2100, ⌨ www.cottages4you.co.uk – part of the Holiday Cottages Group, see below) – offers a selection of cottages in France, Spain, Portugal, Croatia and Italy; extensive TV advertising;

- **Easycottages** (UK ☎ 0870-197 2799, ⌨ www.easycottages.com – part of the Holiday Cottages Group, see below) – offers a selection of cottages in the UK, Ireland and France;

- **French Affair** (UK ☎ 020-7381 8519, ⌨ www.frenchaffair.com) – operating in France since 1986, with villas in Dordogne, Lot, Provence, Languedoc-Roussillon, Pays Basque, Atlantic coast area and Corsica;

- **French Country Cottages** (UK ☎ 0870-078 1500, ⌨ www.french-country-cottages.co.uk, ⌨ www.countrycottagesinfrance.co.uk – part of the Holiday Cottages Group, see below) – 900 French properties at the higher end of the market; 200,000 preview brochures sent to mailing list plus 200,000 main brochures to past and potential customers in November; full back-up for owners including dedicated helpline, bilingual representatives in the UK; annual inspections and regional representatives in France; pays up front any money received (e.g. deposits and balance payments), which is non-refundable in the case of late cancellation by the client; 50 per cent of properties have pools;

- **French Life** (UK ☎ 0870-336 2877, ⌨ www.frenchlife.co.uk – part of the Holiday Cottages Group, see below) – 1,000 cottages and villas, priced between those of French Country Cottages and Welcome Cottages;

- **France Direct** and **Gites Direct** (⌨ www.francedirect.net, ⌨ www.gites direct.com) – offers a booking service on a commission basis, not strictly an agency;

- **Holiday Cottages Group** – one of the largest companies in this field with several brands, including Easycottages, French Country Cottages, French Life and Welcome Cottages (see this section) and Chez Nous (see **Chapter 5**), with varying customer profiles, some well known in their own right before being taken over;

- **Individual France** (UK ☎ 0870-191 7890, ⌨ www.individual travellers.com – formerly Vacances en Campagne, now absorbed by the Holiday Cottages Group. see above) – 160 properties in France;

2

- **Just France** (UK ☎ 020-8780 4480, 🖳 www.justfrance.co.uk – formerly Inghams) – booking via the website and a glossy brochure;

- **VFB Holidays** (UK ☎ 01452-716830, 🖳 www.vfbholidays.co.uk) – properties are mostly French-owned; each property is inspected annually; printed brochure; cleaning included in rental price;

- **Welcome Cottages** (UK ☎ 0870-197 6420, 🖳 www.welcomecottages. com – part of the Holiday Cottages Group, see above) – offers less expensive cottages, villas and apartments across France.

DOING YOUR OWN LETTING

Doing your own letting is time consuming but allows you more control and flexibility over rates, and over who you let to and when, and enables you to use the property yourself whenever you choose. It also gives your clients the personal touch, which can be important. Disadvantages can include the following:

- a lot of time, effort and paperwork;

- fewer bookings than using an agency;

- telephone calls at unsociable hours (particularly from people in distant time zones);

- advertising and other marketing costs;

- the difficulty of handling cancellations and requests for reimbursement, especially if you've established a rapport with the clients.

If you plan to let a home yourself, you must decide how to handle enquiries about flights and car hire (rental). It's easier to let clients make their own bookings, but you should be able to offer advice and maybe put them in touch with airlines, ferry companies, travel agents and car rental companies.

Setting Rates

To get an idea of the rent you should charge, ring a few letting agencies and ask them what it would cost to rent a property such as yours at the time of year you plan to let. They're likely to quote the **highest** rent you can charge. You should also check advertisements in newspapers and magazines and on the many websites dealing in French holiday accommodation (remember that they might not have any bookings, but it can give you a fair idea). Set a realistic rent, as there's a lot of competition. It's better to let 20 weeks at €400 than 15 at €500 (see **Viability** on page 75).

Rental Periods

2

Many owners start out with flexible rental periods but most find it's best to stick with Saturday as the changeover day; this is what holidaymakers are familiar with and what suits most working people, and it makes your life simpler. Some owners (especially French) prefer to have a minimum two-week rental period in July and August, but these weeks are the most likely to be booked anyway so such restrictions are usually unnecessary (although having two-week lets reduces the time and money you need to spend on changeovers and cleaning). If there are many French owners in your area, offering one-week lets in high season gives you an advantage.

There's a large market for short breaks (particularly in northern France), but as these are normally let from Friday to Monday, they will preclude your taking bookings for the whole week either side and you should therefore avoid them in high season. At other times of the year, they may bring in income that you wouldn't otherwise have, but there will always be the nagging feeling that you might have been able to let one or two whole weeks!

Handling Enquiries

Make it as easy as possible for people to contact you, and **be available**. This may seem obvious, but if you don't answer the telephone or don't reply promptly to emails, your potential clients will pass on to the next property on their list. Email can be somewhat impersonal and some clients, especially in older age groups, may not have internet access. Telephoning abroad can also be off-putting, and your advertisements are likely to get more response when enquirers don't have to make an international call. If you're targeting UK customers, you could rent an 0871 number and have it permanently diverted to your French landline. These are available from Adcall (💻 www. adcall.com/adcall0871/index.html) and are connected to your existing number, for a once-only cost of around £40. The caller pays 10p per minute (from the UK only).

A computer is essential, as many people book via websites and email. It's necessary to have an answerphone and a fax machine is useful, although most modern computer systems will have a fax facility so there may be no need to have a separate one. Once potential clients have seen your advertisement, or followed a recommendation, their first impression of you, via the way you handle their enquiries, will reflect on their expectations of your accommodation.

If you have the enquirer's telephone number, consider ringing them, as long as you have good communication skills – it's easier to 'convert' an enquiry if you make it personal, answer questions on the spot and become involved with their choice of holiday. If you aren't at your best on the telephone you might be more comfortable with email where you can take time (not too much!) to compose your reply. Either way, answer queries honestly and give additional positive information – the number of places to visit in the area, how lovely it is to spend long summer evenings in the garden, etc. If they're wanting to book a period that's already let, offer other dates – if you've 'sold' the accommodation they might be prepared to change their holiday dates. Finish your answer with an invitation to further action, e.g. "Would like me to hold those dates", or even "How would you like to pay the deposit?"

Telephone

Smile when you answer the telephone – this might sound silly, but it works! Be friendly, but professional and efficient. Keep your calendar and tariff, a notebook and apen handy, so that you can answer questions about availability immediately. (There's nothing worse for a caller than hearing: "Hang on a minute while I find a pen…") Don't allow small children to answer your calls – whereas some people might find it cute, others certainly won't. It doesn't give a professional impression and customers don't want to spend ten minutes on an international telephone call while a three-year-old chatters or wanders off to find its mother!

Find a happy medium between professional and friendly; you aren't a hotel, you must sound warm and welcoming. Be positive when you talk on the telephone and encourage the caller to make a booking by emphasising the benefits of coming to stay at your property. For instance, if they ask if it's near the sea, give the time it takes to drive there, or if you're a long way from the coast mention river bathing or nearby swimming facilities or your own pool. **Remember, you're selling a product!**

Email

Again, be friendly, but professional and clear. You convey an impression of your business in the way you respond.

- Use a spell-checker and punctuate correctly (don't simply put commas between each sentence).

- Use upper and lower case letters where appropriate (don't use all upper case, as this can be interpreted as shouting).

- Don't use abbreviations, 'textspeak' or 'chatty' language.

- When quoting prices, spell out the currency or use the standard abbreviations (e.g. GBP for pounds sterling, EUR for euros, USD for US dollars), as not all fonts support all currency symbols – you may be able to see them on your monitor, but the recipient might not.

- Likewise, don't use fancy fonts – if the recipient doesn't have the same font installed they won't see your pretty prose.

- Avoid over-enthusiastic spam filters at the recipient's end by using a distinctive subject line (e.g. the name of your property).

- Include a link to your website in case the enquirer has forgotten which property is yours amongst the dozens of enquiries they fired off.

Check emails frequently (at least twice a day) and respond promptly; don't miss the opportunity for a booking. Often people will make a list of all the properties in which they're interested and write to them all simultaneously – be the first to reply, as only one on that list will win the booking!

 Beware of email scams – messages from a large group offering to book all your accommodation for an extended CAUTION stay are usually too good to be true.

They might offer to overpay you by cheque or money order, requesting the surplus to be sent somewhere else and /or the payment may be counterfeit, or claim to be on official business, saying the company will pay. There are many variations. This is known as the '419' scam. Here's one (actual) example, sent in October 2006 to many advertisers on an accommodation site (grammar, spelling and punctuation left as received):

"Hello,
I am Dr Henry .A. Opoko, a medical practitioner and i work with the UNICEF here in Ghana. I will be coming over to France on holiday from the 1st of November to the 30th of November 2006 for (1) month Vacation with my wife Lora.

Could you please send me a more detailed description of your accomodation and What's the cost of rental per week or per day? Unicef will be paying you in advance of our visit so that we can be assured of an accomodation during our stay, because this is our first visit to France. and Unicef is also taking care of all my vacation expenses.

An early reply will be appreciated. Please acknowledge if you can offer this accomodation service and give me a call on my direct line as soon as you receive this email, so we can conclude on all other arrangements ASAP, as time is not really on our side.

Most Respectful,
Dr.Henry Opoko.
Social Work Cordinator,
Unicef Ghana."

'Dr. Opoko' sends a money order or bank draft for far more than the total accommodation cost and asks you to immediately forward the excess – two or three thousand euros – to his travel agent (in Ghana). The money order turns out to be counterfeit, and you lose the 'balance' that you forwarded. Such scams are invariably sent through a free email service such as Yahoo or Hotmail.

Contracts & Deposits

If a (genuine) customer wants to book, you must have an agreement form that includes the property description, dates of arrival, departure and approximate times, financial details and terms of booking. Note that if you plan to let to non-English speaking clients, you must have a letting agreement in the appropriate language(s).

SURVIVAL TIP
It's a legal requirement to have a written agreement for all rentals and it should be signed and dated by yourself and the client. You should check with a lawyer that your agreement is legal and contains all the necessary safeguards.

For example, it should specify the types of damage for which the client is responsible and the conditions under which a deposit will be refunded. All descriptions, contracts and payment terms must comply with French laws (see page 63).

Hold availability for one week, a non-refundable booking deposit to be paid within this time. Request that the balance of payment be made at least eight weeks before the arrival date.

```
┌─────────────────────────────────────────────────────────┐
│                      SURVIVAL TIP                         │
│  Keep detailed records and ensure that you never double   │
│                         book!                             │
└─────────────────────────────────────────────────────────┘
```

For information about methods of payment, see **Receiving Payment** on page 191.

Information Packs

After accepting a booking, you should provide guests with a pre-arrival information pack containing the following:

- a map of the local area and instructions on how to find the property;
- information about local attractions and the local area (available free from tourist offices);
- emergency contact numbers if guests have problems or plan to arrive late;
- the keys or instructions as to where to collect them on arrival.

Arrival & Departure Times

Specify the times when guests may arrive, e.g. between 4 and 8pm, and ask them to notify you what time they expect to be with you, asking them to telephone if there's a change of plan. Be quite firm about this; you'll have a lot to do on changeover day and won't want a car full of holidaymakers arriving at 2pm when you're frantically changing beds or unblocking the drains. Neither do you want to be waiting around until 11pm when they were expected at 5pm but decided to stop for dinner without letting you know.

Departure time is usually 10am, but if you have no guests arriving the same day you can extend the deadline a little; departing guests might spend a little longer cleaning before they leave!

Dealing with Problems

Major problems are unlikely to arise if you've described, equipped and furnished your *gîte* properly. If appliances fail during the guests' visit, do your best to sort the problem out, and assure the clients that you're doing so. If they know it isn't your fault (e.g. a washing machine failure, power cut or septic tank blockage), they're unlikely to complain as long as you deal with it quickly, sympathetically and professionally. If you feel that the problem is your fault, offer some compensation and ask for written assurance that they're happy with this. (It isn't unknown for clients to say they're happy but make a major complaint on arrival home.)

Problems more often arise when the standard of the property doesn't meet the client's expectations. Your advertising and marketing **must** be a true representation of the accommodation.

 Under French law, if you misrepresent your property and make false advertising claims (e.g. 'near the sea' when it's 30km/18mi away) you'll be liable to a very large fine.

If you've let the *gîte* through a third party (e.g. an agency or GdF), clients might complain upon their return. There are, unfortunately, far too many TV programmes featuring problem holidays, showing how easy it is to complain and get your money back, and there are quite a few unscrupulous people who put in spurious complaints with this in mind. Examine the agreement you have with the agency – there's probably a clause which states that any problems must be reported to you (or your caretaker) during the stay. If they cannot contact you, the clients should inform the agency's local representative and, failing that, its head office. If they haven't followed this procedure, they shouldn't be compensated. If the matter escalates, take legal advice.

There are, of course, problem guests! A certain amount of wear and tear is to be expected, but damage caused by guests' negligence and misuse can and should be deducted from their security deposit. Start by asking the guests if anything has been broken or isn't working properly; this puts the onus on them to 'own up' to any damage they've caused. Don't make a fuss about one or two broken glasses, but you're entitled to deduct the cost of more serious breakage and damage – that's what the deposit is for. It can be embarrassing having to inspect the *gîte* while the guests are waiting to depart, but it has to be done unless you have a prior arrangement (in the contract) to refund the security deposit after the guests' return.

Check the accommodation as quickly as possible, concentrating on potential problem areas (e.g. bathroom, oven, WC); if these are clean, the rest is likely to be in good condition. Check that nothing has been left behind (a reason to look inside the bedroom drawers and examine the bedclothes). If you aren't present when guests leave and there is any damage, it's advisable to take photographs and, if you let through an agency, to inform the regional representative.

2

Natural Causes

One problem that frequently occurs in rural properties is invasion by animals, birds and insects. Mice come in looking for food. Beech martens (*fouines*), sparrows, barn owls or other large birds might nest in the eaves or roof space. Obviously, you should make sure that there are no mice actually living in the property, but the occasional incursion is difficult to prevent. You can ask guests not to leave open food (bread, etc.) in the kitchen, and you can set traps when there are no guests. Don't put down poison: children or pets might eat it, or poisoned mice might crawl off and die in inaccessible places, creating very unpleasant smells and attracting large blowflies!

Birds are easier to deal with, as their access can be blocked, but make sure you do this outside the nesting season; some species (e.g. barn owls) are protected.

To deal with hornet and wasp nests, telephone the local fire brigade (*sapeurs-pompiers*), whose job it is to remove them. (Hornet stings, contrary to popular belief, are no more harmful than those of wasps, but the sighting of a hornet can cause panic in a guest who isn't used to the countryside and its inhabitants.) Note that the fire brigade isn't authorised to dispose of bee swarms.

Ants are a frequent problem, but are more easily dealt with – find their route and put down some chilli pepper, they won't walk over it, or you can resort to chemical warfare with aerosols!

Mr & Mrs C. and their daughter took a holiday in a French rural cottage. One sunny day the owner was chatting to them outside and asked where their little girl was. "Oh, she's in the kitchen playing with the mice!" The owner was horrified, but the parents were genuinely pleased that Laura had something to keep her occupied. They stayed again the following year, but Laura was disappointed that her little friends had been evicted…

LONGER LETS

Long-term lets out of the holiday season can be a useful way to earn a little income from a property which may otherwise be sitting vacant for several months. **However, there are important legal implications of long-term letting.** In many areas, including long-term letting, French law has completely different principles from British law, for example, and you must find out **exactly** what's involved before committing yourself to long-term letting. **French law is very much weighted in the tenants' favour and you can find yourself with 'tenants' you're unable to get rid of.**

The first rule is **never** to allow anyone to rent your property, however well you know them or however well recommended, unless you have a proper contract.

Property letting is subject to the regulations in the *Code Civil* (Articles 1708-1762), which can be found on 🖥 www.legifrance.gouv.fr (click on the Union Jack next to '*Les codes*' to find the English translation). The *Code Civil* defines three categories of letting:

- short-term furnished (holiday) letting – less than three months;

- long-term furnished letting – normally for between three months and a year;

- unfurnished letting – normally for a minimum of three years, but under certain circumstances for as little as one year.

Unfurnished letting is beyond the scope of this book (with a minimum contract of three years, the legal ramifications are a minefield and allowable reasons for termination are severely limited), but it's important to understand the differences between letting to holidaymakers for one or two weeks and letting to students, professional people or the homeless for three months or more.

Although you can use a standard *gîte* contract, it's essential to obtain the following:

- proof of identity;

- evidence of employment or at least of sufficient income to pay the rent;

- proof that his principal residence is elsewhere.

The last point is crucial, as those whose principal residence is the property rented are entitled by law to a minimum lease of a year; **there are no exceptions**. (Until January 2005, this applied only to properties let by landlords who habitually let four or more properties; it now applies in all cases.) The lease is automatically renewable for a further year and under the same conditions, and there are stringent regulations, similar to those for unfurnished letting, restricting the landlord's right to reclaim the property. If tenants don't have a principal residence elsewhere, and especially if they have children, it can be impossible to evict them, whatever they've agreed to or signed. **Never** allow anyone to stay in your property (however many promises they give) if they cannot provide proof of their principal residence.

2

You may also wish to check references, which usually include a bank's or accountant's reference to establish a prospective tenant's financial standing, an employer's reference and a character reference, which can be from a previous landlord, employer or solicitor. Don't be taken in by a prospective tenant's appearance or demeanour, as the most presentable and well spoken people can prove to be the most difficult once you hand over the keys.

A furnished let is defined in law as a property containing furniture and household items at the time of letting, into which the tenant can move and live, bringing personal effects only. There must be an inventory. If these conditions aren't met, the tenant can take you to a tribunal and have the premises redefined as unfurnished. You would then be subject to the far stricter regulations imposed on that type of accommodation, with the tenant entitled to a let of at least three years.

To terminate a long-term lease, you must give the tenant three months' notice. If the tenant wants to end it, he has to give only one month's notice.

Contracts

You must have a rental agreement or contract that includes all the relevant details for the category of accommodation. Contracts for lets of more than three months must be in French. You can download various types of rental contract and standard letter from the Groupe Express Expansion website (🖳 www.lentreprise.com), but you should always have contracts checked by a *notaire*. A rental agreement must be signed by all parties involved.

OTHER CONSIDERATIONS

Fire Safety

You should have fire extinguishers and fire blankets (check between lets that they haven't been used and that the use-by date hasn't passed) and smoke alarms (check batteries and test between lets). Check with your insurance company and letting agency (if used) for any further fire safety requirements.

Waste Disposal

2

Provide clear instructions for rubbish disposal (e.g. that it's to be left in tied bags at the end of the stay), including the location of nearest community bin if you're in an area that has that system, the nearest bottle bank, etc. Supply plenty of strong bin bags, with instructions to tie them securely. If you're in a rural area, warn guests that bags may be torn apart by wild animals or stray dogs if left in an exposed position; ask them to put bags out only the night before collection day. In hot weather refuse can become smelly, attract wildlife and rodents, and become a health hazard. If you aren't on site and there's a gap between bookings, ensure that you have someone to put rubbish out.

Keys

You'll need several sets of spare keys, as some will inevitably get lost. If you employ a caretaker, his address and phone number should be on the key fob and not that of the house. If you let a home yourself, you can use a 'keyfinder' service, whereby lost keys can be returned to an agency by anyone finding them, but it's more practical and less expensive to put your mobile phone number on the tag. You should ensure that 'lost' keys are returned, or you may need to change the locks (in any case it's wise to change external locks periodically if you let a home). If you arrange your own lets, you can post keys to clients in your home country, or they can be collected from a caretaker in France. It's a good idea to provide guests with two sets so they can go out separately without leaving your keys under a flowerpot! To avoid problems with keys, it's possible to install a keypad entry system, but you must obviously arrange for the code to be changed after each let and for clients to be advised of the code.

Documentation

Supply a folder containing the following:

- local emergency numbers – fire, police and ambulance – and details of health services such as a doctor, dentist and hospital or clinic. The single emergency telephone number for the European Union is 112 – put this at the top of the list. Using this number helps avoid confusion between the three French emergency numbers (15, 17 and 18) and there's usually an English-speaking operator available.

- other useful local telephone numbers (e.g. taxi service);

- a list of places to visit in the vicinity (in good weather and bad) together with plenty of leaflets and brochures which you can obtain from your local tourist office (it might not open until Easter, in which case ask your departmental office);

- a list of restaurants in the area with a description of each and the type of food they serve (e.g. seafood specialities, local dishes, vegetarian, gourmet), days on which they're closed, their telephone numbers and approximate menu prices. Some might not be suitable for children who aren't used to sitting all evening at the table (unlike French children!), so it's advisable to include some recommendations for those that serve fast(er) food and for those that have children's menus.

- if you aren't on site to handle problems, numbers for general assistance such as a repairman, plumber, electrician and pool maintenance person (you may prefer to leave the telephone number of a local caretaker);

- the location of the nearest petrol stations, with opening times. Be sure to specify normal hours when an attendant is present, as automated 24-hour service stations normally accept only French credit and debit cards (even since the introduction of 'chip and pin' cards in the UK, many non-French cards require signature processing).

- the location of the nearest shops for everyday needs, e.g. the nearest *boulangerie* for bread and croissants, the nearest supermarket, and any hypermarkets in the area for the all-important stocking-up on beer and wine;

- a list of local markets – which days they're on, what hours they keep and the type of merchandise they sell (e.g. live animals, food, fish, fabrics, clothes, gifts, antiques);

- house rules, such as where children (and adults!) are/aren't allowed to go, stressing the safety aspect and possible dangers (e.g. falling into the pool);

- how things work, e.g. kitchen appliances, wood-burning stove, television/video/CD/DVD player, heating and air-conditioning, and pool safety equipment;

- if appropriate, a little history of the area and the accommodation itself;

- maps – national, departmental and local, and guidebooks – e.g. *Le Petit Futé* and a Green Guide. It's surprising how many visitors have inadequate maps and guide books (or none at all!), and providing them helps to forestall a barrage of questions. It's a simple matter to check that they're still on the premises at the end of each let.

- if there are any good car tours, walks or bicycle routes in the area, instructions and maps for these;

Also provide a visitors' book (*livre d'or*) for guests' comments.

Extras

It pays to provide a 'welcome pack' for each set of guests. This can be anything from a bunch of flowers and a bottle of wine to a hamper of food basics – coffee, tea, milk, sugar, cereals, bread, etc. Don't include the provision of a welcome pack in your contract, but make it a nice surprise ('added value'). If you put it in the contract, people will ask you exactly what it contains, e.g. the brand names of the products!

Any other little extras you can think of to increase your guests' enjoyment (and exceed their expectations) will encourage them to return and to recommend your accommodation to others. If you know that one of their children has a birthday during their stay, for example, buy a card and a small present. At Easter, give Easter eggs to children (or follow the French tradition of hiding them in the garden for children to find). Let guests know that you're available to help (if you are!) if there's anything they need or have forgotten to bring, e.g. a plug adapter (don't leave these in the *gîte*, as they will 'disappear').

Smoking

Many holiday lets are now non-smoking, but this limits your letting potential to some extent – smokers won't book a non-smoking property (hopefully!), but non-smokers will probably book even if you don't stipulate that it's non-smoking. You cannot police it, so it might be preferable to have a few restrictions such as no smoking in the bedrooms, or leave some ashtrays out on the terrace or in the garden.

CASE STUDY 4

We ran a successful marketing company in Northamptonshire with 100 employees, but when the opportunity arose to sell the business to a larger American company, we seized the chance to provide our children (then aged eight and six) with a bilingual upbringing and a taste of other cultures. Linguistically, we were well prepared: Tim had a degree in French and economics, while Chloe had A Level and business French qualifications.

Our main business is the running of a *gîte* complex on the Dordogne/Charente border, which we took over in a rundown state and developed. Currently, it consists of three *gîtes*, to which we've recently added an on-site restaurant. This has proved attractive to many British and some French customers. The business is better each year than the last, although we sense that it's getting harder as more rental properties come on to the market.

We had little trouble in making the transition in July 2001, although the timing of sales of three homes in the UK was a challenge. We put this down partly to realising that bureaucracy is really just a matter of understanding a different culture and system. We're sure that anybody arriving in the UK for the first time would struggle similarly with council tax, road fund licences, speed cameras and the Inland Revenue. It's a surprise that émigrés to France don't expect the bureaucracy to be difficult. Difficulties come from not knowing – and you never know what you don't know!

Opening the restaurant brought its own share of red tape. We had to learn about live music licences, the four different kinds of drinking licence, restaurant licences and health and safety inspections by the sapeurs-pompiers. Similarly with the change in the European law on septic tanks and new legislation on pool safety – you just have to discover it somehow and then deal with it.

In addition to running the *gîtes*, Tim manages the letting of properties we own as investments in the UK and US, while Chloe works part-time at a French language school in the local town. Tim also lectures to courses for people considering going into the *gîte* business, from which the following advice to participants has been adapted:

● Make a friend of the mayor, who's responsible for adherence to the laws in his commune. In some senses, what he says goes.

2

2

- Ask for help at the *mairie*, from other *gîte* owners, magazines, websites, helplines, etc.

- Avoid:

  - disregarding all advice given;

  - buying in the 'wrong' area (e.g. with inadequate attractions to prompt return visits or recommendations);

  - buying the 'wrong' property (too big or small, with too much land);

  - overspending on purchase and renovation;

  - not leaving sufficient financial 'cushion' for unexpected expenditure;

  - not allowing sufficient funds to live on while building the business;

  - undertaking too much renovation for the time (or money) available before the first holidaymakers arrive;

  - underestimating the time required for renovation (always more than you think);

  - making economies on furnishings, fittings and appliances;

  - extravagant advertising;

  - inadequate monitoring of advertising response and failure to adjust accordingly;

  - overestimating the length of the rental season;

  - vague rental terms and conditions, which can lead to misunderstandings and disputes;

  - insufficiently clear directions to the property;

  - underestimating the time and energy required for thorough cleaning on changeover days;

  - inattention to detail in presentation, advertising, administration, etc.;

  - neglecting safety issues (e.g. notices around the pool);

  - not having a complaints procedure (e.g. how, how soon and to whom faults should be reported);

  - skimping on insurance, particularly public liability;

- unclear or petty restrictions (e.g. on where to park or sunbathe, and when the pool may be used), which can make guests feel unwelcome;

- expecting the French to do things the English (or any other) way – they won't!

- making too little effort to learn French or improve your French;

- struggling alone;

- forgetting to enjoy the experience!

Tim and Chloe Williams: *Gîtes* (☎ 05 45 78 65 80, ✉ timdwilliams @wanadoo.fr); *Gîte* courses (🖥 www.gitecomplexes.co.uk)

TOP TEN TIPS FOR GITE OWNERS

- Be sure your property is marketable – a lot of time and effort can be wasted if it isn't in a good area for letting and doesn't photograph well.

- Be prepared to limit friends' and family's use – you'll feel obliged to offer free or cheap stays, probably at a time of year when you could let for the going rate.

- Check with your insurer the position regarding vacant periods – in some cases insurance is void if the property is vacant for 30 days or more.

- Make sure you declare your rental income for tax purposes.

- Aim to have a low-maintenance property.

- Make your marketing strategy a priority.

- Focus on your target market.

- Learn to speak, read and write French.

- Don't underestimate renovation costs and time.

- Don't overestimate the income.

- If you handle your own marketing, be professional, i.e. prompt and efficient.

Jo Taylor

3

BED & BREAKFAST

For many foreigners moving to France, running a bed & breakfast (B&B) seems an attractive way of generating an income and it's a particularly inviting option for those who buy large (especially rural) properties and wish (or need) to supplement their income. You can operate on as small a scale as you like, just letting one or two rooms in high season to earn a little extra money or dedicating your entire house to a full-time bed and breakfast business with four or five rooms open all year. If you choose the latter course of action, be prepared to swap your nine-to-five, five-day week for a 16-hours-a-day, seven-day week!

Chambres d'hôtes are the French equivalent to bed and breakfast (B&B) accommodation, although there are some differences between *chambres d'hôtes* and B&B. (*Chambres d'hôtes* literally – and confusingly – means either guests' rooms or hosts' rooms, and is also seen written as *chambre d'hôte*, *chambre d'hôtes* and *chambres d'hôte*, even on official websites and road signs – sometimes all four variations in one place!) B&B, as it's known in the UK and US, wasn't familiar in France until relatively recently, the options for overnight accommodation being limited to hotels (small and large), *logis* (more like lodgings, where you would pay for breakfast separately), and a *pension* (board and lodging).

The concept and the phrase were introduced by the government organisation Gîtes de France (GdF), which was started in 1951, initially for the promotion and marketing of self-catering cottages (*gîtes*). In 1969 separate regulations for B&B accommodation were created.

No authorisation is required to offer B&B accommodation, although if it's your principal source of income it must be registered as a commercial activity with the local Chambre de Commerce.

As with *gîtes* (see **Chapter 2**), you can operate independently, with or without an official tourist board rating, or sign up with one of the recognised organisations – Gîtes de France (see page 135) or Clévacances (see page 136). To be classified as a B&B you cannot offer more than five rooms – six in some areas – or accommodate more than 15 guests; this is strictly regulated. If you wish to let a greater number of rooms, you're considered to be running a hotel, must register as such, and must comply with far more stringent safety, fire, disabled access and hygiene regulations – and different taxes will apply. Running a hotel is covered by this book's sister publication, *Making a Living in France* (Survival Books – see page 314).

ADVANTAGES & DISADVANTAGES

Running a *chambres d'hôtes* with several rooms isn't a part-time activity, at least not in the summer; it's **very** hard work – much harder than managing self-catering cottages. You are, in effect, 'on duty' 24 hours a day; you may have arrivals after midnight and then have to be on hand for people leaving at 6am. Work is also involved in attracting clients – you cannot simply put up a sign and wait for the visitors and money to roll in. The advantages of running a B&B, as opposed to any other business, may include the following:

- flexibility – you choose when you're open;

- no formal qualifications or experience required (but see below);

- no formal registration if it isn't your main income;

- little capital expenditure needed – you can start with one or two rooms and expand as time and money allow;

- meeting interesting people.

3

There are also disadvantages, which may include the following:

- having little free time, especially if offering evening meals;

- working long hours;

- having to share your home with strangers;

- having to put up with people you don't like;

- insufficient income to live on unless you let at least four or five rooms.

Running a B&B is hard work. Running a B&B is hard work. It bears repeating!

CAUTION

QUALIFICATIONS & EXPERIENCE

There are two essential 'qualifications' for running a B&B: you must enjoy meeting people and be able to get on with them, and you must be able to speak French. (A smattering of Italian, Spanish and German can come in handy, too!) These abilities are far more important than when letting a *gîte*, as you will have far more contact with your clients. Quite apart from communicating with guests, dealing with paperwork and officialdom is virtually impossible unless you have a working knowledge of the language. It's vital that at least one of the owners speaks good French; you won't be able to rely on English-speaking guests if you want to have a successful business.

You may find that you cannot register with GdF unless at least one host can speak French, as this is becoming an increasingly common requirement.

A variety of other skills are required: you must act as chambermaids, cooks and bottle-washers, waiters, laundry workers and gardeners and perform routine property maintenance. If you're considering offering evening meals, but your prior experience hasn't extended beyond providing family meals, it might be wise to sign up for a cookery course that's aimed at catering for larger numbers.

THE MARKET

It's impossible to state accurately the number of B&B businesses in France, as many are independently run and not subject to any central registration. B&B businesses vary from a farmer's wife letting out a room for 'pin money' to a dedicated business with five bedrooms let consistently throughout the holiday season and, as yet, there's no obligation to register unless you're in the latter category. The figures below are for B&Bs registered with Gîtes de France (GdF), but of course there are a huge number of B&B businesses that aren't registered with GdF, many of which are run by non-French people – probably more than the number that **are** registered.

- There are currently around 10,000 B&B businesses registered with GdF.

- 500 new addresses are added every year (around 1,500 rooms).

- The average investment is €42,000.

GdF's statistics show that B&B accommodation appeals mainly to couples aged between 35 and 64, without dependent children, most of them being city-dwellers and homeowners. In addition:

- 72 per cent of customers are French, with Belgians the second-largest group.

- 49 per cent are middle managers, senior executives or professional people.

- 26 per cent are retired.

- The average stay is three nights.

- The average charge is €49 per night for two people, including breakfast.

- The average price for an evening meal is €17.

- The average annual occupancy is 16 weeks.

B&B clientele as a whole is divided into two main categories:

- Those who book accommodation in advance, for a day or two during a tour, or for a whole holiday (usually a week or two).

- 'Passing trade', including local recommendations and tourist board referrals, who usually stay for just one night but could end up staying longer if they like what you offer.

3

You might choose to accept only customers who have booked, although this severely limits your market. Many owners prefer to target longer-stay customers, as it's less labour intensive, you can be prepared for your guests' arrival and don't need to be 'on duty' 24 hours a day in anticipation of a car full of happy holidaymakers turning into your drive when you're looking forward to just **one** night off. (It's tempting to put up the 'No Vacancies' sign but even more tempting to think of the cash if unexpected visitors turn up!)

> SURVIVAL TIP
> **Satisfying the needs of both groups maximises
> your letting potential.**

WHERE TO BUY

The criteria for the location of a B&B business are slightly different from those for *gîte* accommodation – location is even more crucial to the success of your business, especially if you wish to attract passing trade (see above).

When buying a property with plans to offer B&B accommodation, make sure it's in a place where there will be demand and that it's easy to travel to and to find. To attract your share of passing trade, you must be near enough to a main road to erect signs. Each department has its own rules about signage, but signs are normally allowed up to 5km (3mi) from a property (see **Signs** on page 211). It's best to be fairly near a large town, preferably a well known one; you can then advertise at the local *Office du Tourisme* to attract visitors. Proximity to a major tourist town or attraction gives you good letting potential.

If you buy in a remote rural location, you'll be reliant almost exclusively on clients who book their accommodation before leaving home, and will therefore be dependent on effective marketing. Some beautiful remote locations, excellent for *gîtes*, are too isolated for B&B. In years when demand is low, places that are more accessible will have a better occupancy rate.

Once you've chosen a region and area, consider the suitability of a property's situation within that area. Although isolated locations aren't always the best for B&B, do make sure the location is peaceful; being near a road or railway line, nightclub, restaurant or bar may be convenient for your guests, but they won't appreciate being unable to sleep for the noise.

Another important consideration to be made when determining your location is whether or not you wish to offer evening meals. If you don't, or you don't intend to cook for guests every night, you **must** be within easy reach of one or more restaurants. On the other hand, if you intend to make evening meals your speciality, and sell as many as possible, having no restaurants nearby will be to your advantage!

If your property is in a popular winter sports area, you might choose to operate as a ski chalet. These can be self-catering and run on the same principles as a *gîte*, or you can cater for your guests. The level of comfort can vary from rough-and-ready youth hostel type dormitory accommodation for younger guests to luxury hotel-standard rooms. You can attract skiers in the winter and walkers and nature-lovers in the summer, thus doubling your season. However, owners of catered chalets don't usually live in the same building, so it isn't quite the same as running a *chambres d'hôtes*.

For further information on where to buy and a guide to the regions of France, refer to *The Best Places to Buy a Home in France* (Survival Books – see page 314).

WHAT TO BUY

There are many factors to take into consideration when choosing your property. Many of the criteria that apply to properties to be used as *gîtes* (see **Chapter 2**) also apply to properties to be used as B&B accommodation. The following points apply specifically to B&B properties.

The house must, of course, be large enough for the planned number of guest rooms and for your own accommodation. Aim for five guest bedrooms, possibly six (see **Number of Rooms** on page 131), ideally with space to install ensuite bathroom facilities. If you're planning on converting a property, keep this number as your target; you can always let one or two rooms to start with and renovate the others as you progress.

If it's a country property, you'll probably have plenty of parking space; if it's in a village, make sure there's sufficient free parking nearby and no restrictions on loading and unloading.

Look for a house with an 'added value factor'. It may not be within your budget to buy and renovate a *château*, but large country *manoirs* or old farmhouses make ideal *chambres d'hôtes* accommodation. Consider the surroundings, the views, whether there's a nearby lake or forest with attractive walks or any other feature that you can promote in your publicity and that will give you a competitive edge. Ask yourself: when people from overseas book holidays, what will attract them to this property rather than all the others they have to choose from?

Choose a house that photographs well. It may be beautiful inside, but in printed advertising and on the internet, the first thing people usually see is the exterior photograph. Try it yourself – look at a page of advertisements or an accommodation website and take note of which advertisements attract your attention.

Another important consideration is space for your own accommodation. The concept of *chambres d'hôtes* is having people stay in your house but, however much fun it seems at first, you'll very soon discover how much you need privacy. It's essential to have your own bathroom and living room, and preferable to have private access to the kitchen or your own kitchen. (If you fancy a cup of tea in the middle of the night, you won't want to meet guests whilst trotting around in your pyjamas!) In any case, the kitchen must be of an adequate size for preparing meals, even if you decide only to provide breakfast.

> **SURVIVAL TIP**
> **It's essential to have your own
> private accommodation.**

BUYING A BUSINESS

You can buy an existing business rather than setting one up from scratch, and there are advantages and disadvantages in doing so. The main disadvantage is, of course, the cost, as you're paying for a going concern (*fonds de commerce*), as well as the building itself (*murs*). Assessing the value of a *fonds de commerce* Is a difficult process, often involving more art than science, but it's **essential** to obtain at least one professional valuation and to check the value yourself. (French property agents may be able to give you a more accurate idea of the value of a *fonds* than a foreign agent.) A guide to assessing the value of a business can be found on the website of the magazine *ICF l'Argus des Commerces* (💻 www.cession-commerce.fr).

Whereas the value of the building is usually easily comparable with other buildings in the area, the value of the business may be impossible to relate to anything and you must make your own assessment of whether it's reasonable or not. If not, it may be worth negotiating rather than simply looking elsewhere. The cost of a *fonds de commerce* varies between around €300 and €2,000 per m² (€650 to €6,500 in Paris) according to a number of factors. Sometimes the building is included in the price, although rarely in Paris.

Another disadvantage of buying an existing B&B is that you won't have the freedom to style and decorate the accommodation as you would wish – unless you spend even more money refurbishing it.

3

On the other hand, there are several advantages to buying a business, including the following:

- You won't have to spend time and money renovating or adapting buildings for use as *chambres d'hôtes*.

- You will (or should, if you buy a successful business) have guaranteed income from the outset, which reduces your marketing costs and lessens the risk.

- You won't be setting up in competition to existing B&Bs and so further diluting the market, but will in effect be buying a slice of the market.

Look for a going concern with room for expansion and improvement, e.g. adding a swimming pool or converting outbuildings into a games or conference room. Make sure the owners aren't exaggerating the existing profits or the potential. In particular, ask the following:

- why they're selling;

- whether there are existing bookings for the coming season (ask to see evidence);

- how they market the property;

- whether they registered with GdF, Clévacances or the tourist board, and whether the registration has been cancelled or you'll be able to take it over;

- whether they keep a database of past (happy) customers;

- whether the price include the fixtures and fittings and any furniture. (If it does, ask yourself whether they're worth buying.)

Also ask for detailed accounts for the past few years. It's essential also to do your own research, particularly with regard to location, potential income and the reason for selling, as the owners may be economical with the truth on certain points. If possible, buy a business in the autumn, to give yourself time to settle in, make any necessary alterations, do some marketing and (if necessary) improve your French before welcoming your first guests the following spring.

CONVERSION

If you want to install ensuite bathrooms (recommended), make sure that the layout of the house allows this. (Bear in mind also that rooms must be soundproofed, especially ensuite bathrooms.) You might need to take advice from a surveyor or architect as to whether it's possible. If you cannot have a water supply and waste outlet in all the rooms, you could consider having two rooms share a bathroom and market it as a family suite; macerating lavatories aren't a good solution, as they make far too much noise. On the other hand, if you're appealing to French clients, bear in mind that they generally prefer the WC to be separate from the bathroom (many French people are disgusted by the idea of having a lavatory in the same room as a bath or shower).

If you're on septic tank drainage (as is the case with most rural properties), check the size of the tank. If it's the original installation, it will be the right size for normal family usage with maybe just one WC. With several lavatories and bathrooms, you'll need a much larger tank. Take advice on this before any unpleasant and expensive problems arise (sometimes literally!).

In an old property, the water heating system will also have been designed for a family and not for guests who want baths or showers daily. **You must have sufficient hot water at all times for your guests** and will probably need to install a larger tank and boiler.

LEGAL CONSIDERATIONS

French rules and regulations are a mystifying maze that most French people – let alone foreigners – find difficult to negotiate, particularly as they can change from one day to the next and from one office to the next. Different official bodies may give you contradictory advice (if they don't know the answer, they're likely to give their opinion – i.e. guess – rather than find out!). Moreover, many regulations are formulated at departmental rather than national level; Gîtes de France, for example, is a national governmental organisation, yet each departmental office is run autonomously and their rules can be **very** different. It's therefore imperative to check the rules and regulations that apply in **your** department.

There's now a legal definition of *chambres d'hôtes*. Law no. 2006-437, passed on 14th April 2006 states in article L.324-3 that *chambres d'hôtes* are furnished rooms, situated at the owner's dwelling, for paying tourists to stay one or several nights. Nothing new there, but Article L.324-4 stipulates that anyone offering *chambres d'hôtes* **must** inform the *maire* of their commune that they're doing so.

To this end, your first port of call (**even before you purchase a property**) should be the local *mairie*. If the *maire* is in favour (e.g. because your customers will also patronise local shops and restaurants), you'll have a lot of help. He can point you in the right direction and even help with the process. If your *maire* isn't in favour of any more tourists, B&Bs or foreign-owned businesses on his patch, you won't find it easy, or he might even refuse permission. There's no reason why you should meet any opposition unless there's a surfeit of French-owned (or other) *chambres d'hôtes* in the commune, but if this were the case there would be little point in continuing anyway.

The most widespread and relevant rules and regulations applicable to B&B accommodation are those of Gîtes de France. Whereas these aren't national law (except the two points outlined above), many departments are now requiring *chambres d'hôtes* businesses to be inspected by GdF or the tourist office and rated before being allowed to trade. The government is considering drawing up standard national regulations for B&Bs; until such rules are drafted, your only legal requirements are those detailed below.

Tax Registration

If running a B&B isn't your principal activity (i.e. it doesn't constitute more than 50 per cent of your income), it can be declared on your tax forms as additional income under *bénéfices industriels et commerciaux* (*BIC*) and is allowed as supplementary income without further registration. If the earnings of your B&B are to be your sole or main income **or** if the annual takings exceed €23,000, however, you must register with the Registre des Commerces et des Sociétés (RCS) and pay contributions (*cotisations* – roughly equivalent to UK national insurance contributions) amounting to around €2,500 in the first year and €3,500 in the second year; in subsequent years you pay a percentage of your income. Registration is made at the Centre de Formalités des Entreprises (CFE), which is part of the Chambre de Commerce et Industrie (CCI).

Number of Rooms

The legal definition of *chambres d'hôtes* is a room or rooms in the owner's house for tourists staying one or more nights, including breakfast. Five is the normal maximum for the number of rooms. In some departments it's six, and in yet others you may have six but the sixth must have disabled access. If you offer more rooms than this, your business won't be defined as a *chambres d'hôtes* by GdF, Clévacances or the tourist board and must comply with stringent fire and safety regulations in line with those for hotels, in accordance with the rules governing 'establishments receiving the public' (*établissements recevant du public*).

3

Tariffs

In line with the law of 18th October 1998, the price of accommodation and meals must be displayed outside the premises and inside – in the reception area and on the door of each bedroom. If there are different prices according to the size or quality of the rooms, all of these must be on the list outside and in the reception area, along with the prices of meals if applicable.

Invoices

An invoice must be given to each client on demand or if the total amount charged is more than €15.24 (which is highly likely!). Invoices must be in duplicate – one copy given to the client, the other kept by the owner for a year – and filed in date order. Invoices must include the date, the name and address of the person paying, the name of the client (if different), the date and place of payment, a detailed breakdown of items charged for and the price of each and the total to be paid.

Foreign Visitors

Since 1999, foreign visitors (including EU nationals) must fill in and sign a 'police card' (*fiche de police*) – obtainable from the *préfecture* – with the following information: their name and surname, date and place of birth, nationality, and the address of their normal residence. In theory, these cards must be handed in on the day of arrival to the local police or *gendarmerie*; in practice, you might be met with a look of bemusement! If this happens, ask if it's necessary to do this; you may be allowed simply to keep the cards on file.

If the procedures regarding tariffs, invoices and foreign visitor registration aren't followed, you can be fined €1,500!

Food & Drink

Table d'hôtes is the term for the evening meal in a *chambres d'hôtes*. Legally (to protect the interests of restaurant proprietors), a B&B must provide *table d'hôtes* only to overnight guests. The menu must be fixed, the meal is to be served at one table, and the seating must not exceed the number of guests staying overnight. **If these rules aren't followed, you're liable to a heavy fine.** Prices of meals must be included on the tariff, see above. You must also adhere to strict hygiene regulations.

You must have a licence to serve drinks, even for tea or coffee at breakfast time. For further details, see page 148.

OFFICIAL ORGANISATIONS

There's no obligation to register with the tourist board or any of the recognised B&B organisations, but depending on your target clientele it may be to your advantage to do so. The two main B&B organisations are Gîtes de France (GdF) and Clévacances (see below). GdF is the clear market leader with over 25,000 *chambres d'hôtes* on its books compared with Clévacances' 5,000, as well as a much higher public profile, but only Clévacances handles B&Bs in urban areas. Both are official government organisations, linked to and working closely with the Comité Régional du Tourisme and the Comité Départemental du Tourisme. Other organisations include Fleurs de Soleil (see page 137), Accueil Paysan and Bienvenue à La Ferme (see **Appendix E**), but the last two, as yet, have few members and are largely unknown, especially to overseas clients.

GdF and Clévacances have a range of quality standards and grade your accommodation according to the following:

● the exterior appearance of the building;

● the quality of the materials in its construction (principally walls, floors and ceilings);

● the standard of decoration;

- the quality of the breakfast;

- the quality of bedding, bathroom facilities, etc..

Great emphasis is also put on the participation and attitude of the hosts; this even appears in GdF's official list of criteria (see **Appendix E**).

Advantages & Disadvantages

You don't have to register with any B&B organisations, but if you want to maximise your income from letting, registration has a lot of advantages, certainly far more than with a *gîte* business (especially if you're relying on passing trade), although there may be disadvantages as well (see below).

3

> **SURVIVAL TIP**
> **To attract passing trade and French customers, it's essential to register with an official organisation; otherwise, it's unlikely you'll get enough business.**

The advantages of registration include the following:

- You're 'buying into' a recognised brand name, which appears on your publicity material and signs. (According to a poll carried out by the Institut Français d'Opinion Publique on the reputation of tourism businesses, the brand name Gîtes de France appeared third, below only Club Méditerranée and Nouvelles Frontières.)

- You'll benefit from the organisation's promotional and publicity material (catalogues, internet site, etc.).

- Your accommodation will be known to meet certain recognised standards, which reassures clients.

- You'll attract a greater number of French visitors (who constitute 80 per cent of GdF's clientele).

- You may not be able to advertise your B&B with the local tourist board unless it's registered.

- You might be eligible for a grant (see **Grants** on page 189).

- You can use the organisation's booking system.

- You're supplied with documentation (e.g. contract forms).

- You can obtain free advice (e.g. on setting up your business).

- You'll have access to financial and legal assistance.

Disadvantages of registering with an officially recognised organisation may include the following:

- the cost of registration (see below);

- the cost of adapting your premises to meet their standards;

- If you take advantage of a set-up grant from Gîtes de France (see **Grants** on page 189), you're tied to the organisation's booking system for a considerable time – up to ten years.

- Clientele are on average 80 per cent French, and the French are 'conservative' in their choice of holiday periods, which may limit the number of weeks you can sell.

- Marketing is mainly aimed at the French, although the major organisations have increased their overseas marketing in recent years.

- Pricing is structured around French holidays, so that high season is limited to around six weeks in the summer.

- Rents are often lower than can be obtained by direct marketing focused on British and other overseas clients. (GdF quotes the average price of a three-*épi* room as €45; for UK-marketed properties the average is closer to €60.)

Tourist Board

If you choose to register with the tourist board (Comité Départemental du Tourisme) or if registration is compulsory in your department, you must apply for an inspection, and you'll be awarded a star rating. (The inspector might be a GdF or Clévacances representative, but there's no obligation to become a member of either organisation.) You should check with your local *préfecture* whether an inspection is required.

The tourist board can help you in the following ways to establish your business:

- analyse your project and advise on adjustments to meet local regulations and requirements;

- provide information and advice on accommodation grading systems and standards;

- provide information about B&B organisations and their requirements;

- provide information and advice on standards and equipment for adapting your accommodation for disabled use;

- provide information on financial assistance, e.g. grants (see page 189);

- provide data from the departmental tourist office;

- help to direct your questions to the appropriate organisations.

3

Gîtes de France

By far the best known French accommodation 'label', Gîtes de France (GdF, ☎ 01 49 70 75 75, 🖳 www.gites-de-france.fr), as its name suggests, was set up in 1951 to regulate *gîtes*, but it added B&B to its operations in 1969; its green, yellow and white *'Chambres d'Hôtes'* signs are a familiar sight throughout the country.

Under the GdF system, the rooms you let must usually be part of your own house but in exceptional circumstances, they may be in an adjoining building. Other requirements vary from department to department, but are generally as follows:

- Five, occasionally six, rooms (depending on the department) is the maximum (the sixth may have to have disabled access), accommodating a maximum of 15 guests.

- The price per room must include breakfast.

- Each room must have a minimum area of 12m² excluding the bathroom.

- If there's no ensuite bathroom, every room must have at least a basin and there must be a WC and bathroom on the same floor.

- Rooms must be cleaned daily, and sheets and towels must be supplied.

- Meals must be freshly prepared, using local ingredients wherever possible.

- In some departments, your property must be located in a commune of fewer than 1,500 inhabitants.

The classification, like the *gîte* system, is by *épis* (corn ears): B&Bs are awarded between one and four.

GdF publishes the following guides (a total of 2m copies are printed annually), in which your accommodation is listed, as appropriate:

- **departmental guides** – one for each *département*;

- **regional guides** – one for each of the following regions: Auvergne, Corsica, Normandy (Upper and Lower combined) and Midi-Pyrénées;

- **national guides** – for the following types of accommodation: near a ski resort (*Séjours à la Neige*); in the mountains (*Vivez la Montagne Autrement*); near fishing water (*Séjours Pêche*); 'charming' properties (*Chambres d'Hôtes de Charme*); accommodation offering evening meals (*Chambres et Tables d'Hôtes*).

Clévacances

Clévacances was set up in 1997 to promote self-catering and B&B accommodation. It has around 3,000 *chambres d'hôtes* properties registered in 80 departments, covering a broader variety of property types than those of GdF, including seaside and mountain properties, villas, apartments and character properties, many of them in urban areas. Accommodation is graded with key (*clé* – hence the name of the organisation) symbols – one to four – according to the following criteria:

- the environment, i.e. the quality of the building, the site and its surroundings and absence of nuisances such as noise and smells;

- the quality of the interior, i.e. comfort, furnishings, decoration, facilities, and the arrangement and function of rooms;

- the welcome and assistance offered by the owner(s).

For a visit from a Clévacances representative, you must apply to the departmental office or your tourist office. After an initial visit in the presence of the owner or caretaker (and possibly an inspector from the tourism office), a report is prepared. This report is submitted to the department's *préfecture* for assessment according to the ministerial decree for standards in tourist accommodation. If these steps are completed successfully, you receive accreditation from Clévacances and a grading of one to four *clés* (keys).

Successful owners receive a sign to fix to the exterior of their property, a certificate stating the number of keys awarded, and documentation (invoices, contracts, etc.) to use. A Clévacances representative visits at least every three years, more often in certain cases (e.g. if you request advice, carry out alterations to your property or have problems with a client). The fees charged for inspection, registration and annual subscription vary by department; ask at your Comité Départemental du Tourisme. Further information is available from the Clévacances website (💻 www.clevacances.com).

Fleurs de Soleil

Fleurs de Soleil is a not-for-profit organisation formed in 1997, under the auspices of the association Les Maisons d'Amis en France, to promote quality *chambres d'hôtes*. Fleurs de Soleil stipulates the following:

- The property should be in a region with cultural, historical and other tourism interest.

- The accommodation must be in a detached house that isn't part of a housing estate.

- If the property is in a village, there must be no noise from passing traffic, trains or neighbours.

- The house must have character or charm, be well decorated, and have an attractive garden.

- The owner cannot run any other business on the same premises.

- Members can let up to five rooms, for a maximum of 12 guests.

- The guest rooms must be in the hosts' own house or in an annexe, and there should be a communal room where guests can have their breakfast, talk, read, listen to music or watch television.

- Rooms must have private bathrooms.

- If further facilities (such as a pool or tennis court) are offered, their use must be included in the price of the room.

- Breakfast must comprise tea, coffee or chocolate, a selection of breads and jams, butter and, if requested, cereals, eggs or yoghurt, and must be included in the price of a night's accommodation.

Great emphasis is put on the quality of welcome from the owners. There are further, lengthy regulations regarding furnishings, facilities, size of beds, etc., some of which are included in **Appendix E** and which can be obtained by contacting the organisation's departmental office, via the head office: Fleurs de Soleil, Domaine du Frère, Les Milles, 1382 Aix-en-Provence, Cedex 3 (☎ 08 26 62 03 22). Details can also be found on the website (💻 www.fleursdesoleil.fr). Fleurs de Soleil publishes an accommodation catalogue (of around 200 pages) but it costs €13, which is typical of French marketing (who is going to pay for it when most companies give out free brochures?).

FINANCIAL CONSIDERATIONS

3

If you already have a main occupation and/or income, your initial outlay need not be large; you could start by converting, decorating and letting one or two rooms, then expand as time and finances allow. If, however, you intend to rely on a B&B business for your main or sole income, you must 'hit the track running', which can require a considerable capital investment – well in advance of your first earnings. You must therefore budget carefully, balancing set-up costs (see below), taxes and social security contributions, and the cost of simply staying alive against your projected receipts, which could take years to reach their potential.

Set-up Costs

Your initial expenses may include the following:

- renovation (including the installation of bathrooms and WCs) and decoration;
- beds and other furniture;
- soft furnishings;
- bed linen and towels;
- kitchen equipment, including a dishwasher (essential if you're providing evening meals – or even two), crockery, cutlery, pots and pans, and table linen;
- books, board games and other leisure equipment;
- swimming pool;
- registration with a B&B organisation (see page 130);

- advertising and publicity;

- printing of brochures, headed paper, business cards, invoices, etc..

Your set-up costs will obviously depend on the number of rooms you equip for letting, the quality of furnishings and equipment you choose, whether you install a dedicated kitchen for preparing guests' meals, and a number of other factors.

Running Costs

3

Your budget must also allow for running costs, which may include the following:

- laundry and cleaning;

- food for breakfasts and possibly evening meals;

- fuel for the daily trip to the *boulangerie* if it isn't within walking distance;

- advertising, publicity and printing;

- extra electricity, gas, heating fuel, water consumption and possibly waste charges;

- maintenance contracts for appliances (you cannot afford to have a broken down washing machine or dishwasher);

- periodic redecoration of rooms;

- renewal of worn furniture, fabrics and fittings;

- new clothes (you must look smart when dealing with guests!);

- swimming pool maintenance (if you have one);

- insurance;

- taxes and social security charges (see **Chapter 6**).

Viabllity

The principles of calculating the viability (or not) of your B&B business are essentially the same as those for a *gîte* business (see **Viability** on page 75). If you cannot achieve 40 per cent occupancy (see below), your business is unlikely to be viable and, even then, much depends on the number of rooms you have to let and what other income you can generate (e.g. by offering meals, courses or local tours).

 You won't earn enough to live on unless you let four or five rooms, offer facilities that enable you to extend the season and carry out effective marketing.

3 Occupancy

Occupancy rates vary according to several factors:

- the type and quality of accommodation you offer;
- its location;
- the time of year;
- your pricing and marketing.

Calculate the amount you would receive with full occupancy over ten weeks (the average summer season). For example, four rooms at €60 per night would generate €16,800 at 100 per cent occupancy. With attractive, well appointed, registered accommodation, a good location and efficient marketing you should be able to achieve between 40 and 60 per cent of full occupancy within two years.

Taking the figures above as an example: at 40 per cent occupancy, your gross income would be €6,720 and at 60 per cent it would be €10,080. Out-of-season occupancy is a bonus.

The Agence Pour la Création d'Entreprises estimates the average occupancy rate across France to be 37 per cent, although this figure includes B&Bs run as a supplement to a main income, sometimes with only two rooms (in which case, if a cancellation is made, occupancy drops to 50 per cent!).

Another factor to consider when estimating your occupancy is that bookings are unlikely to dovetail conveniently – unlike those for *gîtes*, which are normally booked for a week at a time with a regular changeover day. For this reason many owners take short-stay bookings only at the last minute – a one-night advance booking for three rooms in the middle of August might seem a good idea at the time but it will leave you unable to accept longer (and more lucrative) bookings.

Letting Rates

Letting rates vary considerably according to the time of year, the area, and the quality of accommodation. You're free to charge whatever you choose, but don't price yourself out of the local market. Do some research in your area and find out what similar establishments are charging. Look at advertisements in newspapers and magazines and on the internet. In fact, a *chambres d'hôtes* business is more restricted than *gîte* accommodation in terms of pricing, as local competition has a far greater influence on what you can charge. As you **must** display your tariff outside the premises, prospective clients can see your prices. If they're higher than those of the B&B down the road, they will probably go there instead, unless there are other means of comparison. Rather than have a simple price list, therefore, consider a covered notice board with photographs of the rooms, garden and any other 'unique selling points'.

The standard room rate quoted is usually for a room with ensuite facilities, accommodating two people for one night including breakfast. Whereas registering with GdF greatly increases your occupancy rate, its charges are generally lower than you can charge foreign (particularly British) clients booking direct. GdF quotes the average price of a three-*épi* room as €45; for UK-marketed properties the average is closer to €60.

For rooms that accommodate more than two guests you must work out a suitable tariff – for instance a room that is €60 for two people could be priced at €45 for a single occupant and at €75 for three people. You can have a lower rate for children sharing with their parents (e.g. €12 on top of the two-person price), but charge the normal rate if they're in a separate room. Consider discounting the price for stays of more than two nights, tempting guests to stay longer and cutting down on the piles of laundry and cleaning time!

For *gîtes*, most people who let year round have low-, medium- and high-season rates, but this isn't as common for B&B, one reason being that heating costs are higher in mid and low season and these must be covered (*gîte* clients can be charged for heating). If you do choose to have different rates, high season generally includes the months of July and August and possibly the first two weeks of September, mid-season usually comprises June, September and October (and possibly Easter and Christmas/New Year), and the rest of the year is low season.

Additional income can be generated by offering evening meals, but these must be costed very carefully in order to cover the time required to prepare them and make a significant profit without being overpriced. In your calculations, don't rely on all guests taking advantage of the service; depending on your proximity to affordable restaurants, you'll generally find that a quarter to half of your guests will book evening meals.

When comparing your proposed rates against those of other owners, take into account the level of comfort, the market in your area, your location, and whether you offer any additional facilities such as a pool. Set a realistic rent, as there's a lot of competition. **You must make a profit without pricing yourself out of the market!**

Taxation

An important consideration for anyone running a B&B in France is taxation, which includes income tax, property tax and other local taxes. **Bear in mind that you must pay tax in France on all income from property letting.** Before buying a property for letting, you should obtain expert advice regarding French taxes. This will (hopefully) ensure that you take maximum advantage of your current tax status and that you don't make any mistakes that you will regret later.

If you run a B&B, you're also normally liable for *taxe professionelle*, although you may be granted exemption if you let for less than half the year and/or the property is your principal residence. Under certain circumstances you could be required to register for value added tax (VAT) and the local authority may charge you a *taxe de séjour* for each paying guest (see **Chapter 4**).

FACILITIES

Additional facilities can give you a competitive edge and add value to your accommodation. They should give extra value either in monetary terms (for instance bicycle hire) or by improving the level of comfort and service, which will earn you recommendations to guests' friends, relatives and colleagues. If you have enough room outside, a children's play area with swings and maybe a slide is a valuable addition (but check your insurance), or an area set aside for ball games away from your precious garden! You could provide sports equipment – a few badminton rackets and shuttlecocks and other lawn games – and offer other equipment for hire, e.g. bicycles or fishing tackle. (Be careful if charging for extra services; you may be liable to register for VAT – see **Chapter 4**.)

Telephone

A telephone for guests' use is a valuable facility. Although most people now have mobile phones, reception, especially in the more rural parts of

France, can be patchy and calls from a fixed line are often cheaper. Guests can purchase a *Ticket Téléphone International* to make long-distance calls from your fixed line (by keying in a code). These cards are available from France Télécom outlets, *tabacs* and newsagents', in denominations of €7.50 and €15. Alternatively, you can provide a separate payphone or invoice them at the end of their stay by consulting your telephone account online.

Internet Access

So many people now depend on the internet for business and personal needs that it's a huge advantage to offer this facility. Even if they don't need access, many feel bereft without a connection! At the very least, many guests will ask if they can check their email; it's a big plus to be able to offer them a dedicated computer for their use. If you have an unlimited use contract or broadband access, there's no extra cost involved (you could nevertheless charge by the minute); with dial-up access you can easily monitor time spent online and charge accordingly. A relatively inexpensive computer system and a telephone socket in the guests' lounge are all that's needed. If you have a wireless connection, guests could use their own laptops.

Swimming Pool

A swimming pool is desirable, particularly in warmer regions, as properties with pools are much easier to let than those without (unless a property is situated near a beach, lake or river). You can also charge a higher rent for a property with a pool, and you may be able to extend the season by installing a heated or indoor pool. Note that there are new safety regulations regarding pools used by the public, which include pools at private homes that are let for holidays. Make sure that you understand the regulations before installing a pool. For further information about swimming pools, see page 77.

Keys

Guests must have a key to their room and possibly to the front door if they're out late at night. **You might prefer to have a front door key available on request; if there's a fire, you must know how many people are in the building.**

FURNISHINGS, FITTINGS & DECORATION

Many people prefer B&Bs to the anonymity of hotel rooms. In furnishing and equipping your rooms, as in the service you provide, you must strike a balance between being professional and providing a personal and individual service. Make your accommodation welcoming and comfortable, but avoid making guests feel that they're intruders in your home. For example, many owners name their rooms, thus avoiding an impersonal numbering system; you could choose a colour or theme for each (e.g. local flowers, towns or artists).

When letting rooms, don't fill them with expensive furnishings or valuable belongings. While theft is rare, items will eventually be damaged or broken. Bear in mind when purchasing furnishings and fittings that you're buying for others to use; they should be easy to clean and maintain in good condition. In the peak season (and hopefully at other times of the year) you'll have only a few hours between departing guests and the new arrivals to do all that's necessary to restore the accommodation to pristine condition.

When furnishing a room that you plan to let, choose durable furniture and furnishings and hard-wearing, neutral-coloured carpets that won't show the stains. Shops such as Casa and Gifi and many larger supermarkets sell inexpensive and attractive home décor. Decoration should be light and bright, with fresh colours, but not gaudy or too individualistic. Some people like frills and flounces, others clean modern lines, so keep a happy medium. It's best to keep walls white or off-white (*blanc cassé*), as it's then easier to redecorate. Add colour with soft furnishings and rugs, plenty of pictures and a selection of bits and pieces to make the rooms more welcoming.

Central heating is necessary if the property is to be let all year round. Otherwise, convection heaters that can be regulated are usually adequate. Depending on the price and quality of a property, your guests may also expect tea/coffee-making facilities, and covered parking.

Bedrooms

Ideally, all bedrooms should have ensuite bathroom facilities, which are expected by the majority of clients nowadays. Sometimes the layout of the house doesn't permit the necessary plumbing for the water supply and waste outlets, in which case you could have two rooms sharing one bathroom, perhaps marketing them as a family suite. Don't install macerating lavatories, as they're far too noisy.

You should also supply a bedside table and a reading lamp for each guest and a water jug (or a bottle of water) and drinking glasses. A full-length mirror is always appreciated, and there should be an electrical socket nearby for hairdryers and other appliances. Optional extras include an alarm clock (ensuring that guests are up in time for breakfast!), a hairdryer, and a small safe for valuables. Think carefully before installing clock radios, a TV or any other item that might disturb other guests.

Some owners provide a tray with a kettle and cups, teabags, coffee, milk, etc., although this is more appropriate for a hotel room. French clients don't expect this facility. You could compromise by putting them in the dining room so that people can make a hot drink whenever they choose.

Furniture

3

You need solid beds with good mattresses. Give careful consideration to the number and type of beds in each room. Too many double beds limit the permutations of guests. If you have only one room, provide twin beds; if you have just two rooms, make one a double and the other a twin. If the rooms are large enough, you could have a double and a single in each, which allows for various permutations (a couple, separate people or a couple with a child). If there are three or more rooms, you could put bunk beds in one of them for children. (Bunk beds should be used **only** by children.) If you have a small room, consider a single bed; if there's enough space, use a 120cm (4ft) bed – luxurious as a single bed and adequate for a couple provided they know in advance that it's a small double. Have a cot or two available – the collapsible type is the best, as they can be easily stored when not in use (they must have the CE mark, showing that they conform to EU safety standards).

Provide plenty of hanging space and a chest of drawers (or a French wardrobe with hanging space and shelves), plus a small table and chair with an electrical socket nearby for guests to use for writing or to plug in a laptop.

Make sure there's somewhere guests can put their suitcases. If you have room, it's a good idea to have a suitable surface for an open suitcase. Many visitors won't use the hanging space and drawers but prefer to live out of their suitcases, especially if they're staying just one or two nights – if the bed is the only place to put cases, they're likely to dirty and snag your bedspreads or quilts.

If you want to provide antique beds, measure their length before buying, as some older beds are too short for modern mattresses. (Mattresses must not, under any circumstances, be of a similar vintage!) Normandy beds and *bateau-lits* with wooden sides are quaint and typically French, but enormously difficult to make tidily. While comfort is subjective and you cannot please all tastes (some like their beds hard, some soft, some in between), if the mattresses are new there's little that can be complained about. There's no shortage of good mattresses in France; every town has frequent visits from itinerant mattress-sellers, although it may be preferable to buy from an established local business.

Bed Linen

3

It's generally a good idea to use white bed linen (whether real linen, cotton or polycotton). It looks clean and fresh and you can replace it piece by piece if one item is damaged or worn, rather than having to buy a whole new set. Colour can be added with quilts, bedspreads or throws. Always use good quality fabrics; cheap sheets and pillowcases are a false economy, as they wear thin very quickly and can be difficult to iron. The larger supermarkets have sales and promotions for household linens in January, so that's a good time to buy. Mail order catalogues such as *La Redoute* and *Trois Suisses* are also good sources.

When deciding on what to buy, bear in mind how easy or difficult it will be to make the beds. Do you want to wrestle with double duvet covers? You could have sheets and blankets, or instead of putting a duvet in a cover use it like an eiderdown with sheets under it and a bedspread on top – much easier to change (do use a protector, though).

Antique pure linen monogrammed and embroidered sheets can sometimes be found at bargain prices in France. Nothing beats the comfort and quality of real linen, it improves with age, and it's the perfect complement to antique furniture – also an added-value point for your publicity.

Provide two pillows for each person, or a pillow and a bolster (*traversin*). Your guests have chosen to come to France, and typical French items such as square pillows and bolsters are all part of the experience (although you might keep a few British-style pillows handy in case of violent objections!). Use waterproof mattress and pillow protectors, as people dribble in their sleep (not to mention other 'accidents' that can occur). Keep a spare set and clean them between lettings.

Supply at least one bath towel and a hand towel for each guest. For guests staying a week or more, you must change bed linen every five days and towels every three days (they might need drying in between). Have some beach towels available on request, as people often forget to bring them and you won't want your bath towels taken to the seaside. Provide a towel rail to avoid wet towels being draped over your furniture and windowsills.

Bathrooms

Shower cubicles take up less room than bathtubs, and showers use less water than baths. Make sure when installing a shower that you minimise the danger of overflowing water (sliding doors are preferable to a curtain and easier to clean). Fit impermeable flooring – guests won't always take as much care as they would at home – and tile as many surfaces as possible, which makes them far easier to clean. Fit a long mirror so that people of all heights can use it easily, with a light above it and a shaver point nearby.

You might like to keep a selection of small soaps, shower gels, shampoos and toothpastes, as well as shower caps and disposable razors for guests who have omitted to bring their own.

Bathrooms must, of course, have excellent ventilation – an extractor fan and/or a window that opens.

Dining Room

You need a dining room, even if not providing evening meals (unless you have an exceptionally large kitchen!). Whatever you do, don't put carpet in the dining room (a tiled floor is ideal); French bread and croissants generate a huge quantity of crumbs. French guests can be particularly messy, preferring bowls without saucers for their morning *café au lait* or *chocolat*, and they often put plates aside, breaking their bread on the table. Provide plenty of napkins – paper serviettes are acceptable for breakfast, although it's better to use fabric ones for dinner. You could also use a vinyl, paper or authentic waxed (*ciré*) tablecloth at breakfast time.

Under *table d'hôtes* regulations you must have just 'one table' for dinners, but consider having two or three small tables that can be separately laid for breakfast and pushed together for the evening meal according to how many are staying. People come down for breakfast at different times and don't always feel sociable first thing in the morning. Use sturdy chairs; many people have the annoying habit of swinging their chairs and when they're adult paying guests it's embarrassing to have to tell them to stop!

You can also provide tea- and coffee-making facilities and a small fridge/freezer for guests' own cold drinks, snacks and ice blocks. If you don't provide a freezing compartment, you'll find your own freezer permanently full of blue blocks! A microwave oven is a good idea for parents wishing to warm up baby food, but you might want to stipulate that it isn't to be used for cooking meals.

Lounge

A guest lounge should have comfortable seating, a small table and chairs for writing, and something to keep children amused on wet evenings. If you don't have a separate lounge, make sure that guests have somewhere to sit and read or write postcards in their rooms.

There should be a TV in the lounge, preferably with a UK satellite system, as it's possible that this will increase bookings, especially during major sporting events. Cartoons to keep the kids quiet seem to work in any language! Have a video and/or DVD player and a supply of films (see **Television** on page 81).

3

The Société des Auteurs, Compositeurs et Éditeurs de Musique (SACEM, 🖳 www.sacem.fr) has long been pressing for performing rights payments to be made by owners of *chambres d'hôtes* that have a TV for guests' use, so check the latest legislation – or you could face a hefty fine.

Have a bookshelf with a generous selection of paperbacks in good condition (French and English) and some toys, board games and jigsaws. French versions of well known games such as Monopoly and Cluedo are always popular – everyone knows the rules, so it's fun to play in another language.

Guests will appreciate a range of maps, guide books and local interest books and a large selection of brochures – check regularly to make sure they're up to date, and put stickers on ones you want to keep, to discourage guests from taking them home.

MEALS

Breakfast **must** be included in the price of the accommodation. The provision of other meals is optional but can be a useful supplement to your income, as well as attracting more bookings; many clients would rather eat on the premises than travel to a restaurant. A lot of French people stay only in *chambres d'hôtes* that offer *table d'hôtes* (see **Evening Meal** below). Many British and American visitors to a remote area might not want to battle with restaurant menus that don't have an English translation, especially on their first night when they arrive tired and hungry. Guests can have a drink with their meal without worrying about driving home, and young children can be put to bed, leaving parents free to enjoy their evening.

On the other hand, providing meals is time consuming: fresh produce must be bought regularly (you **mustn't** serve prepared or frozen meals), which may entail a long round trip to the shops (and the cost of transport), meals must be prepared and cooked, the table laid and cleared, and cutlery and crockery washed, dried and put away. Imagine catering for a large family group twice a day, every day and you will have some idea of what is entailed (except that you cannot ask your paying guests to 'help themselves' or do the washing-up!)

Breakfast

3

You should restrict the hours at which you serve breakfast – some guests will proudly announce that they get up at 6am every day but not actually surface until 11am. You must then wait while they eat their breakfast, return to their rooms, wash, dress and whatever else they need to do then finally go out at one o'clock, severely limiting the time you have to clear up, clean, make beds and begin preparations for the evening meal, not to mention prepare lunch if you decide to do so. Set a limit according to your needs and preferred routine, for instance you can state that breakfast is served between 7.30 and 9am.

The standard breakfast is fresh *croissants* and bread or *brioches* (which must be bought or delivered first thing every morning) with butter and a selection of (preferably home-made) jams, local honey, etc.. Serve a choice of coffee, teas, *tisanes* and hot chocolate and a range of fruit juices. You can also provide a selection of yoghurts, cereals and crispbreads. Some nationalities might request a different menu – the British like their eggs and bacon, the Dutch and Germans eat cold meats and sausage for breakfast. If you choose to offer a cooked breakfast for a supplementary charge, or provide extras, bear in mind the extra work, and calculate whether or not you'll make a profit.

If you register with Gîtes de France or Clévacances, your breakfasts are 'inspected' in addition to the rooms.

Lunch

Lunch isn't normally offered, although you might like to offer packed lunches as an additional service. If you do so, make it clear (especially to French guests) that it's a light meal, as many French people eat their main meal in the middle of the day and expect a packed lunch to contain starter, main course, cheese and dessert – plus wine and aperitifs!

Evening Meal

The provision of an evening meal in a *chambres d'hôtes* is known as *table d'hôtes*, which literally means 'hosts' table' and implies that your guests eat with you, sharing your table. It isn't a restaurant service and you mustn't offer a choice of dishes for each course; it must be a set menu. You might think that you cannot compete with local restaurants offering three-course menus with alternatives for around €12, but in fact you aren't competing with them; you're offering a different service – dinner *en famille* – and your guests are free to go out to eat if they prefer. In any case, by the time all the extras have been added (aperitif, wine, coffee, etc.) the restaurant meal will add up to far more then €12.

The requirement that you eat with your guests poses a problem: who's going to cook and serve the food? Menus with dishes that can be largely prepared earlier in the day can help overcome this; you can then nip out to the kitchen to add the finishing touches as the meal progresses and clear up as you go, perhaps joining your guests at the table for one or two courses and coffee at the end of the meal. It's unlikely you would want to eat a four-course dinner every night anyway, but it can, in good company, be an enjoyable way of spending an evening.

Consider also the following:

- Although main ingredients **must** be fresh (see **Menu** below), some elements can be prepared in advance for use over two to three days (e.g. stocks and sauce bases), and the cheese board can be carried forward each day (with additions).

- You're more likely to make a reasonable profit if you provide dinners on a regular basis, as it's cheaper to buy catering packs of staple ingredients and larger quantities of others.

- It isn't worth cooking a four-course meal for one or two guests, so you might choose to stipulate that evening meals are available only if there are four or more adults booking together.

- Make sure guests (particularly British and American) know what to expect if they book dinner: some visitors to France aren't familiar with the concept of a meal being a whole evening's activity. "Can we have our tea at six, as the kids have to be in bed by seven?" is a difficult request to answer when you would normally gather for aperitifs at 7.30 to eat at 8, work your way through four courses and finish with a coffee and *digestif* at around 11pm!

- Some people request just a main course for a reduced price, or smaller portions for children. You can either accommodate their wishes (perhaps losing money), or you can politely and apologetically explain that you're obliged to offer a set menu at a set price.

- It's easy to put on a lot of weight if you eat a full meal every night!

Ask guests when they book a meal whether they have any food allergies or strong dislikes and cater accordingly (see also **Catering for Vegetarians** below) – it's too late if they're already sitting at the table.

3

```
SURVIVAL TIP
Budget very carefully: sometimes you'll make only
enough profit to cover the cost of your own dinner.
```

Menu

All food should be home cooked using fresh ingredients and should include regional dishes (a requirement if you're registered with GdF). Dinner in France normally has four courses. The starter (*entrée*) can be soup, a salad, *crudités*, pâté or cold meats (known as an *assiette anglaise*), prepared in advance. For the main course, work out around seven basic dishes that can be prepared in the time allotted and within your budget. You can of course vary these (especially when you want to eat something different!), but having standard menus increases efficiency. Cooking for guests **isn't** the time to start experimenting and time will often be short. Have at least one menu that can be prepared at short notice for last-minute guests.

The cheese course is served before the dessert; serve three to five cheeses, including local varieties, a goat's cheese and a blue cheese. For *le dessert*, again use tried and trusted dishes. Desserts such as chocolate mousse, *crème caramel*, apple tart (there's probably a local version) and *crème brûlée* can largely be prepared earlier in the day. Finish with coffee.

Catering for Vegetarians

Vegetarian catering is a useful service to offer and can be a very valuable marketing opportunity. Vegetarianism is unusual in France, so it's extremely difficult for non-meat-eaters to eat in restaurants unless they eat fish – an endless diet of omelettes soon palls! Strictly, however, under *table d'hôtes* regulations, you aren't allowed to offer alternative menus, so you could do one of the following:

● cater only for vegetarians;

● offer a vegetarian menu on certain nights of the week;

● offer all-vegetarian menus to groups who book together.

Make sure it's clearly stated in your advertising if you provide **exclusively** vegetarian food and note that vegetarian meals won't appeal to many French guests, as most French people feel cheated without a chunk of meat as part of their dinner.

Vegetarians will do their research before embarking upon their holidays. Nowadays the internet is the most usual method of gathering information, so if you target the vegetarian market ensure you have an easily found website (see **Your Own Website** on page 219), swap links with other vegetarian establishments, and advertise in vegetarian magazines.

Vegetarian Vacations (🖃 www.vegetarian-vacations.com/bedbreakfast/france.html) is an online directory for vegetarian B&Bs in France; listings are free in exchange for reciprocal links to the Vegetarian Vacations and Bicycle Beano (?) sites.

CASE STUDY 5

In February 2005 we swapped our home in Sussex, England for a converted farmhouse in the beautiful Lot department of south-west France. The house, which is over 150 years old, is built from local stone and sits high in the hills close to St Céré; it's ideal for the many superb attractions that this part of France has to offer.

We chose to run a B&B partly because we had heard that the market for self-catering accommodation was becoming saturated but mainly because we both felt it would be more fun. But the big question was: how could we be different? Experience had taught us that to have a chance of being successful you need to draw on your own passions, whatever they may be. Of course, it also had to be something for which there was a demand but not yet a plentiful supply.

Our first step was to offer dinner on six nights a week – not that unusual nowadays – but to this we added the extra dimension of providing the option of a full vegetarian menu. Whilst neither of us are

100 per cent vegetarian, Alex always cooked vegetarian whenever she could and we had both witnessed the steady rise in popularity of good, imaginative vegetarian cooking when we lived in the UK. France on the other hand can be like a desert for the vegetarian traveller – despite having some of the best fresh fruit and vegetables in the world – and we felt that with European diets changing there was definitely a market to be tapped. What could be better than the satisfaction of growing all your own ingredients or buying from the myriad of smallholders at the wonderful French markets?

The next challenge was to design some menus. Besides inventing our own dishes, we scoured the many vegetarian cookbooks we had collected over the years. We delved into the excellent 'Cranks' restaurant book and borrowed a few creations from Vegetarian Society publications; and, of course, who could do without a few tips from the ever-reliable Delia?

We did hit a few snags. Some of the recipes called for ingredients that were alien to the average French farmer so a little adjustment here and there was called for – resulting in many delicious tasting sessions. Next came the adjustment from the 'buy anything anytime' culture of the UK. In France, if it isn't in season it probably isn't for sale! The upside was that everything you buy has probably travelled only a few miles from the field via the market. The result was a combination of a different set of menus for each season and storing vegetables that would keep in every available cupboard and drawer.

We will probably always offer both non-vegetarian and vegetarian meals; we feel that even just offering that option makes us different, as you often have to have one or the other. So far we've had nothing but praise from our vegetarian guests and we think we may even have converted a few of our carnivorous guests.

Of course you need more than one string to your bow. With fantastic countryside around us, we also offer walking holidays – another of our passions. This has proved immensely popular and resulted in seven- and ten-night bookings, which are far more cost effective than one-nighters. I suppose we will know we've hit all the buttons when we get a group of vegetarian hikers!

Without doubt, our most effective marketing tool is our website; having a well designed and informative site has meant that many enquiries have come straight from guests searching the internet. After that, it's advertising in specialist UK publications for our target markets and on dedicated holiday accommodation websites. Our choice of sites was largely guided by the opinions of other B&B owners – an invaluable and generally friendly source of knowledge.

The promotion of vegetarian holidays in France is still very much in its infancy, almost a secret! However, there's a growing number of similar establishments and, who knows, one day we might even get the French to sit down to a four-course dinner entirely 'sans viande'.

3 In summing up, do we enjoy our life and would we do it again? The resounding answer to both questions is "Yes". Admittedly, it's hard work but to be told by guests that they've enjoyed every minute of their stay, to be on the receiving end of small 'thank you' gifts, to make new friends from all over the world and to know some will return next year ... what could be more satisfying than that?

Richard and Alex Johnson, Jardin du Segala, Le Bourg, 46190 Lacam d'Ourcet (☎ 05 65 34 47 06, 🖳 www.jardin-segala.com)

Drinks Licences

If operating a B&B, you must obtain a drinks licence, even if you don't provide evening meals. This doesn't mean you're expected to serve wine with breakfast! A licence is required for **any** drinks served with a meal, including coffee, tea and fruit juice. Drinks licences are classified into five categories, but only the first two are readily obtainable:

- **First Category** – mineral water, fruit and vegetable juices, lemonade, fruit syrups, milk, tea, coffee and chocolate;

- **Second Category** – fermented (but not distilled) drinks, including wine, champagne, beer, cider, Perry (*poiré*), and alcoholic syrups (e.g. *crème de cassis*) with up to three degrees of alcohol (if you can find them!);

If you wish to serve spirits (e.g. as a *digestif* or with the after-dinner coffee), you must offer them free (or 'lose' the cost in the overall meal price).

You need a *licence à consommer sur place du premier groupe* to serve first-category drinks (i.e. if you're serving breakfast only). If you provide evening meals and must therefore serve wine (or other drinks in the second category), you need a *petite licence restaurant*.

You must obtain an application form at the *mairie* and the licence itself at the local customs office (*douanes*). If the *mairie* has no knowledge of such a licence, you must go to your departmental *préfecture* for an application form. The licence is free.

Drinks may be served only on the premises, to B&B clients, and with meals. You cannot sell alcoholic drinks without meals; this requires a quite different class of licence that's strictly controlled to protect the interests of bar and hotel owners.

Hygiene Regulations

3

The preparation and provision of meals as *table d'hôtes* are subject to the law of 9th May 1995, which regulates food preparation, kitchen cleanliness, avoidance of food contamination and other matters relating to hygiene. For more information and the full regulations in your area, or advice, contact the Direction Départementale des Services Vétérinaires, whose contact details can be found on 🖳 http://lesservices.service-public.fr/local/index.htm. Alternatively, as with many procedures, contact your local *mairie*.

MAINTENANCE

There's a great deal of everyday maintenance involved in running a *chambres d'hôtes* business, much of which is made up of repetitive household chores. Don't forget to schedule a rest break!

Cleaning

You must clean the rooms and make the beds every day. On a changeover day, allow an hour per room for cleaning and changing the bed linen, replacing towels, soap, etc. – a checklist helps. Time must be allocated for cleaning the dining room and guests' lounge; kitchen and food preparation areas must be kept scrupulously clean at all times.

Exterior

Keep the entrance to your property well maintained – a weed-infested drive, overhanging hedges and rickety gates won't attract custom, however smart the house. Lawns must be cut, gardens kept weed free, patios and terraces swept and cleared of moss. If applicable, you must allow for pool maintenance.

Laundry

Washing and ironing can occupy a huge part of the day; you need a robust washing machine (probably two), a large tumble drier for wet days and a **huge** ironing surface – a table covered with old blankets and a sheet is suitable. Rotary irons are good for items that can be folded flat. It may be worth sending your washing out to the local commercial laundry (*blanchisserie*), though this will obviously eat into your profits. If you do this you must buy a much larger quantity of linen to compensate for turn-around time, allowing also for weekend and public holiday delays, which will further reduce your profit margin. If you have more than one commercial laundry within a reasonable distance, ask for quotes and find out whether they collect and deliver. You should also send a test load to see whether the standard is satisfactory, as laundries sometimes iron in more creases than they remove! If you use precious antique linen or embroidered sheets, it's best to launder them yourself. Nothing beats the smell of sun-dried bed linen.

Cooking & Shopping

If you're offering evening meals, take into account the time required for daily shopping (fresh ingredients are essential). Preparation and cooking may take another two or three hours, then there's the clearing, cleaning, washing up and laying the table for the following morning's breakfasts. **It's a long day!**

CASE STUDY 6

We moved from Newcastle-upon-Tyne in the UK to Dordogne, where we now run a B&B. The house was bought in 1983, but we didn't start running it as a B&B until 1989. My father had restored the house but, owing to unforeseen circumstances, never ran it as a B&B himself. We had holidayed in the area for many years before we settled here and knew it well.

We didn't hate the UK, our jobs or lives, but we had the opportunity to do something different and our children were young enough (four and seven) to adapt to a new life. They fitted into the village school within the first six months and made their ways through the local schools. They're now both at university in Bordeaux.

B&B is ideal for those who aren't fluent in French to begin life in France and make some money at the same time. We had no mortgage, as the property was cheaper than the one we'd sold in the UK, and we had plenty of free time in the winter to learn to be passable at DIY – we weren't very good when we arrived!

The house has plenty of space and there are five bedrooms with a large dining room. The garden was small but, when we bought the house next door (in 1989), we were able to combine the gardens into one large one. This was important, as guests like to enjoy the sun and outdoor life when they come to France. Having the house next door meant that we could keep our guests separate from our growing children and also have some privacy for ourselves.

The house is in a hamlet in the countryside, 2km from the nearest village. This hasn't proved a problem for us, although it might not suit many guests. But we don't hide the fact in our publicity that we're remote, and most guests like the idea of a country holiday.

When we started, we advertised in the Sunday newspapers, at great cost and without great response. We also targeted some advertising at the vegetarian market, which was more successful (we aren't vegetarian, but knew that they find France difficult). Later we got into some guides (published in the UK and abroad, e.g. Holland). This was mostly by recommendation, and they've been the best form of advertising and at a reasonable price – or even free.

Our guests are broken down thus: 75 per cent Anglophone (British, Canadian, South African, etc.); 20 per cent Dutch and Belgian; 5 per cent French – mostly wanting accommodation for weddings, celebrations or summer festivals.

We used to advertise with the tourist office in the nearest town but, because we're so remote, few people found us, so we dropped that. We've been lazy about developing the French market. Our website might be the way forward. It works well; 95 per cent of our enquiries and bookings are made by email.

We're always stony broke, especially in the winter months; there's no significant winter season round here. And social security contributions always hit us hard.

Our guests are always unbelievably good and we've had no serious problems, but in the summer season we stay up late and party a bit too much. Sometimes we work non-stop for weeks on end without free time. We haven't employed staff – we cannot afford to and couldn't really justify it. The kind of B&B we run demands our presence – we couldn't really ask someone to do it for us.

We both enjoy it still. The winter gives us time to recover, although I could do without the financial hardship. We used to worry too much about what people would think, but now we believe you should be honest and offer what you feel to be the right service; if people don't like it, the worst that can happen is that they won't come back.

Jane and John Edwards

HANDLING ENQUIRIES & BOOKINGS

General information about handling enquiries can be found on page 104; the following details apply specifically to a B&B business.

As many B&B bookings are received at short notice, carry a cordless telephone with you at all times so that you don't miss any, and perhaps even have calls diverted to your mobile telephone when you're out.

Beware that French guests, being used to the concept of paying per room rather than per person, may attempt to fit a family of five into one double room! Insist on the names and ages of every person and make it clear when they book how many rooms will be required.

Decide how to handle enquiries about flights and car rentals. It's easier to let clients make their own bookings, but you should be able to offer advice and put them in touch with airlines, ferry companies, travel agents and car rental companies.

Booking Form & Deposits

You must have a simple booking or agreement form that includes the dates of arrival and departure and approximate times, a description of the rooms and beds required, the price and your terms and conditions. You can send this by post, email it or have it as a downloadable document on your website. Clients should return the form to you with their non-refundable deposit;

there's no fixed amount, but 25 per cent of the price of the stay is usual. You might choose to ask for the total price in advance, especially during peak season. A provisional booking shouldn't be held for more than a week or ten days; the deposit must be paid within this time.

Payment & Cancellations

Some cancellations are inevitable but non-refundable deposits and flexible payment methods can help keep them to a minimum. Make it easy to pay – if clients have already parted with their money, they're less likely to cancel. If the booking is made at short notice, take an immediate deposit with a credit card or PayPal (see **Receiving Payment** on page 191). Make it clear that the deposit isn't refundable; if clients cancel as a result of illness, their insurance should compensate.

3

Information Packs

After accepting a booking, you can provide guests with a pre-arrival information pack, though you may decide to do so in the case of longer bookings only. This should contain the following:

- a map of the local area and instructions as to how to find the property;

- information about local attractions and the local area (available free from tourist offices);

- contact numbers if guests have problems or plan to arrive late.

Arrival & Departure Times

Specify the times when guests may arrive, for instance between 4 and 8pm, and ask them to notify you what time they expect to be with you, asking them to telephone if there's a change of plan. Be quite firm about this; you won't want a car full of holidaymakers arriving at 2pm when you're frantically changing beds, unblocking drains, out shopping or (you should be so lucky!) putting your feet up with a well earned cup of tea. Neither do you want to be waiting around until 11pm when they were expected at 5pm but decided to stop for dinner without letting you know. Also specify a departure time, e.g. 10am; you should be flexible, but it's best to state a time so that guests aren't tempted to linger.

OTHER CONSIDERATIONS

Smoking

You must decide whether to allow smoking or not. You might attract clients who prefer a non-smoking environment, or put off others – French people are generally less accustomed than Britons and Americans, for example, to restrictions on their freedom to smoke, although this is changing with the introduction of the law banning smoking in public places. (Note that the new law applies to hotels, as they have bars and restaurants open to non-residents, but not to *chambres d'hôtes* because they aren't open to the public.) You could have some areas where smoking is allowed, such as the lounge or outdoor sitting areas, but forbid smoking in the dining room and bedrooms.

Animals

Allowing animals should be seriously considered, although you must base the decision on whether the layout and soundproofing of your rooms is suitable. Since the introduction of 'pet passports', it has become easy for travellers from the UK to take their dogs and cats on holiday with them. There are several disadvantages, not least that they might mess indoors, bark at night, or decide that your own dog or cat is their worst enemy (or best friend – you must keep an eye on bitches at certain times of the year!). They may leave hairs, causing allergic reactions in other guests. You can ask that dogs be kept on leads when not in their owners' rooms, and ask owners to bring a rug or their animal's bed. Animals shouldn't be allowed to climb on beds or other furniture or cause annoyance to other guests. Bitches on heat shouldn't be allowed as the smell can spread throughout the house and attract all the stray dogs in the neighbourhood – a howling midnight chorus won't go down too well with your other guests! Check with your insurance company if you decide to allow pets.

Children

Not allowing children drastically reduces your letting potential. However, your property might simply be unsuitable. You might have beautifully landscaped gardens or fragile antique furnishings unsuitable for children's play, the property may not be fenced, or you might not want to risk the

© Joe Laredo

© tonidesign (www.bigstockphoto.com)

© Madeleine Openshaw (www.shutterstock.com)

 © Johnson

© Kevin Britland (www.shutterstock.com)

© Survival Books ▲

© Benjamin F. Haith (www.shutterstock.com) ▲

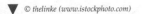
© thelinke (www.istockphoto.com) ▼

© kkgas (www.istockphoto.com) ▲

© Cryrille Lips (www.123rf.com) ▼

© bananaman (www.bigstockphoto.com)

© Norman Pogson (www.shutterstock.com)

© Scott Brandt (www.123rf.com)

© Benjamin F. Haith (www.shutterstock.com)

© Graham

© Iloveotto (www.123rf.com)

© Manic Blu (www.istockphoto.com)

© Christopher Lofty (www.shutterstock.com)

© William Berry (www.shutterstock.com)

© MalibuBooks (www.shutterstock.com)

possibility of toddlers throwing tantrums or babies crying in the night and disturbing other guests. Some people don't allow children under five because of the risk of bed-wetting. If you prefer not to cater for children, make it clear in your advertising, promoting your property as a peaceful adult environment.

If you decide to accept children, you should do your best to make your accommodation child-friendly by providing facilities for babies, such as a cot, highchair, potty, changing facilities, enclosed garden, protected electric sockets and stair gates. **All equipment provided for children must bear the CE mark, indicating that it conforms to EU safety standards.** For older children outdoor play equipment such as swings and a climbing frame, and especially a games room with table tennis, TV, computer games and books, will be appreciated.

It's usually expected that you'll charge less for children if they share a room with their parents (see **Letting Rates** on page 141). If they have a separate room, you may choose to charge full price – after all, they're occupying the same accommodation that could otherwise be let to adults.

Disabled Access

If your property has disabled access, including wide doors, and no steps to at least one bedroom and bathroom, this can be a good selling point. Most agencies have provision for emphasising this in their advertisements, and there are some that specialise in this area, e.g. Access Travel (UK ☎ 01942-888844, ⌨ www.access-travel.co.uk).

Specialist Holidays & Niche Markets

To maximise your bookings, particularly out of season, exploit your location. For example, there may be a large annual antiques fair or a Christmas market nearby. If there are interesting walks in your area, photocopy some local maps, have them laminated and offer them to your guests (and provide somewhere for them to leave their muddy boots!). You can also make tourist route maps for car journeys, or itineraries for a day's sightseeing, mountain biking, horse riding, golf or bird watching – a one-off effort on your part which can lead to repeat bookings and recommendations.

To add to the appeal of your B&B, you might offer accommodation as part of a themed or special interest holiday: painting, cookery, wine tasting, business training, and writing and language courses – the possibilities are endless. If your property is in an area with historical interest (e.g. the D-Day landing beaches, First World War battlefields or Roman sites), or in a wine-growing region, you could arrange guided tours. All these extend your season, as you won't be relying solely on family-summer-holiday visitors. If you have particular skills or qualifications, you could consider running speciality holidays based on your own knowledge and interests. Otherwise, for holidays including tuition (e.g. painting, writing, cookery) you must factor in the cost of hiring instructors and a specialised advertising budget targeting your prospective clientele in the relevant magazines. Catering specifically for vegetarians is an excellent niche market, and can be combined with cookery lessons (see page 148).

CASE STUDY 7

We're migrants from Southampton in the south of England to Aude in the south of France. While in Southampton, we'd been a host family for the Southampton English Language Centre (an organisation that provides English tuition to foreigners) and had always liked having people to stay with us for two main reasons: you meet many very nice people and you learn a lot of things about other cultures. We'd often thought about running a B&B and, as we wanted to start a new life in France, it seemed sensible to try to combine the two.

We searched different regions and areas within regions in France for a long time and finally decided to buy a plot in the village of Granes in Aude, then to design and build the house that would be our new home and hopefully provide an income. We chose this area for its stunning landscape (it's in the foothills of the Pyrenees), varied attractions for holidaymakers and ease of access from the three airports nearby.

We designed the house with B&B accommodation in mind and included a small, two-person gîte, aimed at couples who wanted good quality accommodation for holidays or house hunting. We decided to advertise to a specific market – mainly vegetarian. The reason for this was that we realised how difficult it is for vegetarians to get good quality, varied meals in a mainly carnivorous country.

While the house was being built, we sold our house in Southampton, rented accommodation in Eastleigh and kept our jobs for a year to help finance the project. This turned out to be a good move, as it enabled us to design our brochures and website, spend time on word-of-mouth promotion among friends and work colleagues and take advance advertising space in two specialist magazines. Buying advertising space cost us around £200, but didn't produce a single enquiry; it just generated a lot of interest from other companies trying to sell us much more expensive advertising space with no guarantee of results.

This year of preparation also gave us the chance to visit the area several times to oversee the construction of the house and to stay in various types of B&B to get a feel for what we liked and didn't like, so that we could focus on providing top quality accommodation for our guests. Once we'd moved into our house in France, there was a flurry of activity lasting many months to get the house ready for guests. 2004 was to be our first year of operation.

Our breakthrough came with advertising in the Aude Tourist Board brochure, a full-colour publication available from all the tourist offices. Each advertisement costs €25 and entitles you to two photographs plus supporting text. We took two advertising spaces, one for the B&B and one for the gîte, at a total cost for the year of €50 and the results so far have been very encouraging – in a year when everyone told us that tourism in the area was down by around 30 per cent. Enquiries came from France, Germany and Denmark, and all the enquirers subsequently booked with us. In our small village of around 120 inhabitants, there's also a gîte equestre, which offers horse riding holidays. Having visited us to see what we offer, they often use us for overspill accommodation.

For the B&B, we have one twin-bedded room with full ensuite (shower, WC, washbasin) and one double-bedded room with shower, washbasin and separate WC. Our small, self-contained gîte has a lounge/dining room, bedroom with double bed, ensuite shower and toilet and fully fitted kitchen; gîte users have their own entrance and a private area of the terrace with table and chairs. All visitors benefit from fully non-smoking, no-pets accommodation, this being remarked upon by most guests as an important factor in their choice of accommodation.

If they wish, guests can eat with us 'en famille' and we've already achieved quite a reputation for being able to meet most dietary needs. Perhaps it's a little easier for us, as Suzie has a life-threatening nut and nutmeg allergy, which means that we must be ultra-careful about what we buy and what we eat – especially in an area that uses nuts, nut oils and nutmeg in many foods!

We provide a book for visitor comments plus a handbook for the *gîte*. We're encouraged by the comments that guests write, so we thought it would be a good idea to translate the handbook from English into French and German, thus covering most people's needs. What we didn't realise was that computer translation programmes don't always 'understand' the nuances of English. Given our limited French and even more limited German, it looked reasonable to us; the reality, though, provokes much hilarity and has led us to wonder if we should change it or leave it as a talking point!

We've met many lovely people, have benefited from interesting and varied conversations, have found that people genuinely appreciate the standard of accommodation that we set out to achieve, but haven't yet made our fortune – nor are we likely to.

Mike and Suzie Broderick, Les Tamaris, Chemin du Moulin, 11500 Granes, France (☎ 04 68 20 72 53, ✉ aude@connxns.demon.co.uk, 💻 www. audexperience.com)

TOP TEN TIPS FOR BED & BREAKFAST

- Don't even think about running a B&B unless you enjoy meeting people and are happy about having strangers in your home.

- You must be prepared to work long hours at tasks that can become repetitive and boring.

- You must speak French if you're to attract the maximum number of clients.

- Think carefully whether the layout of your property is suitable for a B&B.

- Make sure your electricity and drainage system will cope with the extra load.

- Consider registering with Gîtes de France or another recognised organisation.

- If in a remote location, you must provide evening meals.

- Make a business plan and budget carefully.

- Check the rules and regulations that apply in your department, as they can vary considerably from one to another.

- Think of ways to give added value, as there's a lot of competition.

3

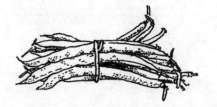

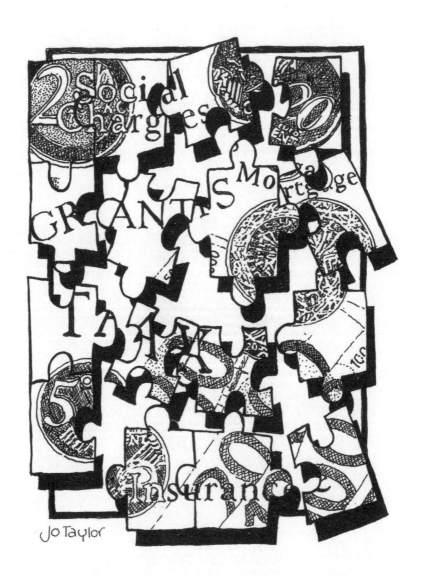

Jo Taylor

4

MONEY MATTERS

Whether you're letting one or two rooms for some extra money or running a fully fledged commercial enterprise, you must understand the financial implications, which may vary according to your situation. This chapter includes a consideration of taxation, social security contributions, mortgages, insurance, grants and (last but not least!) how to receive payments from your clients. Calculating the viability of your letting business and setting your letting rates are covered in chapters 2 and 3 under Financial Considerations, as there are different variables for *gîtes* and B&B.

TAXATION

An important consideration for anyone letting property in France is taxation, which includes property tax, income tax, value added tax (VAT) and capital gains tax – all discussed below. Note that letting tax (*contribution sur les revenus locatifs*) was abolished in 2005.

As you would expect in a country with millions of bureaucrats, the French tax system is inordinately complicated and most French people don't understand it. It's difficult to obtain accurate information from the tax authorities and, just when you think you have it cracked, the authorities change the rules or hit you with a new tax. **With the change of government in May 2007, changes are likely and you should check the latest regulations.** Taxes are levied at national and local levels.

Before buying a property for letting, you should obtain expert advice regarding French taxes. This will (hopefully) ensure that you take maximum advantage of your current tax status and that you don't make any mistakes that you'll regret later.

Income Tax

Whether you're a French resident or not, you must pay tax in France on all income from property letting, irrespective of any double-taxation or other agreements.

Letting furnished premises (including bed and breakfast and *gîte* accommodation) is regarded as a business activity; therefore income from it is taxed as business income and classed as *bénéfices industriels et commerciaux* (*BIC*). This section deals only with the taxation of furnished letting income.

The letting of unfurnished property is regarded as a civil activity, classed as *revenus fonciers*, and very different tax rules apply, in addition to different rules and regulations regarding leases – for further information see *Earning Money from your French Home* (Survival Books – page 314).

Domicile & Residence

Domicile and residence have different meanings in the laws of some countries – for instance the UK definitions are extraordinarily complex; they're explained in HM Revenue and Customs (HMRC) booklet IR20, which is available online at ▣ www.hmrc.gov.uk/pdfs/ir20.htm. (UK law states you can have only one domicile but may have more than one residence for tax purposes.)

The French view is less complicated (for a change!). You're domiciled, and therefore tax resident, in France if **any** of the following three statements apply:

● You live there for 183 days or more each fiscal year (see **Residents** below).

● Your spouse and family live there for 183 days or more per year.

● You derive the majority of your income from French sources – e.g. if you're retired and your *gîte* business earns more than your UK pension, you're classed as tax resident in France, even if you live in the UK.

However, if you let property in France (even if domiciled elsewhere) the letting income is taxable in France. **Note that tax legislation is constantly changing.**

Residents: As a French resident, you must declare to the French tax authorities **all** your income, wherever it originates and wherever it's paid. Note that you won't necessarily be sent a tax form – it's your responsibility to obtain, complete and return a tax form, normally before the end of April (see **Declaration** on page 174); ignorance is no excuse!

Non-residents: If you spend less than 183 per year in France you must still declare any letting income and pay tax on it in France **even if you're paid by UK clients in UK currency into a UK bank account**. If you don't complete a tax return (see **Declaration** on page 174), there are penalties. Overdue tax gathers interest at 0.75 per cent per month, and if you file late there's a penalty of 10 per cent rising to 40 per cent if you fail to respond within 30 days of the first reminder. If a second reminder is sent and ignored, the penalty can rise to 80 per cent. **Recently, the tax authorities have been checking on foreign-owned properties in search of undeclared revenue.**

Non-residents must declare any income received in France on their tax return in their country of residence, but tax on French letting income is normally paid only in France (see **Double-taxation treaties** below). However, if you pay less tax in France than you would have paid in your home country, you must usually pay the difference there. On the other hand, if you pay more tax in France than you would have paid on the income in your home country, you aren't entitled to a refund.

If you're a non-resident of France but own residential property there through a company or *SCI* (see below) that's available for your use, you're liable for French income tax on the basis of a deemed rental income equal to three times the rental value of the property. This is usually calculated to be 5 per cent of its capital value. There are, however, exceptions, e.g. if you have French income that exceeds this level or if you're protected by a double-taxation treaty (see below). Consult a tax accountant to clarify your position.

If you're a British national, information can be obtained from the centre for non-residents in the UK (☎ 0151-210 2222, 🖳 www.inlandrevenue. gov.uk/cnr).

Double-taxation treaties: Double-taxation treaties mean that citizens of most countries are exempt from paying taxes in their home country when they spend a minimum period abroad, e.g. a year. According to the Convention for the Avoidance of Double Taxation and the Prevention of Fiscal Evasion, France has double-taxation treaties with over 70 countries, including all members of the European Union (EU), Australia, Canada, China, India, Israel, Japan, New Zealand, Pakistan, the Philippines, Singapore, Sri Lanka, Switzerland and the US. Treaties are designed to ensure that income that has already been taxed in one treaty country isn't taxed again in another treaty country. The treaty establishes a tax credit or exemption on certain kinds of income, either in the country of residence or the country where the income is earned. Where applicable, a double-taxation treaty prevails over domestic law. The US is the only country that taxes its non-resident citizens on income earned abroad, although there are exclusions on foreign-earned income (around $76,000 per spouse; check the exact current figure).

If you're in doubt about your tax liability in your home country, contact your nearest embassy or consulate in France.

Calculation

The rate(s) at which you pay tax depend on whether you're resident or non-resident in France, as follows.

Non-residents: If you're non-resident in France and your letting income is less than €76,300 per year you can benefit from the *micro-BIC* régime (see page 172). You'll pay a flat rate of 25 per cent tax on 32 per cent of your gross income. For example, if your gross takings are €40,000, you're taxed on €12,800 at 25 per cent, which comes to €3,200.

Residents: If you're tax resident in France, your letting income is added to any other taxable income you have, subject to any deductions and allowances, and is then taxed at the following rates (2006/07 income):

Taxable Income	Tax Rate	Tax Amount	Cumulative Tax
Up to €5,614	0%	€0.00	€0.00
€5,615 to €11,198	5.5%	€281.40	€307.06
€11,199 to €24,872	14%	€1,914.22	€2,221.28
€24,873 to €66,679	30%	€12,541.80	€14,763.08
Over €66,679	40%		

4

The taxable unit is the household. The figures above are for each 'part': a single person is one part; a married couple is two parts; if there are any children, the first two have 0.5 of a part each, any further children one part each. For example, a household of a couple with three children will add up to four parts. The number of parts is known as the 'family quotient' (*quotient familiale/QF*). The total household income is split across those four parts, each of which is separately taxed according to the bands in the table above, the sum of these being added together to result in the amount of tax payable.

If our theoretical family's income totals €72,000, it will be taxed on €18,000 four times, the amount of tax due being calculated as follows:

0 per cent of the first €5,614 = €0

5.5 per cent of the next €5,583 = €307.06

14 per cent of the next €6,803 = €952.42

Total €1,259.48 x 4 = €5,037.92

By way of comparison, a couple with no children (two parts) earning the same amount will be taxed on €36,000 twice, as follows:

0 per cent of the first €5,614 = €0

5.5 per cent of the next €5,585 = €307.06

14 per cent of the next €24,803 = €3,472.42

Total €3,779.48 x 2 = €7,558.96

Obviously this is a simplified example and your circumstances may have a bearing on the calculation of your tax liability (e.g. if you're over 65). The first website listed below has a 'practice' form to fill out.

Further information on French income tax can be found on the government website (🖥 www.impots.gouv.fr) and on the vast and complicated Service des Impôts website (🖥 www.impotrevenu.com) as well as in *Living and Working in France* (Survival Books – see page 314). There's also an excellent booklet, *VO Impôts* (in French), published by La Nouvelle Vie Ouvrière, which is available for €6 from newsagents' (*presse*) in France, or you can order it from the website (🖥 www.vo-impots.com).

Tax Regimes

Individuals with income from letting property must choose between two tax 'regimes' (*régimes*), depending on the type of property, the level of income and the status of the owner:

● **mini-regime** (*régime micro*) – known as a 'forfeit basis' regime, which means that you forfeit the right to claim actual expenses in exchange for a fixed deduction, which you hope is more than your actual expenses! (This regime is subdivided into *micro-BIC* for furnished property, which applies here, and *micro-foncier* for unfurnished property.) For details, see below.

● **'real' regime** (*régime réél*) – whereby you claim actual expenses, where these are or are expected to be higher than the fixed deduction applicable to the mini-regime. This is subdivided into the 'simplified real regime' (*régime réel simplifié*), for businesses with a low turnover and 'normal real regime' (*régime réel normal*), for businesses with a higher turnover. For details, see below.

Régime micro-BIC: If you receive total gross property income of less than €76,300 per year, you can opt for the *micro-BIC* tax regime (*BIC* stands for *bénéfices industriels et commerciaux*) and qualify for a 68 per cent tax deduction to cover expenses, paying tax on only 32 per cent of the total income. This regime is obviously beneficial if your actual profit exceeds 32 per cent of income after expenses. It's a simple system: no formal records have to be kept, just a simple account of receipts with dates. You file one tax return per year giving your gross rental income. If you opt for the *régime micro-BIC*, you're tied to it for five years, provided your income doesn't exceed the threshold during that time, in which case you are automatically subject to the *régime réel* (see below).

If you're resident in the UK, and your actual profit is more than 32 per cent, take advice when filling in a UK tax return, as the *micro-BIC* system isn't recognised by the British tax authorities and you could find yourself taxed twice.

Note also that you cannot show a loss – there will always be a taxable profit – and you cannot use the *régime micro-BIC* if you purchased your property using an *SCI* (see page 174).

4

 If an *SCI* lets furnished property, it's classed as a commercial activity and you cannot use the *micro-BIC* tax regime.

CAUTION

Régime réel: The *régime réel* is sub-divided into *simplifié* and *normal*, the difference between the two being the level of gross income, as explained below.

- **régime réel normal** – If your letting income exceeds €763,000 (lucky you!), you **must** use this system, which requires the services of an accountant.

- **régime réel simplifié** – If your gross letting income exceeds €76,300, but is less than €763,000 excluding VAT (*TVA*), you **must** be registered as *régime réel simplifié*.

If your gross letting income is below €76,300, you can choose to register under this system rather than *micro-BIC* (see above), but it would be to your advantage only if the costs incurred on your property exceeded 68 per cent of your rental income. Other advantages of this system over the *micro-BIC* regime are that you can offset any annual losses against other income, e.g. a salary; and a tax loss can be carried forward for the next five years and offset against other furnished rental income or business activity.

If you have a choice, you must opt in to the *régime simplifié* before 1st February of the tax year and remain opted in for a minimum of two years.

Under the *régime simplifié*, you deduct from your rental income the actual costs incurred on the property and must provide all invoices relating to these costs. You must prepare accounts quarterly.

Property owners can deduct from their income expenses such as repairs, maintenance, security and cleaning costs, mortgage interest payments, management and letting expenses (e.g. advertising), local taxes and insurance fees. There's also an allowance to cover depreciation. Capital expenses (e.g. installation of a swimming pool) aren't deductible.

If you live in the property for part of the year, only a proportion of charges can be deducted. For instance if you let the property for 13 weeks, you can deduct only 25 per cent of the expenses above. You should seek professional advice to ensure that you're claiming everything to which you're entitled; contact your local tax office (don't rely on your accountant).

4

Société Civile Immobilière

Many people, especially from the UK, buy their property as a *société civile immobilière* (*SCI*) in an attempt to circumvent French inheritance laws. An *SCI* is a company, usually with family members as shareholders. In France, an *SCI* is a transparent entity for tax purposes, which means that the shareholders are taxed as individuals. If an *SCI* lets furnished property, however, it's classed as a commercial entity and **cannot** use the *micro-BIC* tax regime. Furthermore the UK and French tax authorities differ on the status of the *SCI*, the UK's Inland Revenue and Customs authorities regarding it as a company subject to corporation tax rather than income tax, which may lead to double taxation. They will also tax you on perceived benefits provided by your company, which can include a substantial sum for all the weeks when the property isn't let, as it's a company asset.

> **SURVIVAL TIP**
> **It's essential to take legal advice (in France and in your home country) before buying property through an *SCI*.**

Declaration

The French tax year is the same as the calendar year (1st January to 31st December). You must complete tax form 2042 (the main tax form). From

2006 there are two versions of this – 2042 DPR, the standard form, and 2042S DPR, which is simplified. However, the simplified form is for those with no income other than a salary, so won't apply in your case. If you've previously filed a tax declaration in France, your 2042 will come partially completed with your name and address and details of your main income, and any supplementary income – for instance letting income (*gîte* or B&B activity) – will appear on form 2042C. There are other forms for declaring pensions from other countries, investments, capital gains, etc.

If you have income from outside France (e.g. a foreign pension), you may be required to complete other forms (e.g. 2047 for the details of your foreign income and 3916 for foreign bank account information). Everyone's tax liabilities and declarations differ, being dependent on the source(s) of income and many other variables, so you should consult an accountant or other financial adviser before completing your tax declaration.

You must normally submit your tax return by mid-March, but in both 2006 and 2007 the deadline was extended to the 31st of May. They are specified on the official website (see above), as are the deadlines for online submissions; the latter are dependent on where you live (by school zone!).You can now complete your tax returns online (💻 www.impots. gouv.fr) and even earn a concession of €20 if you opt to pay by direct debit (monthly or quarterly).

Non-resident property owners who earn letting income must file form 2042/2042C, which must be submitted to the Centre des Impôts de Non-Résidents (10 rue du Centre, 93465 Noisy le Grand, ☎ 01 57 33 85 00). Deadlines vary according to whether you live – see the official website (💻 www.impots.gouv.fr). It's wise to keep a copy of your return and send it by registered post (so that there's no dispute over whether it was received).

Some months after filing you receive a tax assessment detailing the tax due. There are penalties for late filing and non-declaration, which can result in fines, high interest charges and even imprisonment. The French tax authorities can impose tax on 52 weeks' letting income and cancel your entitlement to tax deductions in the future. **The tax authorities have many ways of detecting people letting homes and not paying tax and have been clamping down on tax evaders in recent years.**

Late payment of any tax bill usually incurs a surcharge of 10 per cent. Changes in your tax liability may be made by the tax authorities up to three years after the end of the tax tear to which the liability relates, so you should retain all records relating to the income and expenses reported in your tax returns for at least three years. **Ignorance is no defence – it's your responsibility to declare all taxable income!**

Property Taxes

Taxe d'habitation (residential tax) and *taxe foncière* (property tax) are roughly similar to community tax (formerly rates and poll tax) in the UK, funding local services and including a contribution towards regional and departmental expenses. They're both based on a notional rental value of the property (*valeur locative cadastrale*), i.e. the assumed value of the property if it were let on the open market, which obviously varies according to the size and type of the property and its location. The rates calculated are set by region, department and commune, and vary **enormously** from one place to another, generally higher in towns and cities and lower in rural areas and villages, although rates don't necessarily reflect the salubrity of the location: St Germain-des-Prés, which is one of the most expensive suburbs of Paris, has some of the lowest property tax rates!

Tax rates rise each year. (An overall review of prices was last carried out in 1974 – if the tax authorities were to update their survey again, the resulting figures would probably be a nasty shock for many taxpayers!)

Taxe Foncière

Taxe foncière is payable by the person who's the owner of the property on 1st January. It's divided into two parts, for developed and undeveloped land (*le bâti* and *le non-bâti*). Any development (e.g. conversion, installation of a pool, change of use) must be reported to the tax authorities – so that they can increase your tax!

The amount payable varies by up to 500 per cent with the region, and even between towns or villages within the same region, and may be as little as €300 or as much as €1,500 per year, although there are plans to make the application of the tax 'fairer'. (Strangely, the Paris area has some of the country's lowest rates.)

Taxe d'Habitation

Taxe d'habitation is payable by the occupier of a property (who may or may not be the owner) on 1st January of each year, irrespective of whether he's actually staying in the property on that particular date. If the property is furnished, has water and electricity supplies and is available for occupation, the tax is payable.

Even if you vacate or sell a property on 2nd January, you must pay residential tax for the whole year and have no right to reclaim part of it from a new owner.

Residential tax is levied by the town where the property is located and varies by as much as 400 per cent from town to town. As with *taxe foncière* (see above), the Paris area has some of the country's lowest rates. Generally, you should expect to pay around half the amount paid in *taxe foncière*. Residential tax is usually payable in the autumn of the year to which it applies.

If you have a *gîte* registered with Gîtes de France (or another official organisation), you may be exempt from this tax if the *gîte* is part of the property that's your principal residence (e.g. an outbuilding on the same site as your house).

Taxe Professionelle

'Professional tax' (*taxe professionelle*) is normally payable by individuals and companies carrying out non-salaried work. It's levied at between around 15 and 20 per cent (the exact percentage varies with the commune) of a 'base', which is currently 8 per cent of your annual income, including VAT. For example, if you earn €30,000 per year, your tax base will be €2,400; if *taxe professionelle* is levied at 20 per cent in your commune, you'll pay €480 per year.

Taxe professionelle is assessed as follows: in your first year of French residence, you pay nothing; in your second year, you pay according to your earnings in Year 1 (pro rata if you moved to France part way through the year); in Year 3, your tax is again based on your Year 1 earnings, in Year 4 on your Year 2 earnings, and so on.

A *gîte* owner is exempt if the property is registered with Gîtes de France or another official organisation, e.g. Clévacances or the Comité Départemental de Tourisme. Exemption also applies where the property is your principal residence, provided the rental you charge is 'reasonable'. In effect, most B&B, *gîte* and letting businesses aren't liable for *taxe professionelle*, but check with your accountant or local *trésor publique*.

Taxe de Séjour

The local commune may charge you a 'holiday tax' (*taxe de séjour*) for each paying guest. The commune fixes the rate of tax, which varies from €0.20 to

€1.50 per person per night according to the standard of accommodation. This might sound like a small sum, but if you have eight people staying for a week at the higher rate it adds up to a not insubstantial €84; multiply this by 30 weeks and your annual bill will amount to €2,520. Children under a certain age (check the age limit locally) aren't counted, and there may be concessions for French families on certain social benefits and those paying with *cheques-vacances* (see page 191). Some communes charge a lump sum per year.

Find out from your *mairie* whether or not this tax is applicable in your commune and, if so, the rates – ignorance is no excuse for not paying! It's up to your *mairie* to charge you, but you'll have to declare how many 'people nights' you've let. Don't forget to check the age limit for 'children'. The tax is paid to your local *trésor public*, usually located in your *canton* capital.

4 Value Added Tax

Furnished rentals are generally exempt from VAT (*taxe sur la valeur ajoutée/ TVA*) if you're operating under the *micro-BIC* tax regime (see page 172). If your income exceeds €76,300 and you therefore aren't eligible for the *micro-BIC* scheme, your income may be subject to VAT. This applies if you offer 'hotel' services, namely three or more of the following:

- bed linen;
- a reception desk;
- daily cleaning;
- breakfasts.

This means that a B&B business (generating over €76,300) is almost certainly subject to VAT and must therefore charge its clients VAT, whereas most *gîte* businesses are exempt. If your business is subject to VAT, the accommodation itself is taxed at 5.5 per cent and other services (e.g. meals) at 19.6 per cent.

SURVIVAL TIP
You should take advice from an accountant as to whether you're required to register for VAT.

Capital Gains Tax

Capital gains tax (*impôt sur les plus-values*) is payable on the profit from sales of certain assets in France, including property worth over €15,000 – i.e. anything other than a caravan! (Income tax treaties usually provide that capital gains on property are taxable in the country where the property is located.) Gains net of capital gains tax (CGT) are added to other income and are liable to income tax (see above). If you're a French resident, capital gains are also subject to social security contributions at 8 per cent. Changes to the capital gains regulations were made in the Finance Act, 2004, which also requires a *notaire* handling a property sale to calculate and pay CGT on behalf of the vendor.

Principal Residence

4

CGT isn't payable on a profit made on the sale of your principal residence in France, provided that you've occupied it since its purchase (or for at least five years if you didn't occupy it immediately after purchase). You're also exempt from CGT if you're forced to sell for family or professional reasons, e.g. the death of a bankrupt relative.

If you move to France permanently and retain a home abroad, this may affect your position regarding capital gains. If you sell your foreign home before moving to France, you're exempt from CGT, as it's your principal residence. However, if you establish your principal residence in France, the foreign property becomes a second home and is thus liable to CGT when it's sold. **EU tax authorities co-operate in tracking down CGT dodgers.**

Second Homes

Capital gains on second homes in France worth over €15,000 are payable by residents and non-residents up to 15 years after purchase (until 2004, the period was 22 years). The basic rates of CGT are 26 per cent for residents, 16 per cent for non-resident EU citizens, and 33.3 per cent for non-resident non-EU citizens. Any inheritance or gift tax paid at the time of purchase is taken into account when determining the purchase price, and there are certain exemptions to the above tax rates, as follows:

● If you've owned a property for more than five years, but less than 15, you're entitled to a 10 per cent reduction in CGT for every year of ownership over five (i.e. 10 per cent for six years' ownership, 20 per cent for seven years', etc.).

● If you've owned a property for at least five years and can produce proof of substantial expenditure on improving it (e.g. receipts for work done by professionals), you can claim a further deduction of 15 per cent of the property's purchase price against CGT (irrespective of the actual cost of the work), but you're no longer entitled to claim for work you've done yourself, nor any materials purchased for DIY improvements.

However, the purchase price of a property is no longer indexed to increases in the cost of living. Note also that, if you make a loss on the sale of a second home, you cannot claim this against other CGT payments, nor against income tax!

Before a sale, the *notaire* prepares a form calculating the tax due and appoints an agent (*agent fiscal accrédité*) or guarantor to act on your behalf concerning tax. If the transaction is straightforward, the local tax office may grant a dispensation (*dispense*) of the need to appoint a guarantor, provided you apply **before** completion of the sale. If you obtain a dispensation, the proceeds of the sale can be released to you in full after CGT has been paid. The *notaire* handling the sale must apply for the dispensation and must declare and pay CGT on your behalf; you're no longer required to make a CGT declaration.

SOCIAL SECURITY

France has a comprehensive social security (*sécurité sociale*) system covering healthcare (plus sickness and maternity care), injuries at work, family allowances, unemployment insurance, and old age (pensions), invalidity and death benefits. It's a generous and generally excellent system – social security benefits are among the most generous in the European Union (EU), the average household receiving around a third of its income from social support payments such as family allowances, state benefits and pensions – but, for this reason, it's **very** expensive. France has one of the highest levels of social security contributions in the EU.

Total contributions per employee (to around 15 funds) average around 60 per cent of gross pay, some 60 per cent of which is paid by employers (an increasing impediment to hiring staff). The self-employed must pay the full amount. The good news is that, with the exception of sickness benefits, social security benefits aren't taxed.

French social security is an extremely complex subject, and the following is the briefest summary of relevant aspects of it. For further information, refer to *Living and Working in France* (Survival Books – see page 314). There are also a number of books (in French) about social security, including *Tous les Droits de l'Assuré Social* (VO Editions), and consumer magazines regularly publish supplements on various aspects of social security, particularly pensions and health insurance. Some information is available in English on the Service Public website (🖳 www.service-public.fr) and the Assurance Maladie site (🖳 www.ameli.fr – it stands for *Assurance Maladie en ligne!*).

Registration

If you're working in France, you must register at your local social security office (Caisse Primaire d'Assurance Maladie/CPAM). Your town hall will give you the address of your local CPAM or you can find it under *Sécurité Sociale* in your local yellow pages.

You must provide your personal details, including your full name, address, country of origin, and date and place of birth. You must also produce passports, *cartes de séjour* (if applicable) and certified birth certificates for your dependants, plus a marriage certificate (if applicable). You may need to provide copies with official translations, but check first, as translations may be unnecessary. You also need proof of residence such as a rental contract or an electricity bill. When you've registered, you receive a permanent registration card (*carte d'assurance maladie*, known as a *carte Vitale*), which looks like a credit card and contains an electronic chip (*puce*), and a certificate (*attestation*) containing a list of those entitled to benefits on your behalf (*bénéficiaires*), i.e. your dependants, and the address of the office where you must apply for reimbursement of your medical expenses.

Within a limited period of starting a business, you must also register with the Caisse d'Allocations Familiales/CAF (family allowance), the Caisse Nationale de l'Assurance Maladie/CNAM (sickness), and the Caisse Nationale d'Assurance Vieillesse/CNAV (old-age pension).

Contributions

Social security contributions (*cotisations sociales* or *charges sociales*) are calculated as a percentage of your taxable income, although for certain contributions there's a maximum salary level. Note that contributions start as soon as you're employed or start work in France. Social security contributions are paid to the Union de Recouvrement des Cotisations de Sécurité Sociale et d'Allocations Familiales (URSSAF), which has 105 offices throughout France. Other contributions are paid to the Caisses listed above.

Self-employed

As a self-employed person you're treated as an employer and must deduct social security contributions from your own earnings and pay them directly to URSSAF. Once registered, you may choose from a selection of recognised organisations providing pensions and health insurance.

Recent legislation has provided some more-than-welcome respite for the newly self-employed, who, instead of making crippling social security contributions from their start-up, now make contributions (as well as paying income tax) as their business generates income. If you're registered under the *micro-BIC* tax regime (see page 172), you may be entitled to exoneration from part or all of the social security contributions on your letting income.

Payment

Contributions are payable in two lump sums on 1st April and 1st October each year. It's possible to pay contributions monthly (actually, you pay ten monthly instalments from January to October based on an estimated total contribution; any necessary adjustment is made in November or December); you must apply before 1st December of the year preceding the payments.

Employing Others

If you employ full-time staff, you must make social security contributions for your employees equivalent to over 35 per cent of their salary. If you employ someone to undertake work for you, you should ensure that he has adequate insurance (e.g. accident and third-party liability) and is registered as self-employed and therefore making social security contributions.

Casual Employees

If you pay someone to do a job on a casual basis (e.g. gardening) and he isn't registered as self-employed, you can make the necessary contributions on his behalf in order to ensure that both he and you are insured in the event of an accident. This can be done by using the *Chèque Emploi Service Universel* system (ask your bank for details).

If you agree to pay anyone in cash or by ordinary cheque and he has an accident on your premises, you can be sued for a very large sum of money – it's your responsibility to check that a worker is registered.

MORTGAGES

Mortgages or home loans (*hypothèque*) are available from all major French banks (for residents and non-residents) and many foreign banks. If you require a mortgage to buy your French property, where and how you obtain it depends first on whether you're resident in France or in another country.

If you're resident and your main income is earned in France, you should normally take out a French mortgage. 'Buy-to-let' mortgages aren't a familiar concept in France, with the exception of leaseback schemes, which aren't relevant to running a B&B or *gîte* business.

French mortgages are normally granted only for residential properties, which can include second homes. They may be granted for properties used for holiday letting, but the (estimated) letting income won't usually be taken into account (it's usually only taken into consideration if the property is rented on long-term contracts) and you must provide proof of other income, e.g. a pension, to obtain a loan.

If you're a foreign resident, you have three options:

- borrowing against assets in your home country;

- taking a second mortgage on (or re-mortgaging) your principal residence in your home country;

- raising a mortgage in France.

For the first two options, you obviously need to take the advice of your existing lender (see **Re-mortgaging** BELOW). It's also wise to do this if you opt to raise a mortgage in France, as many foreign lenders have reciprocal arrangements with French institutions. Many even have French sister companies such as the UK's Abbey National (see 💻 www.abbey-national-france.com) and HSBC, whose French equivalent is Crédit Commercial de France (CCF).

When you let the property, you can deduct the mortgage interest from your French tax declaration. Your assets and liabilities will be in the same currency, so fluctuating exchange rates won't result in negative equity.

For example, HSBC/CCF offers a capital repayment mortgage over 5 to 15 years, with variable, fixed or capped rates. The minimum you can borrow is €50,000, and this can be up to 80 per cent of the purchase price or the estimated value of the property (excluding legal fees), whichever is lower. The arrangement fee is generally 1 per cent of the amount borrowed.

It's possible to obtain a foreign currency mortgage, other than in euros, e.g. GB£, Swiss francs or US$. **However, you should be extremely wary of taking out a foreign currency mortgage, as interest rate gains can be wiped out overnight by currency swings and devaluations.** It's generally recognised that you should take out a loan in the currency in which you're paid or in the currency of the country where a property is situated. In this case, if the foreign currency is devalued you'll have the consolation of knowing that the value of your French property will have increased by the same percentage when converted back into the foreign currency.

When choosing between a euro loan and a foreign currency loan, be sure to take into account all costs, fees, interest rates and possible currency fluctuations. However you finance the purchase of a home in France, you should obtain professional advice from your bank manager and accountant. Most French banks offer euro mortgages on French property through branches in other countries. Most financial advisers recommend borrowing from a large reputable bank rather than a small one. Crédit Agricole is the largest French lender, with a 25 per cent share of the French mortgage market.

Both French and foreign lenders have tightened their lending criteria in the last few years, as a result of the repayment problems experienced by many recession-hit borrowers in the early '90s. Some foreign lenders apply stricter rules than French lenders regarding income, employment and the type of property on which they will lend, although some are willing to lend more than a French lender. It can take some foreigners a long time to obtain a mortgage in France, particularly if they have neither a regular income nor assets there. If you have difficulty, you should try a bank that's experienced in dealing with foreigners, such as the Banque Transatlantique (🖳 www.transat.tm.fr).

Further information about French mortgages can be found via the internet (e.g. 🖳 www.europelaw.com, 🖳 www.frenchentree.com and 🖳 www. french-mortgage.com) and in *Buying a Home in France* (Survival Books – see page 314).

Types of Mortgage

All French mortgages are repaid using the capital and interest method (repayment); endowment and pension-linked mortgages aren't offered.

Interest rates can be fixed or variable, the fixed rate being higher than the variable rate to reflect the increased risk to the lender. The advantage of a fixed rate is that you know exactly how much you must pay over the whole term. Variable rate loans may be fixed for the first two or more years, after which they're adjusted up or down on an annual basis in line with prevailing interest rates, but usually within pre-set limits, e.g. within 3 per cent of the original rate. You can usually convert a variable rate mortgage to a fixed rate mortgage at any time. There's normally a redemption penalty, e.g. 3 per cent of the outstanding capital, for early repayment of a fixed rate mortgage, although that isn't usual for variable rate mortgages. If you think you may want to repay early, you should try to have the redemption penalty waived or reduced before signing the agreement.

Terms & Conditions

French law doesn't permit French banks to offer mortgages or other loans where repayments are more than 30 per cent of your net income. Joint incomes and liabilities are included when assessing a couple's borrowing limit (usually a French bank will lend to up to three joint borrowers). Note that the 30 per cent limit includes existing mortgage or rental payments, in France and abroad. If your total repayments exceed 30 per cent of your income, French banks aren't permitted to extend further credit. Should they attempt to do so, the law allows a borrower to avoid liability for payment.

To calculate how much you can borrow in France, multiply your total net monthly income by 30 per cent and deduct your monthly mortgage, rent and other regular payments. Note that earned income isn't included if you're aged over 65. As a rough guide, repayments on a €60,000 mortgage are around €600 per month at 6 per cent over 15 years. There are special low mortgage rates for low-income property buyers in some departments. In November 2004, the maximum interest rate a bank could charge on a fixed-rate mortgage was 6.56 per cent and the maximum on a variable-rate mortgage 5.85 per cent.

As a condition of a French mortgage, you must take out a life (usually plus health and disability) insurance policy equal to 120 per cent of the amount borrowed. The premiums are included in mortgage payments. An existing insurance policy may be accepted, although it must be assigned to the lender. A medical examination may be required, although this isn't usual if you're under 50 years of age and borrowing less than €150,000.

French mortgages are usually limited to 70 or 80 per cent of a property's value (although some lenders limit loans to just 50 per cent). A mortgage can include renovation work, when written quotations must be provided with a mortgage application. Note that you must add expenses and fees, totalling around 10 to 15 per cent of the purchase price on an 'old' property, i.e. one over five years old. For example, if you're buying a property for €75,000 and obtain an 80 per cent mortgage, you must pay a 20 per cent deposit (€15,000) plus 10 to 15 per cent fees (€7,500 to €11,250), making a total of €22,500 to €26,250.

Mortgages can be obtained for any period from 2 to 20 years, although the usual term is 15 years (some banks won't lend for longer than this). In certain cases, mortgages can be arranged over terms of up to 25 years, although interest rates are higher. Generally, the shorter the period of a loan, the lower the interest rate. All lenders set minimum loans, e.g. €15,000 to €30,000, and some set minimum purchase prices. Usually there's no maximum loan amount, which is subject to status and possibly valuation (usually required by non-French lenders).

Note also the following:

- It's customary for a property to be held as security for a loan taken out on it, i.e. the lender takes a charge on the property. Note, however, that some foreign banks won't lend on the security of a French property.

- In France, a mortgage cannot be transferred from one person to another, as is possible in some countries, but can usually be transferred to another property.

- The deposit paid when signing a preliminary property purchase contract (*compromis de vente*) is automatically protected under French law should you fail to obtain a mortgage.

- A borrower is responsible for obtaining building insurance (see page 188) on a property and must provide the lender with a certificate of insurance.

- If you fail to maintain your mortgage repayments, your property can be repossessed and sold at auction. However, this rarely happens, as most lenders are willing to arrange lower repayments when borrowers get into financial difficulties.

Procedure

To obtain a mortgage from a French bank, you must provide proof of your monthly income and all outgoings such as mortgage payments, rent and other loans or commitments. Proof of income includes three months' pay slips for employees, confirmation of income from your employer and tax returns. If you're self-employed, you require an audited copy of your balance sheets and trading accounts for the past three years, plus your last tax return. French banks aren't particularly impressed by accountants' letters. If you want a French mortgage to buy a property for commercial purposes, you must provide a detailed business plan (in French).

It's possible to obtain agreement in principle to a mortgage, and most lenders will supply a guarantee or certificate valid for two to four months (in some cases subject to valuation of the property), which you can present to the vendor of a property you intend to buy. There may be a commitment fee of around €150.

4

Once a loan has been agreed, a French bank sends you a conditional offer (*offre préalable*), outlining the terms. In accordance with French law, the offer cannot be accepted until after a 'cooling-off' period of ten days. The borrower usually has 30 days to accept the loan and return the signed agreement to the lender. The loan is then held available for four months and can be used over a longer period if it's for a building project.

If you're buying a new property off plan, when payments are made in stages, a bank will provide a 'staggered' loan, where the loan amount is advanced in instalments as required by the *contrat de réservation*. During the period before completion (*période d'anticipation*), interest is payable on a monthly basis on the amount advanced by the bank (plus insurance). When the final payment has been made and the loan is fully drawn, the mortgage enters its amortisation period (*période d'amortissement*).

Fees

There are various fees associated with mortgages, which include the following:

- All lenders charge an administration fee (*frais de dossier*) for setting up a loan, usually 1 per cent of the loan amount. There's usually a minimum fee, e.g. €350 (plus value added tax/VAT) and there may also be a maximum.

- Although it's unusual to have a survey, foreign lenders usually insist on a 'valuation survey' (costing around €250) before they grant a loan.

- If a loan is obtained using a French property as security, additional fees and registration costs are payable to the notary (*notaire*) for registering the charge against the property.

If you borrow from a co-operative bank, you're obliged to subscribe to the capital of the local bank. The amount (number of shares) is decided by the board of directors and you're sent share certificates (*certificat nominatif de parts sociales*) for that value. The payment (e.g. €75) is usually deducted from your account at the same time as the first mortgage repayment. When the loan has been repaid, the shares are reimbursed (if required).

If you have a foreign-currency mortgage or are non-resident with a euro mortgage, you must usually pay commission charges each time you make a mortgage payment or remit money to France. However, some lenders will transfer mortgage payments to France each month free of charge or for a nominal amount.

Re-mortgaging

If you have spare equity in an existing property, in France or abroad, it may be more cost-effective to re-mortgage (or take out a second mortgage on) that property than to take out a new mortgage for a second home. Re-mortgaging involves less paperwork (and you therefore incur lower legal fees) and, depending on the equity in your existing property and the cost of a French property, may enable you to pay cash for a second home. The disadvantage of re-mortgaging or a second mortgage is that you reduce the amount of equity available in a property.

French lenders have traditionally been reluctant to re-mortgage, but new rules introduced in spring 2006 mean that 'equity release' mortgages should be available by the end of 2007. There will be two types of 'product': a *crédit hypothécaire rechargeable*, which allows you to re-borrow the amount you've already paid off on an existing mortgage, and a *prêt viager hypothécaire*, which enables you to release the 'capital' tied up in a property as a result of an increase in its value. Before taking out either type of mortgage, you must visit a *notaire*, who will warn you of the risk you're undertaking!

INSURANCE

You must notify your insurance company that you're letting your property and obtain appropriate cover for your *gîte* or B&B. Policies vary between insurance companies, so discuss with your insurer your particular circumstances and needs. It's a legal requirement to have adequate public liability (*responsabilité civile*) and fire insurance once you've bought your property. This should cover your clients, but check whether it includes a guarantee for *recours de locataires contre le propriétaire*, which covers you if the client suffers water or fire damage caused by faulty maintenance.

> ### SURVIVAL TIP
> **When running a B&B business it's essential to have cover against food poisoning (*le risque d'intoxication alimentaire*).**

You should also have comprehensive household insurance (*assurance multi-risques habitation*) and should check that this includes theft cover.

4

Notwithstanding the above, it's wise to advise your clients to have an adequate comprehensive insurance policy, including public liability, personal injury, loss/theft of property, holiday cancellation and vehicle breakdown. (French residents usually have a clause called *villégiature* in their own household insurance policies, which covers them while on holiday.)

Extra insurance is required for swimming pools – consult your insurance company. Further information about insurance can be found in *Buying a Home in France* (Survival Books – see page 314) and general information regarding insurance can be obtained from the Centre de Documentation et d'Information de l'Assurance (CDIA), 26 boulevard Haussmann, 75311 Paris Cedex 09 (🖥 www.ffsa.fr).

GRANTS

Grants may be available for converting a property to *gîtes* or *chambres d'hôtes* in certain areas. Grants may be funded by the Conseil Général, the Conseil Régional, and even the European Union. The availability of grants, conditions of eligibility and amounts offered vary greatly from one department to another. In many departments, there's no provision for grants whatsoever, whereas in other areas, especially those that are seeking to extend their tourist appeal, you may receive from €7,500 to €10,500 per room for a *chambres d'hôtes*, or 30 per cent of the cost of setting up a *gîte* business. As a general rule, to be eligible for a grant a property must be in a commune of fewer than 1,500 inhabitants.

Generally, grants are available in areas designated as *Zones de Développement Régionales* (*ZDR*). Sometimes these are simply poor areas looking for money from tourism, and if you're in one of these areas (or considering buying property in one) you must do your homework carefully – if there's a lack of tourist accommodation, it could very well be because no one wants to visit the area!

The award depends not only on your location, what budget for grants is available in your area and whether any more tourist accommodation is needed, but also on your financial contribution to the work; generally, the more you invest, the bigger the grant you're eligible for. There are usually further amounts allowed for buildings 'of character' and facilities for disabled clients.

In all cases, applications must be made through Gîtes de France. The first step is to contact the departmental office of Gîtes de France, a list of which can be found in **Appendix E**, which handles all grant applications irrespective of where the funds originate. There's a catch – or rather, several – the biggest of which is that once you've accepted a grant you're obliged to register with GdF, usually for ten years, and must use its booking service for some or all of this period (the exact period varies by department). If you sell the property, if your business fails, or if you simply decide to cease operating during this period, the grant received must be paid back in full or part. **Grants are counted as income and are therefore taxable.**

GdF sends an inspector to evaluate the property's suitability and advise you on all aspects of running a letting business, including the demand for rental accommodation in your area. He prepares a dossier with your proposals and presents it to the main office. You must await the decision of the organisation **before** starting work. Once approval is granted, you must comply with GdF standards and have the work carried out by registered tradesmen, submitting the bills before the grant is paid. In some cases, it's acceptable to do the work yourself, submitting the invoices for materials, but ask first! **Note that the money might not be forthcoming until long after work is completed.**

Work that can be taken into account for a grant includes the following:

● building work;

● interior alterations;

● improvements to the fixtures and fittings (not furnishings and decoration).

Certain conditions usually apply:

- Applicants must be permanent residents of the department.

- The property must be in a rural location.

- Work associated with a grant must be completed within one or, sometimes, two years.

- Grants are usually paid only on completion, although 50 per cent is sometimes paid halfway through a project.

- Grants are conditional on the accommodation provided meeting certain standards (see **Appendix E**), and properties are assessed annually.

- For a *gîte*, the typical basic grant is equal to around 30 per cent of the cost of work (up to a maximum of €5,000) excluding taxes.

- B&B rooms must be in an existing building (not newly built) and in a house (not a flat).

- B&B rooms must graded at least at level three (*épis*, *clés* or *étoiles*) with one of the recognised organisations when completed.

- Grants from GdF are conditional on the property being available to rent by them for a set period – usually ten years, but longer or shorter in some departments. If you sell within this period or the property is unavailable for letting, you must repay the grant.

For further details, contact Gîtes de France, La Maison des Gîtes de France et du Tourisme Vert, 59 rue Saint-Lazare, Paris 75439 Cedex 09 (☎ 01 49 70 75 75, 💻 www.gites-de-france.fr).

SURVIVAL TIP
A grant isn't an easy way of paying for renovations.
Carefully weigh up the pros and cons of obtaining a grant
before committing yourself.

RECEIVING PAYMENT

When running a holiday accommodation business, it's important to be able to offer various methods of payment. For *gîtes*, most of your bookings will be made in advance by post or online. For B&B, bear in mind that you'll have a lot of smaller transactions to handle – far more than if you're running *gîtes*. Whichever method(s) of payment you choose to accept, carefully weigh up the convenience (both for you and, especially, for your customers) and cost and don't forget to include the cost of processing transactions in your budget.

Cheques

If guests are British and you have a UK bank account, the easiest way for them to pay is with a sterling cheque. Ask French guests to send a cheque in euros. Note, however, that although other European countries (except the UK) are in the euro currency zone, most French banks make a hefty charge for banking any cheques in euros from outside France – similar to the fee they would charge for a US or UK cheque.

Bank Transfer

A more frequent method of payment from one European country to another is a direct bank transfer. With this method you give the customer your IBAN and BIC codes (your bank will advise you of these if they aren't printed in the back of your chequebook or on your statement) and they arrange a transfer, which takes just a few days. Make sure the customer pays in euros and opts for 'shared charges', which will minimise the bank's fees. If this isn't done, you can add the bank charge to the final bill. Payments from outside Europe attract higher charges. Ask your bank for details.

Online Payment

For payments from most countries across the world, PayPal is immediate and easy (🖳 www.paypal.com, 🖳 www.paypal.co.uk, 🖳 www.paypal.fr). This is an online payment method whereby clients can pay by credit card. You (the owner) must open an account, for which there's no charge. The fee structure varies according to where your account is based, and on the volume of payments received. For example, if you register with an address in the UK and have average monthly receipts of up to £1,500, you pay 3.4 per cent plus £0.20 per transaction; for monthly receipts between £1,500 and £6,000 the fee is 2.9 percent plus £0.20 per transaction. Details can be found on the above websites.

Western Union

If the client doesn't want to enter financial details online, another efficient method is a Western Union Money Transfer. The clients pay cash at their nearest Western Union (WU) agency, and you pick up cash at your nearest main post office (after filling in a long form and providing proof of identity). From some countries funds can be sent online. A list of locations and further information can be found on the Western Union website (🖳 www. westernunion.com). Despite media scare stories, WU money transfer is perfectly safe – the company is long established and highly reputable. The scams which mention WU are those where the 'customer' offers to send a WU money order which turns out to be counterfeit, or transfers are made to unscrupulous recipients who don't send the goods ordered. It is, however, an expensive method of being paid.

4

Credit Cards

If your business grows, you can apply for your own merchant account so that you can take credit card payments (Visa, MasterCard, etc.) directly. You must be registered as a business with the Chambre de Commerce and have a business account with your bank, which provides you with the card machine for a monthly fee and charges a small percentage of each transaction. You must be able to accept transactions when the customer isn't present (for deposits). This is called *vente à distance* and incurs an additional small monthly charge. Ask your bank for details.

Chèques-vacances

Many French employers give their low-paid workers a form of holiday voucher called a *chèque-vacances*. Each voucher is worth €10 or €20 and can be used to pay for holiday accommodation, as well as leisure activities, restaurant meals and other holiday 'entertainment'. They're valid for two years from the date of issue. If you decide to accept these, you must register with the Agence Nationale pour les Chèques-Vacances (ANCV, 36 boulevard Henri Bergson, 95201 Sarcelles Cedex, ☎ 08 25 84 43 44, 🖳 www.ancv.com). Registration is free (details of how to register can be found on the website), but you're charged a 1 per cent fee on the redemption of vouchers, with a minimum of €2. You're paid the value of the vouchers (less the fee) by bank transfer within 21 days.

ACCOUNTING

French accounting principles derive from the *Code de Commerce* and the *Plan Comptable Général*, which are amended and updated periodically by the Conseil National de la Comptabilité, as well as from the *Code Général des Impôts*. The French make much of the supposed differences between 'French accounting' and what they call *la comptabilité anglo-saxonne*. In practice, however, they aren't all that different, although French accounting – in true Gallic style – involves a host of complex rules that must be observed, and certain accounting requirements vary according to the type or size of business.

Generally, it's a legal requirement that accounting records be in French. The principles also specify not only the names, but also the method of numbering for business accounts. Although this can be a nuisance, it simplifies many of the tax reporting requirements, as the instructions refer to the number of a particular account, making it easy to identify. The initial digit of an account number indicates the type of account, as follows:

1. Capital accounts (shareholder equity)

2. Fixed assets (property, plant and equipment)

3. Stock, including raw materials, work in progress and finished goods

4. 'Third-party accounts' (*comptes tiers*), which include all parties to which the business owes money or from which it's due money (separate accounts and account numbers are required for each social security agency and each taxing authority)

5. Bank and other treasury accounts

6. Expenses

7. Sales and other income

There are three legally required journals: *le livre-journal*, *le livre d'inventaire* and *le grand livre*, which roughly correspond to 'general journal', 'inventory journal' and 'general ledger', respectively, as detailed below:

● **Livre-journal** – The 'general journal' is a chronological list of operations (i.e. journal entries) that track the daily sales and expenditure of the business. The French tend to divide the general journal into sub-journals, dealing with sales, purchases, treasury (i.e. the bank accounts) and 'miscellaneous operations' (*opérations diverses*).

- **Livre d'inventaire** – The 'inventory journal' isn't strictly speaking confined to inventory or stock taking. It's more of a trial balance, a listing of each account and its balance as of a specific date. Under French accounting law, you're allowed to review the trial balance at the end of the year, and make adjustments, up and down, to those assets and liabilities that have fluctuated in value. This requirement includes the need to verify the status of your stock (of merchandise, raw materials, work in progress and finished goods) and to verify your fixed assets (property, plant and equipment). You must maintain a year-end inventory journal, documenting the final balances in each account, which serves as the basis for your balance sheet.

- **Grand livre** – The 'general ledger' is the document where the transactions from the general journal (or from the various sub-journals) are summarised and sorted by the accounts affected.

4

Accountants

French accountants (*experts comptable*) vary greatly in their expertise, helpfulness and cost. Like *notaires*, they tend to view their responsibility as to enforce the letter of the law, rather than to assist their clients. For example, there are very few (if any) accountants in private practice who do 'write-up' work for clients (i.e. where the client puts all his receipts and invoices in a shoebox and takes them to the accountant every fortnight or so for the accountant to transcribe into the relevant books). In France, you risk being charged by the invoice if you ask your accountant to do this sort of bookkeeping work for you!

For the same reason, you shouldn't expect much in the way of tax saving or tax planning assistance from an *expert comptable*. This is due, in part, to the fact that changes are often made to the current year's tax law as late as October or November in the year, which makes tax planning almost impossible. Bear in mind also that, if your accountant makes a mistake, e.g. in calculating your tax, you must pay the correct amount and he's under no obligation to compensate you for his error.

Many small businessmen complain bitterly about how expensive their accountants are, and especially how much they charge for miscellaneous tasks, such as determining which account an invoice should be charged to. (The standard joke is that they charge €60 to tell you which account a €20 invoice should go to – and you must still book the entry yourself!) The chances are an accountant won't save you money on a day-to-day basis, but he can save you hassle with the tax authorities – if only by having the forms correctly filled out. It can also be an advantage to have accountant-prepared financial statements if you need a bank loan or credit of any kind.

French accountants are an excellent source of information on the technicalities of the law, especially tax and accounting law. They may be more knowledgeable than many lawyers when it comes to knowing the various forms of business that are possible, and can advise you about the various social security regimes.

CASE STUDY 8 (Part 1)

Like many people, we had been toying with the idea of moving to France for a number of years before we finally committed ourselves. Eventually, finding ourselves with no mortgage and having decent pension funds for the future, we decided in 2003 to sell our property in the UK and move to our favourite holiday destination, where we would open a small bed and breakfast to supplement our savings until we reached retirement age (still some way off as we were in our mid-40s).

Having decided to turn our lives upside down and chuck in two well-paid jobs (bank manager and market research consultant) to create a B&B from scratch, there were three BIG challenges facing us:

● finding the right property;

● financing the purchase and any work required;

● getting people to pay good money for the pleasure (?) of staying with us.

Each of these could have been divided into a dozen or more separate tasks, but concentrating on the bigger picture made the whole project look a lot less daunting.

We had holidayed in France for two decades so we knew a few areas superficially, and we had used our holidays and weekend breaks during the previous two years to refine our target area. At the same time we had gathered notes about the B&Bs we stayed in – 'no maps or information on the area', 'nice terrace to sit and relax', 'Gordon Bennett – how old were those croissants?', etc. We finally narrowed our focus to two patches of Normandy and we thoroughly briefed a couple of property-search agents as to our requirements. We were careful to stress our budget and the type of property we were seeking – both agents promised that our plan was feasible for the kind of money we were talking about.

In March 2004 we crossed to Normandy full of hope mixed with a little fear: after four days of trailing around with the agents, the hope had all but evaporated and we feared the worst. However, when we saw the last house on the last day we knew we had found the right place — the following day we put in an offer and it was accepted. On reflection, we realise we were lucky to have found what we were looking for so quickly, with a price under our budget. All it required was for the first floor to be converted into guest bedrooms and bathrooms and we would be in business.

We took possession of 'La Basse Cour' in August 2004 and there followed six months of planning and thumb twiddling — but mainly thumb twiddling as we waited for our plans for the house to be drawn, revised, submitted and, hallelujah, finally approved.

When we bought the house we had a budget for the total cost of purchase and refurbishment. We also had a pot of money put aside which, if nobody came to stay, would see us through the first five to ten years (so long as we went without luxuries like food and drink and we grew our own clothes!) while we worked out what to do. However, when we approached Gîtes de France in order to enquire about registering with them, they mentioned that there was the possibility of obtaining a grant from the Conseil Général towards the cost of the conversion work to create our chambres d'hôtes.

This wasn't an offer to be sniffed at, as they said we could get a grant to meet 30 per cent of the building costs up to a maximum of €2,400 per room. The work had to be carried out by registered tradespeople and covered building and decorating only — not furnishing. Two further conditions had to be met: we had to get a Gîtes de France classification of at least three épis (or a Clévacances classification of three clés) to qualify for the grant, and we had to operate our chambres d'hôtes for ten years; otherwise a commensurate proportion of the grant would have to be repaid. All this seemed fine to us, as that was what we were planning anyway.

It was as well that we asked our local Gîtes de France office to check our floor plan before we began work — one of our planned rooms was too small to meet their requirements. However, a meeting with our architect and an adjustment to the position of a couple of walls soon fixed that problem. Easily fixed, but an important point – if we hadn't done this then we wouldn't have been able to obtain our classification or our grant.

In March 2005 serious work began and that spring saw the first floor completely gutted, rebuilt and decorated. (Warning: knocking holes in a roof encourages heavy snowfalls.) By June 2005 we were ready to open for business and welcome the crowds of happy holidaymakers who would come flocking to our doors, if only they knew we were here... (continued on page 226)

Phil and Jude Graham, La Basse Cour, 3 rue de l'Oisellerie, 72610 Ancinnes, France (☎ 02 33 82 01 19, UK ☎ 0844-837 8419, 💻 www. normandie-chambres.co.uk)

4

TOP TEN FINANCIAL TIPS

- Make a business plan and calculate the viability of your business when setting your rates; don't just hope for the best.

- Whether you're tax resident in France or not, you must declare your property-letting income in France.

- Ensure that you're declaring your income through the *régime* that's most beneficial for your circumstances.

- Submit your tax return on time to avoid penalties.

- Make sure you have appropriate insurance.

- Ask at your *mairie* whether you'll be liable for *taxe de séjour*.

- Obtain expert advice if you own property through an *SCI*.

- Take advice as to whether you must register for VAT.

- Make it easy for your clients to pay.

- If in doubt, ask an accountant.

4

JoTaylor

5

MARKETING

As with any enterprise, effective marketing is crucial to the success of your business – and marketing doesn't just mean advertising.

Marketing strategies for B&B and *gîtes* differ slightly. When marketing a B&B, you must throw your net wide and catch customers from every possible source. You aren't marketing a relatively small quantity of discrete units (weeks), as with a *gîte*, but a variable product; you're chasing goals as diverse as a fortnight's family holiday and a one-night business stopover.

Monitor the effectiveness of your marketing by asking anyone who makes an enquiry where it was they found information about your property, although they may say, "On the internet", which can be a less than useful answer! Also make sure you obtain feedback from your customers (see **Monitoring & Follow-up** on page 225).

DEFINING YOUR MARKET

Begin by asking yourself what your target market is; e.g. what type of customers do you hope to attract? "As many as possible! Everyone!" is, understandably, the answer most owners initially give. But your marketing must be efficient in terms of time and money, and it isn't possible to promote your property to 'everyone' without vastly overspending. To help define your market, ask yourself the following questions:

● Who will my property appeal to – e.g. families, young couples, older people or wealthy people?

● Who is it most suited to (not necessarily the same)?

● What type of customer would I rather attract (possibly different again!)?

Having decided on your target market(s), ask yourself:

● How do these people prefer to communicate?

● What are they looking for?

● Which advertising medium are they most likely to see?

For example, you wouldn't advertise (nor let) a €4,000-per-week apartment near Cannes to the same people as you would a €300-per-week cottage in Brittany; a family with two children on a low to medium income will opt for the €300 cottage, whereas the €4,000 apartment (for which a cleaning lady alone may cost you €300 per day!) will appeal to an entirely different socioeconomic group. Likewise, a €300-per night suite in a chateau won't sell to the same people as a €50 per night room in a farmhouse.

Different sections of the population have different criteria when booking a holiday. Your advertising must be targeted at your preferred customer profile, without excluding the wider market. Ask yourself whether you can target more than one group? Don't limit yourself to a single customer type: a property suitable for a family in the high season might attract older couples or younger couples without children at other times of the year.

A key decision is whether to target mainly French or English-speaking people. It can be easier to look to the English-speaking world, especially if your French isn't fluent, but you'll have fewer guests, particularly in a B&B. The Anglophone marketplace is much bigger (including all of the US and Canada, South Africa, Australia and New Zealand, for example, as well as the Netherlands!), its marketing techniques generally more effective, its booking systems more efficient and the holiday season is less restricted, but it's much more widely spread, whereas the French are all around you. Moreover, the French (and other continental Europeans) make frequent use of *chambres d'hôtes*, especially those that are registered with Gîtes de France. Advertising through UK publications and websites will attract visitors from the US, Australia, Canada and other Anglophone countries. Advertising with Gîtes de France or Clévacances will attract mostly French visitors, but also a number of other (mainly) Europeans.

5

SURVIVAL TIP
Remember to monitor your enquiries and bookings so that you know where your customers and potential customers are coming from and can adjust or focus your marketing effort accordingly.

Another key question to ask yourself is: Does your property have a 'unique selling point' (USP) and, if so, how can you best exploit it? This might be the nature of the property itself, or its location.

Generally, the more effort you put into marketing, the more income you're likely to earn. Bear in mind, however, that marketing takes time, which is in effect money.

ADVERTISING

Advertising can bring you success (if your advertising is reasonably priced and effective) or failure (if you spend a lot of money on ineffective advertising), and you should make your advertising strategy (and budget) one of your highest priorities. It need not be astronomical; effectiveness is the key.

Advertising doesn't just mean insertions in glossy magazines. You can advertise among friends and colleagues, in company and club magazines (which may even be free), and on notice boards in companies, shops and public places. It isn't necessary to advertise only locally or even to stick to your home country; you can extend your marketing abroad.

There's no need to spend a fortune on advertising, although some expenditure is almost inevitable (see below) and it's essential to allow for advertising in your budget. Don't skimp on your advertising budget, but on the other hand don't throw too much money at it without first doing some research. There are many ways of promoting your accommodation cheaply (and not so cheaply!), some of which are detailed below. **The most expensive advertising is that which doesn't produce results!**

Tourist Offices

5

Regional and departmental tourist boards can be particularly useful for generating B&B business, although some are inevitably more efficient and 'proactive' than others. They maintain lists of holiday accommodation and publish widely distributed brochures, in which a listing may cost as little as €15. (The costs, as with so many things, vary by department.)

In recent years, however, the regional tourist offices have become far more stringent in respect of whose holiday accommodation they promote; most now advertise only premises that have been inspected and rated by their own representatives or those of Clévacances or Gîtes de France. Ask your local Comité Départemental du Tourisme whether or not your accommodation must be inspected and graded to qualify for entry and for details of any other requirements.

Most people book their summer holidays in January, and the deadline for an entry in printed brochures is typically the previous August, so be sure to carry out your enquiries well in advance.

Newspapers & Magazines

There's a wide range of French and foreign newspapers and magazines in which you can advertise, e.g. newspapers such as the *Sunday Times* and the *Observer* in the UK, although advertising a single property might be prohibitively expensive. You must experiment to find the best publications and days of the week or months to advertise. Most of the English-language newspapers and magazines listed in **Appendix B** include advertisements from property owners.

You might have a particular special interest group in mind; for example, if your property is near Le Mans, you might want to target car and motorbike enthusiasts and advertise in their magazines. If you're in an area of outstanding natural beauty where there are good routes for hiking, aim your advertising at walkers. If you're near sites of historical importance such as the D-Day Landing beaches, the First World War battlefields or Roman remains, try to target people with an interest in such things. The same strategy applies if you're in an area with interesting wildlife and birds, outstanding sporting facilities, steam railways, gourmet restaurants or any other interest with a large number of devotees and dedicated publications. A glance at the shelves of any large newsagent will reveal a wide range of special interest magazines; an internet search will disclose even more.

The most obvious special interest group is those who love France! There are many magazines specifically catering for Francophiles, which are packed with holiday accommodation advertising (see **Appendix B**).

Guidebooks

As far as *gîtes* are concerned, the internet has largely displaced guidebooks as the preferred medium for advertising properties to let (see below), although a few specialist publications remain in print, most notably Alastair Sawday's *Special Places to Stay – French Holiday Homes, Villas, Gites & Apartments* (UK ☎ 01275-464891, 🖳 www.sawdays.co.uk), in which entries (for properties that meet the criteria) cost from €200.

On the other hand, entries in guidebooks are one of the most effective methods of advertising a B&B, as many people use a guidebook to plan their holiday itinerary. The disadvantage is that there are so many titles that it's difficult to choose which one(s) to advertise in. Also, you must plan your advertising well in advance – in most cases at least a year in advance for the following season's edition, and it takes some time after that to fully reap the rewards, as even the most fervent guidebook user won't buy a new copy every year. Popular English-language B&B guidebooks include the following (there are also several published in French):

● **AA Bed & Breakfast in France** – This guide, which has over 3,000 entries, is a joint promotion with Gîtes de France, incorporating GdF properties with a grading of three *épis* and above. Arranged by region, it includes contact details, prices, and local facilities and attractions.

- **Alastair Sawday's Special Places to Stay – French Bed & Breakfast** – a popular UK-published guide. Entries cost from €200 (UK ☎ 01275-464891, 💻 www.sawdays.co.uk).

- **Karen Brown France Charming Bed & Breakfasts** – a prestigious US-published guide. Listings are free, but by invitation only once the property has been visited by their research team/author (💻 www.karenbrown.com).

Internet

The internet is replacing travel agents as the most popular way to book holidays. A report by the Office of National Statistics in the UK states that the most common purchases on the internet are travel, accommodation and holidays (52 per cent). Thomson, for example, now sells 50 per cent of its holidays online, its high street outlets increasingly becoming advice and guidance centres to help customers book on the internet. A survey by Nielsen/NetRatings in December 2006 reported that 55 per cent of internet users book their holidays directly online. A further 17 per cent gain their information through a web search but make the booking by telephone, and another 9 per cent research online then book at a high street travel agent, making a total of 81 per cent.

In January 2007 there were over 37.6m internet users in the UK (62.3 per cent of the population), 57 per cent of individuals using the internet regularly (at least once a week). Over 75 per cent of connections are now via broadband. These figures can only increase.

Advertising on the internet is an increasingly popular choice for property owners; indeed it's essential nowadays. There are two options: set up your own website (see **Your Own Website** on page 219); or take an entry on a commercial site. You can, of course, do both.

Commercial websites fall broadly into two categories:

- those that simply carry advertising – the clients contact the owners direct to book (see **Deal-direct Sites** below);

- those that act as agents, handling bookings as well as advertising your property, usually on a commission basis. As these are mainly for self-catering accommodation they're dealt with in **Chapter 2** (see **Using an Agency** on page 96 and the list of websites in **Appendix C**).

Note that Brittany Ferries, one of the best-known holiday accommodation companies, offers a choice between an agency scheme (called 'Holiday Homes') and an advertising-only arrangement ('Owners in France').

Some deal-direct sites (e.g. Chez Nous) also have a printed catalogue or brochure. Their rates may include brochure entry or this might be optional.

A new and increasingly popular concept, owing to the advent of widespread broadband access, is the online video brochure, which can be updated and amended easily and instantly. It can either be viewed online or delivered by email. See, for example, ⌨ www.webtvmarketing.tv.

Deal-direct Sites

Internet sites that simply carry advertising – the properties are let directly by the owners – are known as 'deal-direct' sites. There are dozens, even hundreds, of such sites, which simply display your advertisement on a website (and sometimes in a catalogue or brochure) for a one-off or annual fee. Some are excellent; many are a complete waste of money. The potential holidaymaker contacts you directly and you handle the transaction, which gives you complete control over your bookings.

Advantages & disadvantages: Advantages may include the following:

- high visibility on search engines and therefore exposure to a large number of potential clients;

- flexibility as to how much you can charge and which weeks you offer;

- the opportunity to vet clients – if you don't like the sound of someone making a telephone enquiry, you can choose not to accept their booking!

Disadvantages may include the following:

- the cost (although some sites offer free listings – see below);

- the time and effort producing an advertisement, which are much the same as those required for doing your own letting;

- no guarantee of attracting bookings.

Choosing a site: Every day someone sets up a new holiday accommodation website, and these are now so numerous that you cannot rely on clients coming across a particular site when searching the web. Some sites will produce few or no bookings. Try a search engine (e.g. ⌨ www.google.com) with various related keywords and phrases that a potential customer might use and see which sites appear in the top ten. If a company is exclusively web-based, the search result is important – most people won't look further than the first page or two.

Note, however, that some of the market leaders in holiday property advertising may not always appear high in search results. However, their strengths lie in their strategy of consistent press marketing campaigns in conjunction with a well organised, easily navigable, informative, well maintained and user-friendly website – the essential factors which attract clients.

Look for sites where you can browse the properties, as many (particularly French) sites require you to enter the exact number of people, bedrooms, the area, the date and the precise length of stay before showing any properties, which won't attract any 'window-shoppers'. Some offer a free entry for a limited period (when they have a certain number of properties on their sites, they start charging).

SURVIVAL TIP
Free is worth a try; cheap is a false economy.

---

5 The best companies are those with the greatest coverage (e.g. number of brochures distributed, TV and press advertisements) and a known brand name, such as Chez Nous or Brittany Ferries, who also produce a glossy colour catalogue with wide distribution via travel agents and ferry ports and advertise in national newspapers. They're far more expensive to advertise with, but the returns are usually worth it.

You should bear in mind that catalogues and brochures are easier to browse than websites and choose a company that publishes these, as despite the meteoric increase in holidays booked via the internet, there are still many people who don't use computers, have no internet access, mistrust this method of making their holiday arrangements or simply prefer to do things the 'old-fashioned' way. There are still plenty of high street travel agents, and your property needs to be seen by their customers.

Leading companies: The major sites for advertising holiday accommodation in France include the following:

- **Bonnes Vacances** (UK ☎ 0870-760 7073, 💻 www.bvdirect.co.uk) – advertises in national newspapers and offers travel discounts and an insurance service. Full details on how to advertise available on the website. Listing cost: from £85 plus VAT per year.

- **Brittany Ferries Owners in France** (UK ☎ 0870-901 3400, 💻 www. ownersinfrance.co.uk), to be re-branded **Holiday France Direct** in autumn 2007 – has an easy-to-navigate site and a widely distributed brochure, and offers ferry fare and other travel discounts. Downloadable advertisers' guide on the website. Listing cost: brochure (one-sixteenth page) **or** website only – from £190 + VAT per year; brochure (one-eighth page) **and** website – from £425 + VAT.

- **Chez Nous** (UK ☎ 0870-197 1000, 💻 www.cheznous.com) – has an easy-to-navigate site and a widely distributed brochure listing over 4,000 properties. Brochure also available to download in PDF format. Advertises in the UK national press. Discounts with continued advertising. Travel offers, discounts for owners on cottage holidays through sister companies. Downloadable advertisers' guide on the website. Listing cost: website only – from £179; brochure only – from £299 to £1,899 (full page advert); website and brochure – from £418 to £1,978 (full page ad in the brochure). All prices plus VAT.

- **France Direct** & **Gites Direct** (☎ 05 53 07 17 75, 💻 www.gitesdirect.com, 💻 www.francedirect.net) – a British company, also registered in France (95 per cent of advertisers are English-speaking). Booking service on a commission basis. The website is easy to navigate (there's no brochure). Several levels of advertising. Listing cost: from €125 per year.

- **France One Call** (☎ 05 53 90 49 76, UK ☎ 0871-717 9092, 💻 www. franceonecall.com) – self-catering only. Web-based advertising business with a referral system, whereby members refer enquirers to France One Call if they're unable to accommodate them, who then pass them on to other members. Listing cost: £180 per year for one property; £25 for each additional property.

- **French Connections** (💻 www.frenchconnections.co.uk) – has a fast, easy-to-search site including plenty of details. Over 3,000 properties. Listing cost: from £149 plus VAT per year.

- **Guide Vacances** (💻 www.guidevacances.com). French holiday listing site. Listing cost: basic listing free, with several optional paid extras (e.g. €15 for a photograph).

- **Homelidays** (☎ 01 70 75 34 03, 💻 www.homelidays.com) – the site is available in French, Spanish, German, Italian and Portuguese. Listing cost: first month free, but you pay a €20 'inscription' when renewing; the renewal fee is then €75 for four months, €105 for eight months or €125 for a year.

- **Le Petit Futé** (☎ 01 53 69 65 35, 💻 www.lepetitfute.com) – a well-known French guide (website only). Listing cost: €220 including five photographs.

5

- **Vacation Rentals by Owner/VRBO** (🖳 www.vrbo.com) – a fast site providing comprehensive details of accommodation worldwide; France can be searched by region. Listing cost: US$149 per year (includes three photographs).

- **Visit France** (UK ☎ 0870-350 2808, 🖳 www.visitfrance.co.uk) – has an easily navigated site listing over 500 properties, including *gîtes* and B&B. Listing cost: from £99 plus VAT.

PROMOTION & PUBLIC RELATIONS

Look for opportunities for joint promotions or 'tie-ins', such as promoting a local attraction, in return for which the attraction lists your establishment in its own promotional material, or displays your poster. The attraction may even offer your guests a discount on admission or products purchased there.

Contact companies that organise tours (e.g. wine, shopping, motorcycling) in your area and invite them to list your establishment in their documentation or even include your accommodation in their tours.

It also pays to work with other local people in the same business and send surplus guests to competitors (they will usually reciprocate).

Look for opportunities for free publicity (in terms of money, not necessarily time!), such as spreading the word via friends and family, putting up cards in local supermarkets and petrol stations, and contacting local estate agents (people who are on house-hunting trips may be looking for somewhere to stay).

Newspaper & Magazine Articles

The many magazines about France (see **Appendix B**) and even national newspapers and television companies are constantly looking for feature articles on unusual properties abroad – and properties in unusual locations. You could even write about the local area and include a mention of your establishment; they may not pay you for an article, but it could generate business.

Business Name

You need a name for the signboard outside the property and for your letterheads and publicity material. In rural areas, several properties may share an address, the postman distinguishing between them by the names of the occupants. Choose a name with the help of an intelligent French person; you don't want something that sounds peculiar (or utterly nonsensical) to French people. Don't choose an English name that means something quite different in French; in fact, it's best not to use an English name at all. Don't choose a name that could be mistaken for another type of business, e.g. *La Boulangerie* for a property converted from an old bakehouse – clients looking for your B&B will be directed to the nearest baker's shop! It should be easy to pronounce by people of all nationalities, and short to stand out on signs.

Signs

If you want to erect signs on a main road, your property must generally be within 5km (3mi) of it. If it's a national road (*route nationale*, prefixed by N), you must contact the Ministère des Transports, de l'Equipement, du Tourisme et de la Mer (🖳 www.equipement.gouv.fr); if it's a departmental (D) road, contact your local Direction Départementale de l'Equipement (DDE), which controls not only the roads themselves, but the land within 3m of it (unless private property); if it's a communal (C) road, ask at your local *mairie*.

One of the major benefits of GdF registration is that you're provided with signs: directional signs with arrows on for the road and circular signs for your gatepost or wall. Whether or not they're installed for you depends on how keen the regional, departmental or communal administration is to promote tourism, but it's as well to ask – if only to find out where they may and may not be sited. Clévacances also supplies signs, but these are less familiar to holidaymakers and consequently of less marketing value.

For a B&B business your signs have two functions – to attract passing trade (thus a marketing opportunity), and to help guests who have booked to find your property (also important for *gîtes*). Therefore a sign must be attractive but also clear and, above all, visible (check regularly that plants or trees aren't obscuring it).

At the entrance to your property, the sign should be large and clear, visible to traffic passing in both directions. Test its position and visibility by driving past. Often, signs are just too small to be noticed, the lettering is too thin to be read from a moving car, or the sign doesn't actually say what it's advertising!

If you're catering to passing trade and there's strong competition in your area, you must find a way to entice guests to stay at your establishment rather than passing on to the next one down the road.

For B&B, remember to target different nationalities – your sign could read, for instance: "B&B – Chambres d'Hôtes – Gastzimmer", one of which will be understood by most people. Once people have arrived at your entrance, they will see your price tariff, which must, by law, be displayed there. Use this as a marketing opportunity by having a display board with photographs of your rooms and facilities and a description of the accommodation in French and English (and any other language relevant in your area). Replace the photographs regularly, as they will fade and discolour quickly.

PRINTED MATTER

Make sure that all your documentation reflects your desired image and be consistent in your style of presentation in brochures and leaflets as well as on signs, letterheads, advertisements, your website, etc. You may wish to design (or have designed) a logo, incorporating the name of your establishment with a simple image.

It's highly recommended that you have your literature professionally designed unless you have the necessary skills to produce your own (see below). Remember that owning a desk-top publishing (DTP) program on a computer doesn't magically bestow graphic design skills on the user (just as having a spreadsheet program doesn't transform anyone into an accountant, nor having a pencil make someone an artist!).

Although it works out cheaper to have a large quantity printed at once, this can prove a handicap. A big advantage to printing as needed is that you can make any necessary amendments in the light of experience and keep tariffs, directions and other information up to date.

While you're having leaflets and headed paper printed, it may be cost-effective also to print some simple flyers (hand-outs – see **Flyers & Posters** below) and business cards, which you should always keep in your wallet or handbag – you never know when you might run into potential clients!

There are online producers of business stationery such as Vistaprint (💻 www.vistaprint.co.uk, 💻 www.vistaprint.fr); you choose from stock layouts, inputting your own details. This can work out cheaper than using a local printer, but you're limited in your choice of design unless you pay a supplement to upload your own logos, pictures, etc. It's worth experimenting to see what you can come up with, or to give you some ideas, without going as far as pressing the 'pay' button!

SURVIVAL TIP
Make sure your documentation is regularly updated; there's nothing more off-putting than out-of-date information or a document amended by hand.

5

Creating Your Own Documentation

Keep things simple if doing your own designs on a computer – just because you have 100 pretty fonts you don't have to use them all. A good rule of thumb is not to use more than two different typefaces on a page, and no more than two sizes or styles of each. Don't get carried away with myriad colours, either. If in doubt, keep it plain. **The information is the most important thing.** If you aren't completely confident of your spelling and grammar, have someone with good language skills check the text before you print it. It's always a good idea to do that anyway, as even glaring mistakes can easily slip through and will make your material (and, by implication, your business) look unprofessional.

To make a good job of it you'll need a desk-top publishing (DTP) program. This is a program that enables you to manipulate, collate and place the elements of your layout (text, graphics, photographs) on the page. A word processing package (e.g. Microsoft Word) is **not** a DTP program. Microsoft's equivalent is Publisher, which is user-friendly for the amateur and offers templates for different projects. The two leading professional DTP programs are QuarkXpress and Adobe InDesign (formerly PageMaker), but they can be very expensive; there are less expensive alternatives such as Serif PagePlus.

If you decide to produce publicity material in languages other than English (if that's your native language), it's essential to have it translated and proofread by an educated native speaker. Automated and online translators (e.g. 🖳 www.google.com/language_tools) are useful **only** to help you understand foreign-language text; they cannot handle complicated constructions or colloquialisms, and usually make a bad job even when the original is fairly simple.

5

A restaurant in a well known tourist town generously provides an English version of its menu. The result of using an automatic translation program, however, is somewhat less than helpful: 'Foie gras frais maison et sa petite salade' has been transformed into 'Liver greasiness cool house and his small salad', while 'Pigeon à la croque de caramel et son jus parfumé" has become "pigeon to her crunches of toffee and his fragrant juice".

Leaflets & Brochures

The standard format for leaflets is a sheet of A4 (297mm x 210mm) paper folded into thirds, which fits into a standard business envelope (DL: 120mm x 220mm). On the front, have the name and address of your property, any logos of organisations to which you belong (e.g. GdF) and a picture. Inside, include the following:

- exterior and interior pictures;
- the location and details of how to get there (with a small map);
- local attractions and other reasons for staying in your accommodation;
- the name, address and telephone number of your caretaker if applicable;
- any other important details, e.g. the number of rooms and a brief description of each including how many they sleep, your star/*épi*/*clé* rating, and what types of meals you serve (if any).

On the back page have your contact details: name, address, telephone and fax numbers, email and website addresses.

It's necessary to make a property look as attractive as possible in a leaflet or brochure without distorting the facts or misrepresentation (you can be fined heavily for this). Advertise honestly and don't over-sell your property.

5

Flyers & Posters

It's useful to have a small poster or flyer for the purpose of advertising your property on notice boards in local shops, the tourist office, etc., and for satisfied customers to take home and put up in their workplace or give to friends and relatives. You could have the same layout on both A4 (297mm x 210mm) and A5 (210mm x 148mm) sheets. Keep the design simple and eye-catching – its purpose is to attract the viewer to find out more. You need to say what it's advertising and give the location, your contact details and a very brief description. The main selling point (e.g. 'Holiday Accommodation in France' or 'Cottage in Provence to Let') should be visible from a distance. It's pointless having the name of the property in large letters as it won't mean anything to anyone. Include a good picture of the property and maybe a banner highlighting special offers.

Business Cards

Business cards are small (around 85mm x 55mm) so the content needs to be concentrated! Don't be tempted to make them an unusual size or they won't fit in people's wallets. If you intend pinning them up on notice boards, include the essential information as for flyers (see above) but don't include too much text – it's better to have a separate card for this purpose, maybe A6 size (148mm x 105mm).

It's strongly recommended that you have business cards professionally printed and **not** to use coin-operated machines in supermarkets, as they'll be far better quality and more durable, with a superior finish and thick card. You can buy sheets of business cards for inkjet printers but the finish is inferior and the ink will usually blur or run if it becomes damp. If you decide to print them yourself, avoid cards with perforated edges, which look shoddy, and if you're including a graphic or a photograph choose a gloss finish.

A business card should have your name, address, telephone number and maybe email and website addresses. A logo or photograph adds colour and interest, and you should include a brief description (tagline – e.g. 'French Holiday Accommodation').

YOUR ADVERTISEMENT

A catalogue, directory, guidebook or press advertisement will be small (unless you want to spend a fortune); it needs to be concentrated and effective. Think about what you look for when flicking through holiday advertisements – and, more importantly, what you **see**. Most people see the following in this order:

1. the picture;

2. the price;

3. the capacity of the accommodation;

4. the written description.

5

All these aspects are important, but it's the picture that will sell your property. The location is obviously significant, but if people are looking for a holiday 'in France' they will want to window shop and browse all advertisements. You **should** include the price in your advertisement – that's the first thing people ask anyway (once they've seen the picture!). French advertisements often don't show prices – the attitude being that one must establish a relationship with the other party before discussing the vulgar matter of money – which people of most other nationalities find irritating. This may therefore give you an 'edge' when competing against French businesses for your slice of the foreign market.

Head your advertisement with the nature of the accommodation (e.g. '*Gîte*' or 'B&B' or both), a well known town or area, such as 'near Bayeux',

'Charente coast' (rather than a small town whose name is unknown outside the area), and the name of your property.

The text of your advertisement should describe the main selling points of your property – whether this is the property itself (e.g. 16th-century mill), its location (e.g. by a lake or river), proximity to tourist attractions, wonderful restaurants or sites of historical interest nearby, or facilities for walking, cycling and other sports. Focus on the reasons why a holidaymaker would want to choose your accommodation over all the others available – not just in your area but in the whole of France!

If space allows, include a list of the facilities available and main appliances, information about the pool and garden, distances from the nearest towns and/or village shops, a breakdown of the accommodation (number of bedrooms, type of beds), and any facilities such as disabled access or children's play equipment.

PHOTOGRAPHY

5 If you let through an agency, it may send a representative to take them. **Ask the agency to send a proof of the photo for your approval.** You may be able to submit your own photographs. If you aren't confident of your ability as a photographer, or don't have a good enough camera (especially for interior shots), hire a professional. As stated above, **the photograph is the most important element of your advertising, so don't skimp.** If it's for print, a high-resolution digital image (at least 3 mega-pixels) is normally required, although you may be asked for good 35mm prints or transparencies; ask the publisher what he prefers. For internet advertisements, a lower resolution is adequate (and may even be required, in order to maximise upload speed) although if it's for an online directory the publisher might want to adjust the resolution himself, so you should still supply a high-resolution image. It's best to have the highest quality image you can manage – resolution can always be reduced, but you cannot improve the quality of a digital image.

The main photograph (of the front of your property) is the most important, as it must catch the eye of the magazine, catalogue or website browser and stand out from hundreds of others.

Advertisements that don't display an exterior shot rarely attract bookings, as the impression given is that there's something unattractive about the property or its surroundings.

Many people book their summer holidays in January; the deadline for an entry in printed brochures is typically the previous August, or even earlier. If your property renovation isn't yet completed, this can be a problem – concentrating on finishing the roof and facade and strategically positioning container plants to get an attractive photograph might be a solution! (Interior photographs can always be added to the related website at a later date, when you actually have an interior…)

Tips

When taking photographs yourself, bear in mind the following points:

General

- Don't make the common mistake of centring the focal point (i.e. the main element the eye is drawn to when viewing the finished image) but have it slightly off-centre (either horizontally or vertically).

- Take plenty of shots with various settings and choose the best. If you're using a digital camera there's no limit to how many you can take, so there's no excuse for not producing a superb picture!

5

Exterior Shots

- Choose a sunny day with a blue sky (a few fluffy white clouds are permissible!).

- Choose the time of day when the sun is on the facade you want to photograph.

- The quality and colour of light is usually better in the early morning or early evening than in the middle of the day. The 'golden hours' are one hour after sunrise and one hour before sunset.

- Test unusual views and angles. If you can, erect a ladder and look down on the property or lie on the ground and look up.

- Dress your property. Even if you hate net curtains and wouldn't normally have them in your windows, nevertheless hang some before taking exterior photos, as they brighten the facade and prevent the 'empty eyes' effect.

- Introduce plenty of colour with pots of flowering plants and hanging baskets.

- For a *gîte* advertisement, don't include people, cars or pets. The viewers must be able to imagine themselves staying in the property – if there are other people in the photograph, they will be subconsciously seen as intruders.

- Include pretty garden furniture – viewers can envisage themselves basking in the sun.

- Include the pool if you have one.

Interior Shots

- Photograph the most attractive parts of the prettiest rooms.

- Use a wide-angle lens if possible, in order to make rooms look larger. (Fish-eye lenses are to be avoided unless you're experienced in using them, as they can produce a highly distorted image.)

- Dress the rooms with big pots of fresh flowers and colourful accessories.

- Give your picture a focal point, e.g. an open fire (lit), a window with a view or an antique bed, but don't centre it (see **General** above).

- Switch on wall lights, table lights, etc..

- Let in as much natural light as possible.

- Use a stepladder to find a good angle.

B&B

For the most part, the criteria for good photographs of your B&B are the same as for *gîtes*, but there are a few significant differences:

- Include people in exterior shots (this is an advantage for a B&B as guests will be expecting to mix with others), but make sure they're the right sort of people!

- For interior shots, create a mood in keeping with your chosen image – whether you're selling a romantic getaway or a fun family holiday, try to convey that impression in the photographs.

- Include a shot of your dining table laid with plates full of food, lighted candles, and glasses of wine ready for drinking.

YOUR OWN WEBSITE

Although it may initially be more expensive to set up your own website than to advertise on existing sites, the cost of maintenance is low compared with continual advertising. You can have a site professionally designed (**recommended**) or do it yourself, although if you're a complete 'dummy', it's much better pay someone else to do it for you. Avoid asking a friend's 12-year-old daughter do it; she might be a whiz with computers but is very unlikely to have any knowledge of design and marketing.

From the outset, bear in mind that you're selling a product and will be up against stiff competition; gear your efforts towards achieving bookings. You must include everything that the potential client needs to know in order to make a decision – this might seem obvious, but too many people design websites that don't include the essential information. However pretty and well designed your site is, clients will move on to another, more informative website if you don't them what they **need** to know, namely:

5

- what you're offering;

- where it is;

- how to get there;

- how much it costs.

Even if your website isn't the main booking source, it can be useful for clients' reference – they can download pictures, information, directions, maps, etc. after having made contact by telephone or email or having seen a magazine or internet advertisement.

A good website should be easy to navigate (don't include complicated page links or indexes) and must include contact details, preferably via email. Flashing red text on a black background won't sell your property; a clean, simple, easy-to-navigate site with plenty of content will. Look at other owners' sites in order to evaluate what features and designs are the most effective; what would prompt you to make an enquiry to one owner but not another? Incorporate ideas (but don't copy them!) from sites you like.

Consider registering your own domain name (e.g. www.bellemaison.net). This isn't essential and is an additional cost, but it's easier for people to remember and looks far more professional than a long name provided by your internet service provider, e.g. www.freeinternet.com/bellemaison. There are numerous books about website design, although some are incomprehensible by the novice.

Creating Your Own Website

If you choose to create your own website, keep it simple.

Although there are 'idiot-proof' website design packages (some of which are free), these often create more problems than they solve; to create a professional-looking site, it's best to have at least a basic knowledge of HTML (Hyper Text Mark-up Language). You don't need any special programs to write HTML; this can be done in simple text programs such as Windows NotePad. Go to any website and (using Internet Explorer) click on View > Source (there will be a similar function on other browsers). This will show you the HTML in NotePad. A basic HTML tutorial for building a web page can be found on 💻 www.davesite.com.

It's useful to be able to see what you're doing as you progress by viewing your results in a browser, so a simple HTML editor is the next step. A free HTML editor is available at 💻 www.arachnoid.com.

The most sophisticated tool is known as a WYSIWIG ('what you see is what you get') editor; one of the best is Macromedia's DreamWeaver (💻 www.macromedia.com).

Another way to do it is to subscribe to an 'off-the-shelf' website builder such as MrSite (e.g. 💻 www.mrsite.co.uk). The package includes the registration of a domain name and hosting (the web space where your files are stored). You pay around £35 for the first year and £2.50 per month thereafter. You can either use the builder's templates and tools or upload your own HTML.

Photographs & Graphics

Unless your photographs are perfect, you'll need an image editing program, to make them fit the space available and look as 'professional' as possible. You might already have one on your system (they're often packaged with scanner or digital camera software). If not, there's a huge choice available and you needn't spend a lot – or even anything; a free program is IrfanView (💻 www.irfanview.com). At the other end of the spectrum is Adobe PhotoShop (💻 www.adobe.com) – the professionals' choice, but with a professional price tag! The same company's PhotoShop Elements is adequate for the amateur user, and is often one of those included with camera or scanner software. A good middle-ground program is Corel Paint Shop Pro (⌨ www.corel.com), which costs around £50.

Pictures speak louder than words, but photographs and logo graphics must be kept to a reasonable size – if people have to wait too long for a page to appear, they will lose patience and move on to the next property on their list. To make picture files smaller, use the resize option in your graphics program (specifying pixel dimensions in HTML won't reduce the file size!).

You'll no doubt want to include quite a few photographs (remember – they're what sells your product) and graphics (e.g. maps, your logo). For a large number of photographs, consider using thumbnail images, each of which is linked to a bigger image. Remember that many people don't yet have broadband access. Include exterior and interior shots (see **Photography** on page 216).

For information about scanning and image manipulation, visit ⌨ www. scantips.com.

SURVIVAL TIP
The purpose of your website is to convey information and present your accommodation in the most attractive possible light, not to dazzle your potential customers.

5

Text

Keep to standard fonts such as Arial, Helvetica or Verdana (sans-serif) and Book Antiqua, Century or Times New Roman (serif). You might have some exotic fonts on your system, but if the people viewing the site don't have the same fonts installed on theirs, they won't see them and your carefully arranged text might appear misaligned or even with characters garbled or missing. In any case, fancy fonts are often difficult to read. Use a graphic for logos or any other items that you want to appear in a specific typeface.

Don't make text too small – many of your potential customers may no longer have perfect eyesight! Try viewing at different text sizes within the browser (e.g. in Internet Explorer: go to the View menu > Text Size > Largest / Larger / Medium / Smaller / Smallest) to see what works best.

Appearance

If you want a coloured background, choose a plain, light, neutral colour or a tiny tile in a subtle pattern that loads quickly and doesn't make the text difficult to read. Use dark text on a light background – you want people to read what you've written, not be dazzled.

Do **not** use flashing or scrolling text, music, trailing mouse pointers or any other embellishments, as they make pages load more slowly, look tacky and are irritating to most users. You're targeting adults who want to book a holiday, not trying to impress teenagers with a 'cool' site!

If possible, view your finished pages using several browsers (e.g. Firefox, Internet Explorer, Netscape and Opera) and at different screen resolutions. Not everyone has the same system or settings and this can cause huge variations in the way a page appears. Make sure each page appears in its entirety without the necessity for lateral scrolling (set widths as percentages rather than pixel dimensions). Many people have their screen resolution set at 640 x 480 because that's how it was set when they bought the computer.

Each page should have the most important information at the top as viewers are often lazy and won't bother to scroll down if the initial portion doesn't catch their interest. **If in doubt, keep it plain and simple!**

5 Structure & Content

Make sure you give each page an appropriate title (this is what shows in the bar at the top of the screen). 'Gîte and B&B in Anyville, France' is preferable to 'Home Page' or 'Page 1'.

Keep pages fairly short, with links to other pages for details of the accommodation, its location, how to book, more information, maps, etc. Include a link back to the home page on each.

The most important information should be on the first screen at the top of the first page. It shouldn't be a slow-loading photograph or graphic logo. You need to catch the attention of potential clients immediately, entice them to read and explore the rest of your site, absorb what they read and then encourage them to make a booking. This first paragraph is often what is found by search engines, so incorporate plenty of key words.

You can include a downloadable booking form – a PDF file is best. If you don't have the necessary software to create PDF files, use RTF (rich text format) files, which can be opened with any word processing or text program. Avoid using frames, as viewers might have difficulty in printing the page, and they might prevent search engines finding the page.

Include comprehensive information about your property, with directions and maps that customers can print off and bring with them when they travel. If you receive repeated questions, add the information to your site.

If you aren't confident of your writing and spelling abilities, hire the services of a copywriter or at least have someone with good language skills read it carefully before uploading.

Remember that you're projecting an impression of the product being sold -- you don't want it to look shoddy and unprofessional. Professional doesn't mean impersonal – use 'we' and 'you' when extolling your accommodation.

Include plenty of text, which increases search engine visibility, as well as selling your property. You can provide information about flights, ferries, car rental, local attractions, days out, sports facilities and links to other useful websites. (Have external links set to open in a separate window; you don't want visitors to wander away from your site).

> **SURVIVAL TIP**
> **Your site should provide a precise description of what you're selling: where it is, how much it costs and why people should want a holiday there.**

- The first (home) page should contain an overview of the property, the accommodation available and its main features – e.g. historic building, proximity to the sea, tourist attractions or airports, or friendly welcome by fluent French-speakers. This page should contain links to all the other pages, plus contact information, and the best photograph you have, as well as an introductory paragraph containing key words and phrases. The file name should be index.htm or index.html to make it more 'visible' to search engines.

- The next page could be a general information page with exterior pictures of the house and garden. Describe the facilities available – garden, terrace, play equipment, guest lounge, swimming pool, etc.. If you want to display more than two or three photographs, use small (but visible) thumbnails that link to a larger version.

- Provide information about the area, the nearest tourist attractions, sports and leisure facilities and any other unique selling points (USPs) that will attract people to book with you rather than with another establishment.

- Include a contact page with your address, telephone number and email address (or an email form). It **is** wise to include your telephone number, but also to include a table comparing time zones in a selection of countries, as you won't want telephone calls from the US in the middle of the night. If you speak to a potential client, you immediately establish a relationship and will be better positioned to convert the enquiry into a sale. Email is more convenient, but impersonal; the person browsing holiday accommodation sites will probably fire off identical emails to several addresses – only one will get the booking, so do your utmost to make sure it's yours!

● Include maps showing the exact location – one of France as a whole, one more detailed showing the nearest airports or ferry ports, and a local map with precise directions for finding your property. Don't simply copy from books or websites, as there are heavy penalties for infringement of copyright on maps. Draw your own (or have someone draw them for you). Alternatively you can link your website to mapping websites (such as 🖥 http://uk.multimap.com) for the larger-scale maps and prepare a simple sketch map for the local details.

● It's important to include a tariff; one of the first questions people ask is the price, so you might as well put the details on your site.

● Use bulleted lists (like this one!) – they're easier to read than long blocks of text, and easier on the eye when reading on a computer monitor.

● Each page should have links to all other areas of the site.

> **SURVIVAL TIP**
> **Make sure your website is regularly**
> **updated; there's nothing more off-putting than**
> **out-of-date information.**

For a B&B, you should provide the following additional information:

● a page for each room, describing it in glowing terms with details of how many people it sleeps and whether a cot is available; if it has stunning views, include photographs of them, as well as of the room itself;

● if you offer evening meals, a page with a photograph of your beautifully laid dining table and a description of your delicious meals, maybe including a typical menu.

Visibility

There's no point in having a beautiful website if no one can find it. Making your website 'visible' is known as search engine optimisation (SEO). This is a vast and complicated area, but there are a few simple rules you can follow to help your website appear when people enter certain words and phrases into a search engine (e.g. 🖥 www.google.com – the most popular).

Google dominates the search engine market in the UK (and the rest of the world), with around 75 per cent of all searches, according to a survey carried out in 2006. The other main engines (Yahoo, MSN and ASK UK) each only represent between 5 and 10 per cent of searches.

As mentioned above, having plenty of text will increase the probability of your site being found by search engines, in particular the opening paragraph on the introductory page. The file name for this page should be 'index.htm' or 'index.html' and its title should be a key word or phrase. A general rule to follow is that search engines only index text, so have plenty of it, including keywords and key phrases (those that people are likely to enter into their search) e.g. 'holiday accommodation', '*gîtes* in Provence', 'B&B in Brittany', 'cottage in France' – think up as many permutations as you can reasonably fit into your text without making it unintelligible. Don't expect your site to appear in the results immediately, it can take some time for the search engines to pick up your keywords.

Another way to increase traffic is to have incoming links from other websites – exchanging links with other websites is a free (although time-consuming) method of increasing your site's visibility. The following sites offer tips on how to make your site more easily found by search engines: 🖥 www.spider-food.net and 🖥 www.wordsinarow.com.

It's also advisable to submit your website to all the popular search engines, although many use automated 'crawlers' to identify new sites, in which case telling them that you exist will make little or no difference to your visibility.

There are specialist SEO services available but costs can be high; you might need to pay upwards of £2,000 for the first year, which may make it uneconomical.

Google offers a 'pay-per-click' advertising system, whereby you write an advertisement and nominate various key words or phrases (e.g. '*gîte*', 'cottage', 'holiday', 'accommodation', 'France') that people might enter when searching for your type of product. Your advertisement appears at the right hand side of the search page each time someone searches on those terms. How often it appears depends on the amount you pay!

MONITORING & FOLLOW-UP

Remember to keep track of your enquiries and bookings so that you know how your customers and potential customers are finding out about you and can adjust or focus your marketing effort accordingly.

Also make sure you obtain feedback from your customers. A visitors' book (*livre d'or*) should always be provided for guests' comments but a confidential and comprehensive comment card will give you more useful information; it shouldn't take customers more than ten minutes or so to complete – but do make it voluntary! As with most surveys, the people most likely to complete a questionnaire will be either those who are very happy or those who have something to moan about, but you might nevertheless pick up some useful pointers from the responses given.

It's much easier (and much cheaper) to obtain repeat business than to constantly find new customers, so make previous (satisfied) clients a marketing priority – bearing in mind nevertheless that most people prefer to holiday in a different place each year. Contact them regularly, but without pestering them: send them a newsletter (by post or email) advising them of any improvements to the property, new attractions in the vicinity or deals you have to offer. Maybe send them a Christmas card each year. If you're a B&B owner, keep a record of any dietary or other foibles your clients have so that, if they book again, you can anticipate them (your guests will be impressed that you've remembered!).

5 OFFERS

Making offers can be a good marketing strategy. Once you've discovered which times of year are low on bookings, you can offer discounted rates at these times to increase your occupancy. If you're near a ferry port, tie your offers in with their fare structures, synchronising your low rates with theirs. Ferry companies often offer five-day return tickets, so you could arrange five nights' stay for the price of three or four nights (B&B) or short breaks for a 'package' price (self-catering) to fit in with these. You could also offer money off on repeat bookings out of season or a percentage discount for friends or family booking on a client's recommendation.

An interesting concept offered by at least one online agency is a 'couples discount' for *gîte* lets – a percentage of the letting rate is discounted for a couple who will use only room (the other bedroom/s can be locked).

CASE STUDY 8 (Part 2, continued from page 198)

On our reconnaissance trips we had asked a dozen guest house owners, plus all the guests we met, how visitors got to hear about the places they stayed. We ourselves had used a variety of guide books over the years, some glossy and full of detail but with limited choice, others packed with properties but short on information, but we had no idea which were most effective for owners. We had never used the internet to search for accommodation, mainly because we always travelled out of season and were happy to take pot luck on availability. We were the type of bed-hunters who turned up unannounced – only now do we realise that owners prefer to know in advance who is coming to stay!

A dozen owners gave a dozen different answers, and twice that number of guests gave another 24. However, some patterns did emerge – a lot of travellers used the internet (obviously we were the exception) and a lot of people used the Gîtes de France guidebook.

In the end, we decided to register with Gîtes de France because not only would they promote us through their own website and guide books (plus AA Bed & Breakfast in France), but also by doing so we could obtain a substantial grant for the work on the guest bedrooms (see page 189). This grant would effectively pay for our subscription to Gîtes de France for many years to come.

We considered a number of other 'paying' guide books, such as Alistair Sawday, but in the end we decided to save our money and see how it would work out promoting ourselves through our own website and locally.

We created our website from scratch during the winter of 2004-05 (when we couldn't do much else) and at the same time set about marketing it. After doing some simple searches we soon found that the internet is littered with innumerable accommodation portals, some paying and some free, as well as a host of directories where you can register your website.

The free listings are usually in exchange for a reciprocal link from your site to their site, so working on the basis that we didn't have anything to lose by doing so (and it would occupy us on cold winter days) we registered with every possible free site dedicated to travel or with an accommodation section. We did this not in the expectation that we would receive many enquiries directly from these sites (we certainly weren't disappointed in that respect!) but because those with 'hard links' to our site would improve our rankings with search engines. For the same reason, we identified as many search engines as possible and submitted our website to them – the main ones like Google, Yahoo and MSN are well known, but there are hundreds of others. You can pay someone to register your site with these, but if you have the time and you don't mind ending up with square eyes there's nothing to stop you doing it yourself.

5

A tip for travel portals and directories: many ask for a description of a certain number of words or characters – so we prepared descriptions of various lengths, which we saved, then copied and pasted the appropriate version into the application forms.

Finally, we chose a couple of paying accommodation portals. To decide which ones, we spent an afternoon trawling the search engines for things like 'B&B in Normandy', 'bed & breakfast in the Sarthe', 'Alençon chambre d'hôte' – just about anything that we thought people might enter if they were searching for a guest house in our area. We noted which sites appeared on the first two pages of Google, Yahoo and MSN and finally chose two which appeared high in the results, were easy to use and whose annual subscription didn't require us to mortgage the house.

Our final marketing strategy was to make ourselves well known locally. We did this through several means:

- a leaflet drop in neighbouring villages and mairies – as a result we get a steady flow of guests who are visiting relatives for parties, weddings, birthdays, and so on;

- registering with local tourist offices – the results of this have been disappointing;

- introducing ourselves to a dozen local restaurant owners and exchanging business cards – we haven't had much return on this;

- contacting the chambres d'hôtes owners in the area – we now exchange overflow bookings with one of these;

- contacting the local paper and persuading the editor to run an article on us – we've managed to get ourselves interviewed for two newspaper articles, which included our business details, though we don't think this has produced any bookings.

Since we opened, we've asked every guest at the time of booking how they found us and we've entered the answer on the spreadsheet we use to manage our bookings. We also track our own website rankings on Google for 20 keyword searches. At the end of 2006 we analysed these data and decided to drop the two paying websites because (a) although they did bring in some business, the return on investment didn't make it worthwhile, and (b) as our website has become established and we've tweaked its content, it now appears on the first page or two for almost all of our keyword searches (and usually above the accommodation directories we were paying for!). We've also dropped two of the three tourist offices, as they produced only a handful of enquiries between them – and only one booking.

Phil and Jude Graham, La Basse Cour, 3 rue de l'Oisellerie, 72610 Ancinnes, France (☎ 02 33 82 01 19, UK ☎ 0844-837 8419, 🖳 www. normandie-chambres.co.uk)

TOP TEN MARKETING TIPS

- Decide on your target market; don't try to attract 'everybody'.
- Advertising should be one of your priorities – and your advertising budget the subject of careful consideration.
- Research your advertising options – then research them again.
- It's essential to advertise on the internet.
- If in doubt, have your publicity designed and photographs taken by professionals.
- If you write your advertisements yourself, have them proofread.
- Don't dazzle potential clients with a flashy website – the information is all-important.
- Keep all your publicity up to date.
- Always include an exterior photograph in your advertisements.
- Exploit every opportunity for free publicity.)

5

6

OTHER CONSIDERATIONS

This chapter covers various aspects of running a business in France that may help you to maximise the income from your property, including communications, employing staff, finding help and advice, learning French and setting up a company.

OBTAINING HELP & ADVICE

There are numerous organisations that can provide help and advice to supplement the information in this book.

General Information

Your first stop should be the French government's 'Public Service' website (🖳 www.service-public.fr), which contains a wealth of general information in English (and French, German and Spanish) about many aspects of France and details about doing business, including statistical, legal and administrative information. The site isn't just aimed at big business, but also at the small entrepreneur who needs simple, basic information. It also contains links to the sites of regional, department and local administrations.

6 Chambers of Commerce

Among the best sources of help and information is your local chamber of commerce (*chambre de commerce et d'industrie/CCI*), of which there are over 160 and at least one in each department (listed on 🖳 www.cci.fr). The website includes a long list of schemes designed to help in the creation or development of a business activity. Most *CCI*s have good libraries of books, magazines and documents relevant to setting up and running small businesses in France, all of which can be consulted free of charge. Most publications are in French, but some *CCI*s have information in English. Many *CCI*s organise regular conferences (e.g. once a month) and training programmes on starting a business, business practice, financing, etc. free of charge or for a nominal fee (e.g. €10). However, chambers of commerce aren't professional associations made up of businesses and business owners in France, as chambers of commerce are in the UK and US, but departmental government offices. For further information contact the Assemblée des Chambres Françaises de Commerce et d'Industrie, 45 avenue d'Iéna, 75116 Paris (☎ 01 40 69 37 00, 🖳 www.acfci.cci.fr).

Government Agencies

Information about industry and trade sectors can be found on the websites of the relevant government ministries: enter 💻 www.[name of ministry]. gouv.fr (e.g. 💻 www.agriculture.gouv.fr). The website of the Agence Pour la Création d'Entreprises (💻 www.apce.com – see also below) contains a wealth of information (in French) about all the major business areas (e.g. hospitality and leisure); click 'Informations sectorielles' for lists of relevant organisations, publications and exhibitions and links to related sites.

Market studies are undertaken by the Centre de Recherche pour l'Etude et l'Observation des Conditions de Vie (CREDOC), 142 rue du Chevaleret, 75013 Paris (☎ 01 40 77 85 06, 💻 www.credoc.asso.fr). The website lists the studies available, which can be purchased or consulted at CREDOC's offices, although you must make an appointment, as only a few people are admitted at a time; waiting lists are long. More general economic and demographic studies are available from La Documentation Française, 29 quai Voltaire, 750007 Paris (☎ 01 40 15 70 00, 💻 www.ladocfrancaise.gouv.fr).

Statistical information is available from the Institut National de la Statistique et des Etudes Economiques (INSEE, ☎ 08 25 88 94 52, 💻 www.insee.fr – the site is available in English and lists INSEE's regional offices), the Association Française de Recherches et d'Etudes Statistiques Commerciale (AFRESCO), 46 rue de Clichy, 75009 Paris (☎ 01 48 74 32 80), and Documentation d'Analyse Financière (Dafsa), 117 quai de Valmy, 75010 Paris (☎ 01 55 45 26 00, 💻 www.dafsa.fr). The 25 Agences Régionales d'Information Scientifique et Technique (ARIST) – which aren't strictly regional, as there are only 22 regions – provide scientific and technical information; contact details are listed on 💻 www.arist.tm.fr. There's also a network of Centres Techniques Industriels; contact CTI Réseau, 41 boulevard des Capucines, 75002 Paris (☎ 01 42 97 10 88, 💻 www.reseau-cti.com).

For information about French and European standards, contact the Association Française de Normalisation (AFNOR), 11 avenue Francis de Pressensé, 93571 Saint-Deni-la-Plaine Cedex (☎ 01 41 62 80 00, 💻 www.afnor.fr).

Legal & Professional Advice

Paperwork for almost everything is notoriously complicated and time-consuming in France – so much so that most French people who can afford to, pay someone to do it for them. This not only reduces your stress, but also means that your chance of presenting the right papers to the right people at the right time are greatly increased. In any case, if your French is anything less than fluent, you shouldn't contemplate doing the paperwork for your property business yourself.

The only professionals qualified to give legal advice in France are lawyers (*avocat*) and you should take legal advice from no one else. Legal advice is highly recommended when you're buying property and essential if you're buying land.

The best way to find an 'expert' (as many professionals are called) is via personal recommendation – ask others who run a similar business or who have had comparable experiences. In small communities, finding someone with a good reputation is relatively easy, as only the best practices last. If you're in an area where there's a large foreign population, many of the advisers you come into contact with will speak good English (and often other languages as well). They will also be used to foreign clients and so be familiar with the kind of advice and help you need.

Fees vary; those for some services are regulated by the professional associations while others are set by the individual professional. For a property purchase, lawyers usually charge between 1 and 1.5 per cent of the property's price, but their fees may depend on the work involved. It pays to shop around and compare fees, bearing in mind that cheaper fees often mean a less professional service and paying more doesn't necessarily mean you receive the best service. It's often cheaper to negotiate an annual fee for services than to pay one-off charges.

6

EMPLOYING OTHERS

Hiring employees shouldn't be taken lightly in France and must be taken into account before starting a business. There are around 1.4m companies in France without employees – and not without reason, as many successful small businesses become less so as soon as they start to recruit!

Hiring employees is complicated and expensive. You must enter into a contract under French labour law and employees enjoy extensive rights. In addition to salaries, you must pay a 13th month's salary, five weeks' annual holiday and 40 to 60 per cent in social security contributions, although there are reductions for hiring certain categories of unemployed people (see below).

There are tax 'holidays' for limited periods for newly formed companies, particularly regarding the first employee. During their first two years' trading, most new businesses are required to pay only around 10 per cent of their first employee's wages in social security contributions. Note, however, that the managing director's spouse doesn't count as a first employee!

Regulations & Employee Rights

General rules and regulations governing the employment of staff are set out in the French Labour Code (*Code du Travail*) as well as collective agreements (*conventions collectives de travail*). Employees have extensive rights under the French Labour Code. The Code details required conditions of employment, including maximum working hours, overtime payments, holiday, trial and notice periods, dismissal conditions, health and safety regulations, and trade union rights. The French Labour Code is described in detail in a number of books, including the *Code du Travail* (VO Editions), and is available online at the Legifrance website (🖳 www.legifrance.gouv.fr).

Specific rules are contained in an individual employee's contract (*contrat de travail*) and the employer's in-house rules and regulations (*règlements intérieurs/règlements de travail*), but employment laws cannot be altered or nullified by private agreements. Anything in contracts contrary to statutory provisions and unfavourable to an employee may be deemed null and void and any exclusion clauses must be 'clear and comprehensible'. In general, French law forbids discrimination by employers on the basis of sex, religion, race, age, sexual preference, physical appearance or name, and there are specific rules regarding equal job opportunities for men and women. It's some consolation for employers that French courts are hesitant to interfere with hiring practices. It's virtually impossible to bring a discrimination action against an employer for not hiring someone. Although discrimination on the job is severely dealt with in the courts, the courts won't normally interfere with the employer's free choice of candidates.

Salaried foreigners are employed under the same working conditions as French citizens, although there are different rules for certain categories of employee, e.g. directors, managers and factory workers. Part-time employees are entitled to the same rights and benefits (on a pro rata basis) as full-time employees.

6

Recruiting

You're required to notify the government employment service, the Agence Nationale Pour l'Emploi (ANPE, 19 boulevard Gambetta, 92136 Issy-les-Moulineaux, ☎ 01 46 45 64 85 or 08 10 80 58 05, 🖳 www.anpe.fr), which has some 600 offices throughout France, of all job vacancies, but you're generally free to recruit staff as you wish. You can, of course, make use of the services of ANPE or you can place job advertisements in newspapers, on the internet and even on television and radio. (There's a cable/satellite channel, *Demain*, devoted to career information and job opportunities.) But most recruiting in France is done on a 'word-of-mouth' basis, so local networking should be an essential part of your early business plan.

Whichever method you use, you must be **absolutely sure** you're engaging the right person, as firing employees is difficult and normally expensive. The hiring process (*embauche*) in France can take several months from initial application to job offer and may involve several visits for interviews, testing, etc. You should take full advantage of this practice and not attempt to short-cut the system, which could be a costly error.

A recruit must be declared to URSSAF (see page 181) using a *document unique d'embauche* (*DUE*), which must be submitted not more than a week before the employee is due to start work. This is known as the *déclaration préalable à l'embauche* (*DPAE*), which must be acknowledged by URSSAF before employment can start. URSSAF pass the *DUE* on to the organisations responsible for registering the employee with social security – for health, unemployment and pension benefits (you'll be told which fund you must contribute to on behalf of your new employee) and for health and safety. The only time you might need to contact any of these organisations directly is if there's a change in status of one of your employees, e.g. you promote him from 'rank and file' to management, in which case his state pension, for example, would be administered by AGIRC instead of ARRCO. Details of the *DUE* can be found on URSSAF's dedicated website (🖳 www1. due.urssaf.fr).

Incentives

There are various incentives for employing certain categories of people, including those listed below. Categories and incentives vary from area to area, the latter being most generous in regeneration zones (*zones de redynamisation*). Details of those that apply in your area are available from local offices of ANPE or the Direction Départementale du Travail, de l'Emploi et de la Formation Professionnelle (DDTEFP). Further general information about recruitment incentives can be found on the government website 🖳 www.travail.gouv.fr.

● **Trainees** – people between 16 and 25 who are studying for a vocational qualification. You must give them a contract for between one and three years (subject to a two-month trial period) and pay them between 25 and 78 per cent of the minimum wage (depending on their age and the number of years they've worked for you). You receive an annual payment of between €1,000 and €5,000 (depending on the location of your business) and you don't need to pay the trainee's social security contributions. The trainee must obviously be allowed time off for studying. This is known as a *contrat d'apprentissage*.

- **Long-term unemployed** – people over 25 who have been unemployed for at least 18 months (12 months if they're over 50). You may give them a fixed term or indefinite contract (see **Contracts** on page 241) and pay them at least the minimum wage. You receive a payment of €330 per month for the first one or two years of employment (€500 per month for up to five years in the case of the over 50s), and the employee may be entitled to continue claiming unemployment benefit. This is known as a *contrat initiative emploi* (*CIE*) and is currently available only to certain types of business, including associations.

- **Young people** – unemployed people between 16 and 23 who haven't passed their *baccalauréat*. You must give them an indefinite contract, although this can be for part-time work, and pay them at least the minimum wage. You receive a payment of between around €250 and €300 (depending on the employee's salary) per month for the first two years of employment and half of this for the third year. This is known as a *contrat jeunes en entreprise* (*CJE*).

6

Stagiaires

Many French employers 'hire' students on training courses (*stagiaires*). Nearly all training programmes, including those at university level, involve several periods of 'employment' – usually for a period of three to six weeks, but sometimes as long as six months. In the vast majority of cases, these short-term 'employees' aren't allowed to accept payment (or only a limited amount, e.g. the statutory minimum wage) and their social charges are covered by the school or university (or their parents). This is therefore a cheap (and legal) way of engaging staff for what amounts to a trial period, and many *stagiaires* are highly trained.

At certain times of the year, most small businesses receive telephone calls, letters and even emails from students who must arrange a course (*stage*) related to their study programme. It's up to the *stagiaire* to contact employers and to negotiate the functions they should do to fulfil the requirements of their school or university. Some schools and local governments send out appeals to small businesses to offer internships, summer jobs and other types of employment to various categories of young people.

There are some tax benefits to hiring *stagiaires*. Businesses often re-engage the same *stagiaire* for the whole of their training/school career and then make them an offer of permanent employment when they finish school. By the time they graduate, they know your business reasonably well and can do 'real' work from the moment you start paying them 'real' money!

Titre Emploi Entreprise

A new recruitment system called *Titre Emploi Entreprise* was pioneered in the catering trade and has recently been extended to other sectors. The system offers employers a simplified recruiting procedure for employees on a short-term (less than 100 days in a year) contract, known as *occasionnels*. Pay slips and social security contributions are handled by a centralised office, which provides a standard contract. Further information on this service can be obtained by telephone (☎ 08 10 12 38 33).

6   Salaries & Minimum Wages

It isn't common practice to specify a salary in a job advertisement and you should negotiate with a prospective candidate according to what you think he's worth! There has been a statutory minimum wage (*salaire minimum interprofessionnel de croissance*, known as *le SMIC*) since 1950. The cost of living index is reviewed annually and, when it rises by 2 per cent or more, the minimum wage is increased. (In practice, the minimum wage rises every year, usually in July and especially when elections are coming up!) The minimum wage is currently €8.27 per hour, equal to gross pay of €1,254.28 per month for 151.67 hours (the standard under the terms of the 35-hour working week).

The *SMIC* is lower for juveniles, those on job-creation schemes and disabled employees. Unskilled workers (particularly women) are usually employed at or near the minimum wage, semi-skilled workers are usually paid 10 to 20 per cent more, and skilled workers 30 to 40 per cent more (often shown in job advertisements as '*SMIC + 10, 20, 30, 40%*'). Details of the legislation relating to minimum wages can be found on the INSEE website (🖥 www.insee.fr/fr/indicateur/smic.htm).

CAUTION

Although many employers pay less than the minimum wage, the French government is increasingly clamping down on this practice and penalties can be severe.

Unless you're paying the minimum wage, it may be advantageous to 'pay' part of your employees' salaries in kind, i.e. in the form of benefits and perks such as lunch and holiday vouchers, inexpensive or interest-free home and other loans, rent-free accommodation, travelling expenses, a non-contributory company pension, and a top-up health insurance policy, which may qualify you for tax deductions or allowances and mean that you have to pay less in social charges. **The legalities of doing so are complicated and you should take expert advice on the subject.**

An employee's salary (*salaire*) must be stated in his employment contract, and salary reviews, planned increases, cost of living rises, etc. may also be included. Salaries may be stated in gross (*brut*) or net (*net*) terms and are usually paid monthly (see **Payment** below), although they may be quoted in contracts as hourly, monthly or annually. If a bonus is paid, such as a 13th or 14th month's salary (see below), this must also be stated in the employment contract. General points, such as the payment of a salary into a bank or post office account and the date of salary payments, are usually included in a separate list of employment conditions (*règlement intérieur*), which must be drawn up by any company with 20 or more employees.

Salaries in France must be reviewed once a year (usually at the end of the year), although employers aren't required by law to increase salaries that are above the minimum wage, even when the cost of living has increased. Salary increases usually take effect on 1st January.

6

13th Month's Salary & Bonuses

Most employers in France pay their employees a bonus month's salary in December, known as the 13th month's salary (*13ème mois*). A 13th month's salary isn't mandatory unless part of a collective agreement. In practice, however, its payment is almost universal and it's often taken for granted. In the first and last years of employment, an employee's 13th month's salary and other bonuses should be paid pro rata if he doesn't work a full calendar year. Some companies also pay a 14th month's salary, usually in July before the summer holiday period, although this isn't recommended until you're earning millions! Where applicable, extra months' salary are guaranteed bonuses and aren't pegged to the company's performance (as with profit-sharing). In some cases, they're paid monthly rather than in a lump sum at the end or in the middle of the year.

Payment

Salaries above €3,000 per month must be paid by cheque or direct transfer (not cash), although it's never wise to pay salaries in cash, as it makes you subject to scrutiny by the tax authorities! You must issue employees with a pay slip (*bulletin de paie*) itemising their salary and deductions.

Computerised payroll programs are widely available, usually as part of a 'management software' package (*logiciel de gestion*), including accounting, payroll, and *gestion commerciale*, which combines purchasing, inventory, and accounts receivable and payable. Among the cheapest are *Ciel* and *ESB*, which can even be bought in hypermarkets; one of the most popular programs is *Sage* (not to be confused with the English software package of the same name, which is incompatible with French accounting practice!).

It's possible to use a payroll service, such as ADP (🖳 www.adp.com), which takes care of all this for you: prepares pay slips and makes the bank transfers, then sends you a report with totals for the various compulsory insurances and withholdings. Ciel also offers online payroll services (🖳 www.ciel.com) for around €15 per pay slip (cheaper if you agree to sign up for a year at a time): you enter the data and Ciel produces a printable pay slip and transfers the appropriate amounts into your employees' accounts.

Taxes

Employees pay their own tax, as France has no pay-as-you-earn (PAYE) system. (There has been periodic debate on the introduction of a PAYE system, but the idea has had little support, especially from employers, who are reluctant to 'do the government's work for it', and tax authority employees, who don't want to give the government any excuse for thinning their ranks! It's even unpopular with employees, who consider it a violation of their private lives for their employer to calculate how much tax should be withheld from their pay.) As an employer, you must of course declare and pay your own income tax. For details of French income tax, refer to *Living and Working in France* (Survival Books – see page 314).

Social Security

As an employer, you must pay a significant portion of your employees' social security contributions, which can add up to 40 per cent or more of their salaries. Employees are entitled to sickness and maternity, work injury and invalidity, family allowance, unemployment, old age, widow(er)'s and death benefits, most of which an employer must contribute to. However, employees must earn a minimum salary to qualify for certain benefits. Employers normally continue to pay employees who are off sick for short periods, after which they become entitled to social security sickness benefit.

Contracts

Legally, an offer of employment in France constitutes an employment contract (*contrat de travail/d'emploi*), although it's safer to draft a formal contract. Employers usually issue a formal contract stating such details as job title, position, salary, working hours, benefits, duties and responsibilities, and the duration of employment. Employment contracts usually contain a paragraph stating the date from which they take effect and to whom they apply. **Contracts must be carefully worded and you should take expert advice before drafting them.** For example, whether or not an employee can be required to work at a different location than the one he was hired for or to move if the company moves depends on the wording of his contract.

All employment contracts are subject to French labour law (see page 235), and references may be made to other regulations such as collective agreements. In some sectors, e.g. the catering trade, you must use a standard contract. All contracts must be written in French.

There are three main types of employment contract in France: a temporary contract, a fixed-term contract and an indefinite-term contract.

6

Temporary Contracts

A temporary contract (*contrat de travail temporaire*, also known as an *intérim*), which has no minimum or maximum duration, can be issued in specific circumstances only, as follows:

● to replace a staff member who's temporarily absent (except if striking) and whose function is essential to the running of the business;

● to fill a post on an interim basis until a permanent staff member takes over;

● in the case of a temporary, unforeseen and otherwise unmanageable increase in the workload of existing staff;

● if the business is seasonal and requires additional workers at specific times of year (e.g. in agriculture for harvesting or in catering for peak periods);

- for workers in specific sectors (e.g. the theatre), where the use of temporary contracts is habitual.

Any other type of temporary contract is regarded as a fixed term contract (see below). A worker engaged on a temporary contract is known as a *salarié intérimaire* or simply *intérimaire*. Details of the obligations of employer and employee can be found on the website of the Monster Company (💻 www.jobpilot.fr/content/service/channel/interim/pratique/contrat.html).

Fixed-term Contracts

A fixed-term contract (*contrat à durée déterminée/CDD*) is, as the name suggests, a contract for a limited term. This is normally a maximum of 18 months, although it's limited to nine months if a post is due to be filled permanently and can be extended to two years if the post is due to be suppressed (there's no minimum term). A contract for longer than two years comes under the rules for indefinite-term contracts (see below). A *CDD* must be in writing and for a specified period or, in the case of temporary employment, for a specific purpose, which must be stated in the contract. A *CDD* ends on the date specified, although it can be renewed twice for a term no longer than the original contract, provided it doesn't exceed two years in total.

A *CDD* can be issued when a permanent employee is on leave (including maternity or sick leave), if there's a temporary increase in business, to pick up the slack during the summer while various employees are off on holiday, or at any time in the construction industry or for youth employment schemes.

*CDD*s are strictly regulated, mainly because they're considered a contributing factor to the ever-increasing 'precariousness' of employment (*précarité d'emploi*). For example, the salary of an employee hired on a fixed term contract mustn't be less than that paid to a similarly qualified person employed in a permanent job. The employee has the right to an end of contract bonus (*indemnité de fin de contrat*) equal to 10 per cent of his salary, in addition to other agreed bonuses, although this doesn't always apply to seasonal employees.

Contracts for seasonal and temporary workers fall under the same rules as *CDD* contracts.

Indefinite-term Contracts

An indefinite-term contract (*contrat à durée indéterminée/CDI*) is the standard employment contract for permanent employees. Surprisingly, it isn't necessary for it to be in writing (unlike a fixed-term contract), although it's in your interest, as well as the employee's, to provide a written contract.

A *CDI* often includes a trial period of one to three months (three months is usual), depending on collective agreements, before it becomes legal and binding on both parties. The trial period doesn't affect the binding nature of the other terms of the contract, just the initial period during which either side can terminate the contract without severance benefits and notice periods taking effect. There can also be a lower rate of pay during the trial period.

Working Hours

In 2000, France introduced a mandatory 35-hour working week for all large employers, and on 1st January 2002 this became effective for all employers, although the original legislation has since been subject to various amendments, which have 'softened' the obligations of employers and the limitations on employees to exceed a 35-hour week and these are likely to be further eroded by the new government, as President Sarkozy is an outspoken opponent of the 35-hour week.

Since the introduction of the 35-hour week, time keeping requirements have become much more complex and nearly all employees must be tracked to ensure that weekly, monthly and annual hours and days worked don't exceed the legal limits. For example, employers can establish mandatory break periods (*heures de repos*) to adapt working schedules to the new rules. However, drinks or (if allowed) cigarettes can usually be taken at an employee's workplace at any time.

The working week for round-the-clock shift workers is limited to 25 hours, and night work and shift working is usually paid at higher rates, as specified in collective agreements.

Overtime

In principle, if an employee works more than 35 hours per week, he must be paid overtime or be given time off in lieu. Employees can be asked to do overtime, but cannot be compelled to do more than 130 hours per year, although this can be altered by collective agreements. The total hours worked per week mustn't exceed an average of 44 over 12 consecutive weeks or an absolute maximum of 48 hours per week.

The minimum legal pay for overtime is the normal rate plus 25 per cent for the first eight hours above the standard 35-hour week (i.e. up to 43) and plus 50 per cent for additional hours (i.e. above 43). Employees can be granted time off in lieu at overtime rates (i.e. 1.25 hours for each hour of overtime worked) instead of being paid. Employees cannot be obliged to work on Sundays unless collective agreements state otherwise. If an employee agrees to work on a Sunday, normal overtime rates apply.

Holidays & Leave

The French enjoy generous holiday and leave entitlements compared with employees in most other countries (and especially the US).

Annual Holidays

Under French labour law, an employee is entitled to 2.5 days' paid annual holiday (congé/vacances) for each full month he works. Annual holiday entitlement is calculated assuming that Saturdays are work days (a legacy of the time when the usual working week consisted of six days). After working for a full year, an employee is entitled to 30 days off (12 months x 2.5 days per month), which equals five weeks (including Saturdays).

Legally, holiday entitlement is earned over the course of a year that runs from 1st May to 30th April. So, if an employee starts work in January, by 1st May he will have earned ten days of holiday, which he can take during the subsequent year (i.e. starting 1st May). By the next 1st May, he should have accrued a full five weeks of holiday, which is available to him over the next 12 months. Employers cannot include official French public holidays (see below) as annual holidays.

French employees are legally entitled to take up to four weeks' paid holiday in a single block between 1st May and 31st October (known as the période légale), unless business needs dictate otherwise (although other agreements are possible). However, if you oblige employees to take more than two days off outside the période légale, they're entitled to additional holiday: an extra day for three to six days outside the période légale; an extra two days for six or more days outside. Before taking on staff, check what holidays they've booked or planned. If these fall within their trial period, you aren't obliged to allow them.

Public Holidays

Since 2004, there have been ten public holidays in France, which are listed below. Surprisingly, the only public holiday an employer in France is legally

6

obliged to grant with pay is 1st May (irrespective of which day of the week it falls on). Nevertheless, most collective agreements allow paid holidays on several public holidays and it's usual for employers to grant all of them.

Officially, after the heat wave of 2003, which supposedly killed tens of thousands of people, Pentecost Monday was 'sacrificed' to save money to pay for better care for old people (it wasn't clear how). In typical French style, however, employers were offered a compromise: if you don't want to do away with the Pentecost holiday (e.g. because your business is too busy at that time), you can cancel any of the other holidays (except 1st May) instead. The result is that some businesses observe the Pentecost holiday and others don't.

Date	Holiday
1st January	New Year's Day (*Nouvel An/Jour de l'An*)
March or April	Easter Monday (*Lundi de Pâques*)
1st May	Labour Day (*Fête du Travail*)
8th May	VE Day (*Fête de la Libération/Victoire 1945/Anniversaire 1945*)
May	Ascension Day (*Ascension*) – the sixth Thursday after Easter
14th July	Bastille Day (*Fête Nationale*)
15th August	Assumption (*Fête de l'Assomption*)
1st November	All Saints' Day (*Toussaint*)
11th November	Armistice Day (*Fête de l'Armistice*)
25th December	Christmas Day (*Noël*)

6

When a public holiday falls on a Saturday or Sunday, you aren't obliged to offer another day (e.g. the previous Friday or following Monday) as a holiday instead. However, when a public holiday falls on a Tuesday or Thursday, you must decide whether to allow the day before or the day after (i.e. Monday or Friday respectively) as a holiday. This practice is called 'making a bridge' (*faire le pont*) and you may make yourself unpopular with your employees if you don't allow them to do so. (Some even expect to be allowed to bridge from a Wednesday to the previous or following weekend!) Depending on how the public holidays fall (especially in May, when 'bridging' is a national sport), you can gain or lose a significant number of days' work.

Sick Leave

Employees in France don't receive a quota of sick days, as in some countries (e.g. the US), and there's no limit to the amount of time an employee may take off work due to sickness or accidents – and you must pay him for this time, although long-term illnesses or disabilities are covered by social security benefits. For this reason, many French employers take out salary insurance. An employee is normally required to notify you immediately of sickness or an accident that prevents him from working. He must also obtain a doctor's certificate (*arrêt de travail*) on the first day of his sickness; otherwise it counts as a day's holiday.

Trial & Notice Periods

For most jobs in France, there's a trial period (*période d'essai*) of one to three months, depending on the type of work and the employer (three months is usual). The trial period isn't required by law, although there's no law forbidding it. The length of a trial period is usually stated in collective agreements. During the trial period, either party may terminate the employment contract without notice or any financial penalty, unless otherwise stated in a collective agreement.

Notice periods are governed by law and collective agreements and usually vary with length of service. The minimum notice period is usually a month for clerical and manual workers, two months for foremen and supervisors, and three months for managerial and senior technical staff. The minimum notice period for employees with over two years' service is two months.

A fixed-term contract can be terminated before the specified finish date only if the employer or employee has committed a serious offence (*faute grave*), if there's an event beyond the control of both parties (*force majeure*) that nullifies the contract (e.g. your B&B burns down), or with the agreement of both parties. Under recently passed regulations designed to modernise labour law, an employee may terminate a temporary contract without penalty if he accepts a job with an indefinite contract.

BUSINESS COMMUNICATIONS

Although you wouldn't think so from the postal service, communications have improved in France during the last decade but they're still some way behind those of many other developed countries. For example, letters cannot be relied on to arrive unless registered, telephone lines are frequently out of action, and broadband (*haut-débit*, usually known as *ADSL*) connection still isn't available in all areas of France (see page 249). Moreover, as the principal operator of telecommunications systems, France Télécom, is one of the world's most indebted companies, it's unlikely that France will quickly catch up.

The following is a brief guide to telephone and internet services and the postal service.

Telephone Services

The telephone network is operated by France Télécom (FT), which is 55 per cent state-owned, but since 2002 call services have been open to competition, which has resulted in an intense price war. Despite this 'market liberalisation', however, FT is still the only company that offers a complete service, including the installation of telephone lines, others providing only call services. Nevertheless, some other companies may offer call charge packages that suit your business needs and it's worth investigating the alternatives. There's a variety of tariffs, so make sure you thoroughly investigate the alternatives, particularly if your business relies heavily on telephone communications. See also **Telephone** on page 80.

Alternative Providers

6

There are currently around 20 alternative telephone service providers (i.e. other than France Télécom) in France, some of which advertise in the English-language press (see **Appendix B**). If you wish to use another provider (or several providers, for different types of call), you must open a separate account with each one. You must still have an account with FT for line rental.

It's possible to have subscriptions with several telephone providers, and each one will indicate what numbers you must dial to route your calls correctly. Alternatively, you can notify FT of your default provider and they will set up your telephone line to automatically route calls to whichever of the alternative telephone providers you prefer, without having to use the extra numbers. This facility costs around €11 and takes a week or two to set up (during which time you can use a prefix).

If you have all your calls automatically routed via another provider, it's possible to revert to the FT system by dialling 8 before the number. This service, which is useful if there's a problem with your alternative provider, must be ordered in advance from FT and it's free.

To help you find your way through the maze of alternative telephone providers, you may want to consult a service such as Budgetelecom (💻 www.budgetelecom.com), where you can compare the available tariffs based on your calling pattern and review customer evaluations of the services available from each provider.

Installation & Registration

If you're planning to move into a property without an existing telephone line, you'll need to have one installed. In this case, you must visit your local France Télécom agent, which you'll find listed in the yellow pages under *Télécommunications: service*. You must prove that you're the owner or tenant of the property in question, e.g. with an electricity bill, confirmation of purchase (*attestation d'acquisition*) or lease. You also require your passport or residence permit (*carte de séjour*).

> ⚠️ **If you buy a property in a remote area without a telephone line, it may be expensive to have a telephone installed, as you must pay for the line to your property.**
> **CAUTION**

Contact FT for an estimate. You should have trenches dug for the telephone cable if you want a below-ground connection (you may be able to have an above-ground connection via a wire from the nearest pylon). This work can be carried out by FT, but their charges are high and it's possible to do it yourself, although you must observe certain standards. Details of the required depth of trenches and the type of conduit (*gaine*) to use, etc. can be obtained from FT.

When you go to an FT agency, you must know what kind of telephone sockets are already installed in the property, how many telephones you want, where you want them installed and what kind of telephone you want (if you're buying from FT). If you want a number of telephone points installed, you should arrange this in advance. You may also want to upgrade a line (e.g. to ADSL – see **Broadband** below).

You'll also be asked whether you want a listed or unlisted number and must inform FT where you want your bill sent and how you wish to pay it. If you wish to pay by direct debit, you must provide your account details (*relevé d'identité bancaire/RIB*). You can also request an itemised bill.

You may be given a telephone number on the spot, although you should wait until you receive written confirmation before giving it to anyone. It isn't possible simply to take over the telephone number of the previous occupant. You'll receive a letter stating that you have a mixed line (*ligne mixte*), which is simply a line allowing incoming and outgoing calls.

To have a line installed takes from a few days in a city, to weeks or possibly over a month in remote rural areas, although 90 per cent of new customers have a line installed within two weeks. In certain areas, there's a waiting list and you can have a line installed quickly only if you need a telephone for your safety or security, e.g. if you're an invalid, in which case a medical certificate is required. Business lines may be installed more quickly than domestic lines.

Broadband

There are two types of broadband (*haut-débit*) connection: Asymmetric digital subscriber lines (ADSL) and integrated services digital network (ISDN) lines. France Télécom is committed to extending the availability of ADSL, but it isn't available in all areas and may even be available to some properties in a village, but not others! To find out if ADSL is available in your area, go to 🖳 www.francetelecom.fr, click on '*internet et multimédia*' (on the left) and '*abonnement express*' and enter your current telephone number (or a neighbour's) or the number of the department in which you live or intend to live. France Télécom expects broadband to be available throughout France by the end of 2007.

If available, it's possible to upgrade an existing line to ADSL at no extra charge, although you must pay higher line rental charges; if it isn't available and you aren't in a 'cabled' area, ISDN (*RNIS*, but referred to by FT as *Numéris*) is the only option. An ISDN 'line' actually provides you with three telephone numbers, but only two lines (at least, you can use only two at once!) and you must use both lines simultaneously to achieve 128kbps download speed; check whether your internet service provider (ISP) allows this.

France Télécom also offers various combined telephone and internet access packages (see **Internet** on page 252). Installation of ADSL costs the same as a standard line (normally €104), but an ISDN line costs an additional €90 (for private use) or €123 (for business use).

Bills

France Télécom bills its customers every two months and allows you two weeks to pay your bill (*facture*). Bills include VAT (*TVA*) at 19.6 per cent, although an ex-VAT figure (*HT*) is shown as well as the total, including VAT (*TTC*). You can request an itemised bill (*facturation détailée*), which lists all calls with the date and time, the number called, the duration and the charge. This service is free but must be requested a month in advance.

Bills can be paid by post by sending a cheque to France Télécom, at a post office or at your local FT office. Simply detach the tear-off part of your bill and send or present it with payment. You can pay your telephone bill by direct debit (*prélèvement automatique*) or have the payments spread throughout the year. If you pay your bills by direct debit, your invoice specifies the date of the debit from your account, usually around 20 days after receipt of the invoice. Contact your local FT agent for information. France Télécom is trying to encourage customers to pay by direct debit, by telephone, or by *titre interbancaire de paiement* (*TIP*), whereby your bank account details are pre-printed on the tear-off part of the bill, which you simply date and sign and return. Most alternative providers insist on payment by direct debit, and you may be billed monthly.

Charges

Deregulation of the telecommunications market has resulted in an intense price war, and considerable savings can be made on national, as well as international, calls by shopping around for the lowest rates (see **Alternative Providers** on page 247). However, as there are around 20 alternative providers, it's impossible to list all their tariffs here, and only FT's are given in detail. Comparisons between the rates offered by different service providers can be found via the internet (e.g. 🖥 www.comparatel.fr and 🖥 www.budgetelecom.com) or you can contact the Association Française des Utilisateurs de Télécommunications (AFUTT, BP1, 92340 Marne-la-Coquette, ☎ 01 47 41 09 11, 🖥 www.afutt.org) on Mondays to Thursdays between 10.30 and 12.30. Line rental and call charges are explained below; for information about installation and registration charges, see above.

Line rental: A monthly line rental or service charge (*abonnement*) of around €15 is payable to France Télécom irrespective of the service provider you choose. If you use an alternative provider (see page 247), there may be a separate monthly fee in addition to your call charges, although most providers have dropped these.

Domestic calls: France Télécom's tariffs depend on the destination and time of calls. Calls at peak times (*heures pleines*), which are Mondays to Fridays from 08.00 to 19.00 and Saturdays from 08.00 to 12.00, are charged at the 'normal' rate (*tarif normal*); calls at all other times (*heures creuses*), including all day on public holidays, are charged at a reduced rate (*tarif réduit*).

Call charges are based on an initial 'connection' charge (*mise en relation* or *crédit-temps*), which pays for a minute or 39 seconds depending on whether the call is local (i.e. calls to numbers starting with the same four digits as your own) or not, plus a per-minute rate after that time. The term 'unit' (*unité*) is sometimes used for the initial charge, although you may receive different definitions of the term, even from FT staff! France Télécom's current standard charges for calls from and to fixed lines are shown below.

	Initial Charge	Peak Minute	Off-peak Minute
Local calls	€0.09 (60 seconds)	€0.033	€0.018
Other calls	€0.11 (39 seconds)	€0.090	€0.063

France Télécom no longer publicises these rates, however, but offers instead an array of packages (*forfait*), of which there are currently around 20. Packages require a fixed monthly payment (e.g. between €1.50 and €10) in return for 'reduced price' or, in some cases, 'free' calls, which makes it all but impossible to calculate what you're paying for each call or to compare rates with those of other providers. A recent comparison between rates charged by the five major providers showed a price variation between €0.13 and €0.16 for a three-minute, off-peak local call, and between €0.27 and €0.40 for a ten-minute, peak rate local call, with FT's charges – not surprisingly – generally the highest, although if you're a telephone-addict you may find their 'unlimited use' (*illimité*) packages good value.

6

Alternative telephone service providers also offer a variety of call packages, consisting of a combination of varying initial charges and lengths followed by different per-minute charges and, in some cases, a single rate for all times of day and all destinations.

International calls: France Télécom has eight tariff levels for international calls, listed on its website. All international calls are subject to a 'connection charge' (*mise en relation*) of €0.12 (unless you're using the *Option Plus* or *Les Heures* package, in which case it's €0.11 – big deal!). Calls to other western European countries and North America are charged at the cheapest tariff and cost €0.22 per minute during peak periods (see above) and €0.12 per minute off-peak. Calls to Australia and New Zealand cost €0.49/0.34 per minute.

Other telephone providers have different tariff structures for international calls. Most alternative providers also offer a variety of discount plans, such as half-price calls to a designated 'favourite country' or to specific overseas numbers frequently called.

Mobile Telephones

After a relatively slow start in introducing mobile phones (*téléphone portable* or simply *portable*, but increasingly *mobile*), France has one of Europe's fastest growing cellular populations and it's estimated that over 60 per cent of people in France use mobiles. Mobile phones are now so widespread that some businesses (e.g. restaurants, cinemas, theatres, concert halls) ban them and some even use mobile phone jammers that can detect and jam every handset within 100m.

There are currently three mobile phone service providers: Bouygues (pronounced 'bweeg', ☎ 08 10 63 01 00, 💻 www.bouyguestelecom.fr), France Télécom, operating under the Orange trademark (☎ 08 00 83 08 00, 💻 www.orange.fr), and SFR (☎ 08 00 10 60 00, 💻 www.sfr.fr). Buying a mobile phone is a minefield, as there aren't only different networks to choose from, but also a wide range of tariffs covering connection fees, monthly subscriptions, insurance and call charges. To further complicate matters, all three providers have business ties to one or more of the fixed telephone services (SFR with Cégétel, for example) and offer various deals for those who combine mobile and fixed telephone services.

6

Internet

The internet in France got off to rather a slow start due to competition from Minitel (France's pioneering telephone information service) and the market is still expanding rapidly, which has led to a proliferation of internet service providers (*fournisseur d'accès/FAI* or *serveur*), over 200 currently offering a variety of products and prices. France Télécom offers Orange (formerly Wanadoo), a package that includes email (see below). AOL Compuserve France is the other major internet contender. Between them, Orange and AOL have some two-thirds of the market. Contact details of some of the major French ISPs are as follows:

- **Alice France** (formerly Tiscali) – ☎ 1033, 💻 www.aliceadsl.fr;

- **AOL** – (☎ 08 92 02 03 04, 💻 www.aol.fr);

- **Club Internet** – (☎ 3204, 💻 www.club-internet.fr);

- **Free** – (☎ 3244, 💻 www.free.fr);

- **FreeSurf** – (☎ 08 26 00 76 50, 🖥 www.freesurf.fr);

- **Orange** – (☎ 3900 or 08 92 69 91 14, 🖥 www.orange.fr).

For details of all the French ISPs, go to 🖥 www.lesproviders.com; for a comparison of ISP services and charges, consult one of the dedicated internet magazines, such as *Internet Pratique* and *Net@scope*, or visit the Budgetelecom website (🖥 www.budgetelecom.com), which carries a list of internet access providers in France, with information on current offers, customer evaluations and direct links to provider websites.

Charges: France has a number of 'free' dial-up internet access services, where you pay only for your telephone connection time, not for access to the internet provider. Alternatively (and for broadband), most service providers (including the free ones) offer various monthly plans which include all telephone charges for your online connections, usually at a rate that's lower than the telephone charges alone. As with telephone tariffs, it pays to shop around and to find a package that suits your usage pattern.

Postal Services

The French Post Office (La Poste) is a state-owned company, and post offices (*la poste* also means 'post office') in France are always staffed by post office employees, who are civil servants (*fonctionnaires*); there are no post offices run by private businesses, as in the UK, for example. Privatisation of the postal service began in 2003 and La Poste's monopoly on the handling of letters between 50 and 100g ended in 2006. There are around 17,000 post offices, 60 per cent of them in communes of fewer than 2,000 inhabitants and, as in other countries, those in the least populated areas are gradually being closed in order to save money.

In addition to the usual post office services, a range of other services are provided, although post offices generally have fewer facilities than those in the UK, for example. These include telephone calls, telegram and fax transmissions, domestic and international cash transfers, payment of telephone and utility bills, and the distribution of mail-order catalogues. Recently, La Poste has also started offering email services on the internet, including free and permanent email addresses, as well as e-commerce services for small businesses. *La Poste* also provides financial and banking services, including cheque and savings accounts, mortgage and retirement plans, and share prices. Post offices usually have photocopy machines and telephone booths.

6

La Poste produces numerous leaflets and brochures, including the *Tarifs Courrier – Colis*, or you can obtain information by telephone (☎ 08 20 80 80 00 for general information; ☎ 08 10 82 18 21 for information regarding international post). La Poste has a website where you can find information on all its services, although only limited information is available in English (🖥 www.laposte.fr). The site offers a search tool to help you find the address and telephone number of your nearest post office, according to the town name or postcode. The listings don't include the opening hours or the times for the last collection each day.

Note that French companies are usually slow to reply to letters and it's often necessary to follow up a letter with a telephone call.

Letters

Standard letters (up to 20g) currently cost €0.49 within France by 'non-priority' post (*non-prioritaire*) or €0.54 by 'priority' post (*prioritaire*); €0.60 to European Union (EU) countries (plus Switzerland) and €0.85 to the rest of the world. Stamps can be bought only at tobacconists' (*tabacs*) or post offices, some of which have coin-operated machines.

Parcels

The post office provides a (confusing and ever-changing) range of parcel (*colis*) services, domestic and international, now collectively called *ColiPoste*. Since early 2007, parcels must be taken to a post office and 'registered' and cannot simply be put in a post box (if you do so, the parcel will be returned to you or, if no return address is visible, destroyed). You don't need to write anything on the parcel itself but must complete a form, which is affixed to it. Ostensibly a 'security measure', this has been a convenient excuse to raise the charges for parcels, which now cost a minimum of over €4, even within France.

Parcel services are also provided by French railways and airlines and international courier companies such as DHL, Fedex and UPS. First-class parcels are limited to a maximum weight of 3kg, and parcels containing printed matter (e.g. books and magazines) are limited to 5kg. Parcels heavier than 5kg must be taken to a main post office. International parcels are usually limited to 30kg, although there are lower limits, e.g. 20kg, for some countries. Parcels to addresses outside the EU must have an international green customs label (*déclaration de douane*) affixed to them.

6

Registered & Recorded Post

Registered post is commonly used in France when sending official documents and communications, when proof of despatch and/or receipt is required. You can send a registered letter (*lettre recommandée*) with (*avec*) or without (*sans*) proof of delivery (*avis de réception*). This costs from €2.50 in addition to the postage charge. There are three levels of compensation (*indemnité forfaitaire*) for domestic registered letters and parcels. As with parcels, you must complete a form, which is affixed to the registered item, and receive a copy as a receipt and proof of posting.

LEARNING FRENCH

If you don't already speak good French, don't expect to learn it quickly, even if you already have a basic knowledge and take intensive lessons. It's common for foreigners not to be fluent after a year or more of intensive lessons in France; without lessons and regular exposure to the language, it can take years to achieve fluency. **It takes a long time to reach the level of fluency needed to be able to work in French.** If your expectations are unrealistic, you'll become frustrated, which can affect your confidence.

Although it isn't easy, even the most non-linguistic person can acquire a working knowledge of French. All that's required is a little hard work, some help and perseverance, particularly if you have only English-speaking colleagues and friends. **Your business and social enjoyment and success in France will be directly related to the degree to which you master French.** If you don't speak French fluently, you should consider taking a menial or even an unpaid voluntary job on arrival in France, as this is one of the quickest ways of improving your French.

Most people can teach themselves a great deal through the use of books, tapes, videos and even computer and internet-based courses. A good place to start, and a resource you can continue to use wherever you are, is the impressive languages section of the BBC website (🖥 www.bbc.co.uk/languages/french), which is comprehensive and informative. You can test your ability to find out which level is best for you and learn French online at your own pace. The site also contains news and features about France, to help you get a feel for the country and its people, and there's a useful section entitled 'French for Work'. Here, you can find out what it's like working in a French business environment and get help with specialist language for a variety of business situations. Particularly valuable are the experiences of those who have already taken the plunge and the expert tips from those who have been in the world of work in France for some time.

Other websites offering free tutorials include 🖥 www.france-pub/com/french, 🖥 www.frenchassistant.com, 🖥 www.frenchlesson.org and 🖥 www.frenchtutorial.com. There are also self-study French courses you can buy – if you've paid money for a course, you're more likely to see it through! – including those offered by Eurotalk (🖥 www.eurotalk.co.uk) and Linguaphone (🖥 www.linguaphone.co.uk). A quarterly publication, *Bien-dire* (sic), is aimed at adult learners (🖥 www.learningfrench.com).

There are several things you can do to speed up your language learning before and after your arrival in France, including watching television (particularly quiz shows where the words appear on the screen as they're spoken) and DVDs (where you can select French or English subtitles), reading (especially children's books and product catalogues, where the words are accompanied by pictures), joining a club or association, and (most enjoyable) making French friends!

Lessons

Even the best and most dedicated students require some professional help. French classes are offered by language schools, French and foreign colleges and universities, private and international schools, foreign and international organisations (such as the British Institute in Paris), local associations and clubs, and private teachers. There are many language schools (*école de langues*) in cities and large towns, most universities provide language courses, and many organisations offer holiday courses year round, particularly for children and young adults (it's best to stay with a local French family). Tuition ranges from courses for complete beginners, through specialised business or cultural courses to university-level courses leading to recognised diplomas. If you already speak French but need conversational practice, you may prefer to enrol in an art or craft course at a local institute or club. You can also learn French via a telephone language course, which is particularly practical for busy executives and those who don't live near a language school.

In some areas, the *Centre Culturel* provides free French lessons to foreigners. If you're officially registered as unemployed and have a residence permit (*carte de séjour*), you can obtain free lessons (*perfectionnement de la langue française*), although complete beginners don't qualify (contact your local ANPE office for information).

Major French teaching organisations include the following:

- **Alliance Française** (AF), 101 boulevard Raspail, 75270 Paris Cedex 06 (☎ 01 42 84 90 00, ⌨ www.alliancefr.org) – one of the most famous French language teaching organisations, a state-approved, non-profit organisation with over 1,000 centres in 138 countries, including 32 centres in France, mainly in large towns and cities. The AF runs general, special and intensive courses, and can also arrange a homestay in France with a host family.

- **Berlitz** (☎ 01 40 74 00 17, ⌨ www.berlitz.com) – has around 16 schools in France, including five in Paris;

- **Centre d'Échanges Internationaux**, 1 rue Gozlin, 75006 Paris (☎ 01 43 29 60 20) – another non-profit organisation, offering intensive French language courses for juniors (13 to 18 years) and adults throughout France. Courses include accommodation in their own international centres, with a French family, or in a hotel, bed and breakfast or self-catering studio. Junior courses can be combined with tuition in a variety of sports and other activities, including horse riding, tennis, windsurfing, canoeing, diving and dancing.

- CESA Languages Abroad (☎ 01209-221 1800, ⌨ www.cesalanguages. com) – a British organisation offering advice and arranging language courses.

Most language schools run various classes depending on your language ability, how many hours you wish to study a week, how much money you want to spend and how quickly you wish to learn. Language classes generally fall into the following categories: extensive (4 to 10 hours per week); intensive (15 to 20 hours); total immersion (20 to 40 or more).

Don't expect to become fluent in a short time using total immersion courses unless you have a particular flair for languages or already have a good command of French. (Note also that the cost of a one-week total immersion course is usually between €2,500 and €3,000!) Unless you must desperately learn French quickly, it's better to arrange your lessons over a long period. However, don't commit yourself to a long course of study, particularly an expensive one, before ensuring that it's right for you. Most schools offer free tests to help you find your appropriate level and a free introductory lesson.

You may prefer to have private lessons, which are a quicker, although more expensive, way of learning a language. The main advantage of private lessons is that you learn at your own speed and aren't held back by slow learners or left floundering in the wake of the class genius. You can advertise for a teacher in local newspapers, on shopping centre/supermarket bulletin boards and university notice boards, and through your or your spouse's employer. Otherwise, look for advertisements in the English-language press (see **Appendix B**). Don't forget to ask friends, neighbours and colleagues if they can recommend a private teacher.

French lessons by the hour cost from around €50 at a school (less for a long course) or €15 to €35 with a private tutor, although you may find someone willing to trade French lessons for English lessons. In some areas (particularly in Paris), there are discussion groups which meet regularly to talk in French and other languages; these are usually advertised in the English-language press (see **Appendix B**).

Our sister-publication, *The Best Places to Buy a Home in France* (Survival Books –see page 314) includes lists of language schools in the most popular regions of France. A comprehensive list of schools, institutions and organisations providing French language courses throughout France is contained in a booklet, *Cours de Français Langue Étrangère et Stages Pédagogie de Français Langue Étrangère en France*. It includes information about the type of course, organisation, dates, costs and other practical information, and is available from French consulates or from the Association pour la Diffusion de la Pensée Française (ADPF), 6 rue Ferrus, 75683 Paris Cedex 14 (☎ 01 43 13 11 00, 💻 www.adpf.asso.fr).

6 Regional Languages & Dialects

As well as French, there are a number of regional languages in France, including Alsatian (spoken in Alsace), Basque (Pyrénées), Breton (Brittany), Catalan (Roussillon), Corsican (Corsica) and Occitan (Languedoc). Although you're unlikely to have to deal with anyone who speaks **only** a regional language, you should bear in mind that your linguistic life will be even more complicated if you decide to live and work in any of these areas. If you have school-age children, you should note that in some areas, schools teach in the regional language as well as in French.

As well as regional languages, France has a plethora of local dialects (*patois*), which are often incomprehensible even to native French speakers! Add to all this the various accents of 'standard' French, particularly the typical twang of southerners (who pronounce the word *accent* 'aksang') and you'll appreciate the importance of mastering the language before you even **think** about working in France!

6

APPENDICES

Appendix A: FURTHER INFORMATION

Agencies & Advertising Companies

Holiday Letting Agencies

Allez France (UK ☎ 0870-192 1762, 🖳 www.allezfrance.com). A well established company with over 3,000 properties in association with Cottages4you (see below).

Bowhills (UK ☎ 0870-235 2727, 🖳 www.bowhills.co.uk). 300 properties. Colour brochure printed annually. Strongest in the Dordogne, Provence, Languedoc and Brittany. Looking for properties with pools or within 20 minutes of a beach.

Brittany Ferries Holiday Homes (UK ☎ 0870-900 0259, 🖳 www. brittany-ferries.co.uk). The official UK representative of Gîtes de France, with 850 *gîtes* and 450 cottages in its brochure, some villas with pools in southern France. Discounts on ferry fares. Brochure distributed through 6,000 travel agents in the UK and Ireland.

French Affair (UK ☎ 020-7381 8519, 🖳 www.frenchaffair.com). Operating to France since 1986. Villas on the Atlantic coast and in Corsica, Dordogne, Languedoc-Roussillon, Lot, Pays Basque and Provence.

Gites Direct (☎ 05 53 07 17 75, UK ☎ 0871-781 0024, 🖳 www. gitesdirect.com). Booking service on commission basis, owners otherwise liaising directly with clients.

Holiday Cottages Group: One of the largest companies in this field, which also owns Chez Nous (see **Advertising Sites** below). Its brands include:

- **Cottages4you** (UK ☎ 0870-242 3649, 🖳 www.cottages4you.co.uk).

- **Easycottages** (UK ☎ 0870-197 2799, 🖳 www.easycottages.com).

- **French Country Cottages** (UK ☎ 0870-078 1500, 🖳 www. french-country-cottages.co.uk). 900 French lets. 200,000 preview brochures sent to mailing list plus 200,000 main brochures to past and potential customers in November.

Dedicated owner helpline and bilingual representatives in the UK. Annual inspections by regional representatives in France. Full back-up for owners. 50 per cent of properties have pools.

- **French Life** (UK ☎ 0870-197 6675, 💻 www.frenchlife.co.uk). 1,000 cottages and villas, priced between French Country Cottages and Welcome Cottages.

- **Individual France** (UK ☎ 0870-1917890, 💻 www.individual-travellers.com). Formerly Vacances en Campagne. 400 properties, around half of which have pools.

- **Welcome Cottages** (UK ☎ 0870-197 6420, 💻 www.welcome cottages.com). Less expensive cottages, villas and apartments across France.

Just France (UK ☎ 020-8780 4480, 💻 www.justfrance.co.uk). Formerly Inghams. Website booking and printed brochure.

VFB Holidays (UK ☎ 01452-716830, 💻 www.vfbholidays.co.uk). Properties are mostly French-owned. Each property is inspected every year. Printed brochure. Cleaning included in holiday price.

Advertising Sites

Anglo-French Bed & Breakfast (💻 www.anglofrenchbedand-breakfast.com). Bed & breakfast (B&B) for English speakers. €40 for one year's subscription including an advertisement with up to three photographs.

Bedbreak.com (UK ☎ 0871-781 0834, 💻 www.bedbreak.com). B&B in France. Site in six languages and printed guidebook in association with Thomas Cook.

Bonnes Vacances (UK ☎ 0870-760 7073, 💻 www.bvdirect.co.uk). Advertises in national newspapers, offers travel discounts. Listing cost: from £85 per year.

Brittany Ferries Owners in France (UK ☎ 0870-901 3400, 💻 www.ownersinfrance.co.uk). The well known ferry company's agency division with an easy-to-navigate site and a well distributed brochure. Offers ferry fare and other travel discounts.

Café-Couette (🖳 www.cafe-couette.com). B&B advertising free; 'VIP' subscription at €40.

Chez Nous (UK ☎ 0870-238 5830, 🖳 www.cheznous.com). An easy-to-navigate site and a well distributed brochure listing over 4,000 properties plus extensive advertising in the UK national press. Listings can be on the website only or also in the brochure. Listing cost: from £180 + VAT (website only), £300 + VAT (directory only), or £418 + VAT (website and directory).

Clévacances (🖳 www.clevacances.com). Official French organisation for B&B and *gîtes*.

Fleurs de Soleil (🖳 www.fleursdesoleil.fr). Upmarket B&B.

France Direct (☎ 05 53 07 17 75, 🖳 www.francedirect.net). A UK company, also registered in France (95 per cent of owners are English-speaking). Has an easily navigated site but no brochure. A sister company of Gites Direct (see above), its commission-based agency. There are several subscription levels. Listing cost: from €125 per year.

France One Call (☎ 05 53 90 49 76, UK ☎ 0871-717 9091, 🖳 www.franceonecall.com). Web-based advertising with a referral system: when members receive enquiries for weeks that are already booked they give the enquirer the France One Call number or forward the email. Listing cost: £180 per year for one property, £25 for each additional property.

France Renting Abroad (🖳 www.renting-abroad.com). Three-month free trial, then £50 per year. Easily navigable, well designed site.

French Accommodation (🖳 www.frenchaccommodation.co.uk). Privately owned *gîtes*, chalets, villas and B&B accommodation.

French Connections (🖳 www.frenchconnections.co.uk). Has a fast, easy-to-search site including plenty of details. Listing cost: from £150 + VAT per year.

Gite.com (🖳 www.gite.com). Canadian company. Good photography tips on the site. Listing cost: set-up $209 then from $180 for six months.

Gîtes de France (🖳 www.gites-de-france.fr). Official French organisation for B&B and *gîtes*.

Gites-in-France (UK ☎ 0870-720 2966, 🖳 www.gites-in-france.co.uk). Advertise from £75 plus VAT plus commission of 10 per cent of booking fees.

Guide Vacances (🖳 www.guidevacances.com). Holiday listing site. Basic listing free, with several optional paid extras (e.g. €15 for a photograph).

Holidaygites (🖳 www.holidaygites.co.uk). An easy-to-use site with good search engine visibility. Listing cost: £40 per year.

Holidaylets.net (UK ☎ 01234-757281, 🖳 www.holidaylets.net). Easily searched site with good search engine visibility. Listing cost: £100 plus VAT per year.

Holidaylettings (UK ☎ 01865-201444, 🖳 www.holiday lettings.co.uk). Cottages, villas and flats all over France. Listing cost: £1— per year.

Homelidays (☎ 01 70 75 34 03, 🖳 www.homelidays.com). The site is available in French, Spanish, German, Italian and Portuguese. Listing cost: first month free, but you pay a €20 'inscription' when renewing; the renewal fee is then €75 for four months, €105 for eight months or €125 for a year.

Le Petit Futé (🖳 www.lepetitfute.com). Well known French guide. Website entries cost €120 (including a photo).

JML Villas (🖳 www.jmlvillas.com). Holiday villas, apartments and cottages. Listing cost: £11.75 per year.

Owners Direct (UK ☎ 01372-229330, 🖳 www.ownersdirect.co.uk). Easily navigable site with good search engine visibility. Listing cost: £65 per month, £100 per year, extra three months for new accounts.

Paris-Apts.com (☎ 01 40 28 01. 28, 🖳 www.paris-apts.com). Short-term Paris apartment rentals.

Rentals France (🖳 www.rentalsfrance.com). Good site with plenty of additional information and useful links. Flexible payment plans – pay per enquiry (£3) or £10 per month.

Vacances (🖳 www.vacances.com). Advertisements translated into seven languages; from €83 per year.

Vacation France (UK ☎ 023-8081 2162, 🖳 www.vacation france.com). Simple site, easy to use, each property has its own separate page. Listing cost: £100 per year.

Vacation Rentals by Owner/VRBO (🖳 www.vrbo.com). This fast site provides comprehensive details of accommodation worldwide; France can be searched by region. Listing cost: US$180 per year (includes three photographs).

Visit France (UK ☎ 0845-260 2808, 🖳 www.visitfrance.co.uk). Has an easily navigated site (no brochure) listing over 500 properties, including *gîtes* and B&B. Listing cost: from £100 + VAT.

APPENDIX B: FURTHER READING

English-language Newspapers & Magazines

The publications listed below are a selection of the dozens related to France and, in particular, French property. Most of these include advertisements by estate agents and companies offering other services for house hunters and buyers as well as an ordering service for books about France and the French.

The Connexion, BP25, 06480 La-Colle-sur-Loup, France (☎ 04 93 32 16 59, 🖥 www.connexionfrance.com). Monthly newspaper.

France Magazine, Archant Life, Archant House, Oriel Road, Cheltenham,Glos GL50 1BB, UK (☎ 01242-216050, 🖥 www.francemag.co.uk). Monthly lifestyle magazine.

France Magazine (🖥 www.francemagazine.org). Quarterly magazine published in the US by the French-American Cultural Foundation in Washington, DC.

France-USA Contacts, FUSAC, 26 rue Bénard, 75014 Paris, France (☎ 01 56 53 54 54, 🖥 www.fusac.fr). Free bi-weekly magazine.

French Magazine, Merricks Media, 3-4 Riverside Court, Lower Bristol Rd, Bath, BA2 3DZ, UK (☎ 01225-786840, 🖥 www.frenchmagazine.co.uk). Monthly lifestyle and property magazine.

French News, SARL French News, 5 chemin de la Monzie, BP4042, 24004 Périgueux Cedex, France (☎ 05 53 06 84 40, 🖥 www.french-news.com). Monthly newspaper.

French Property News, Archant Life, 3 Oriel Road, Cheltenham, Gloucestershire, GL50 1BB, UK (☎ 01242-265896, 🖥 www.french-property-news.com). Monthly property magazine.

The Irish Eyes Magazine, The Eyes, 2 rue des Lailières, 94300 Vincennes, France (☎ 01 41 74 93 03, 🖥 www.irisheyes.fr). Monthly Paris cultural magazine.

Living France, Archant Life, 3 Oriel Road, Cheltenham, Gloucestershire, GL50 1BB, UK (☎ 01242-216075, 💻 www. livingfrance.com). Monthly lifestyle/property magazine.

Normandie & South of England Magazine, 330 rue Valvire, BP414, 50004 Saint-Lô, France (☎ 02 33 77 32 70, 💻 www. normandie-magazine.fr). News and current affairs about Normandy and parts of southern England, published eight times a year mainly in French, but with some English articles and translations.

The Riviera Reporter, 56 chemin de Provence, 06250 Mougins, France (☎ 04 93 45 77 19, 💻 www.riviera-reporter.com). Bi-monthly free magazine covering the Côte d'Azur.

The Riviera Times, 8 avenue Jean Moulin, 06340 Drap, France (☎ 04 93 27 60 00, 💻 www.rivieratimes.com). Monthly free newspaper covering the Côte d'Azur and Italian Riviera.

French Property Magazines

ICF l'Argus des Commerces (💻 www.cession-commerce.com). Magazine of interest to all businesses.

Immobilier en France (💻 www.immobilierenfrance.com). Magazine with advertisements for property to buy and rent.

Info Presse (💻 www.info-presse.fr). Subscription service for over 5,000 magazines, e.g. *Artisans Magazine*, *l'Officiel de la Franchise* and *l'Officiel des Commerciaux*.

L'Hôtellerie (💻 www.lhotellerie.fr). Magazine for those in the hotel and restaurant industry.

Living France (💻 www.livingfrance.com). English-language guide to France and French property.

Logic-immo (💻 www.logic-immo.com). Monthly magazine with advertisements for property for sale and rent.

Appendix C: USEFUL WEBSITES

Property Websites in English

1st For French Property (🖳 www.1st-for-french-property.co.uk). French property for sale in all regions, from chateaux, *gîtes* and farmhouses to mobile homes; a portal for over 50 agents.

A Vendre A Louer (🖳 www.avendrealouer.fr). Network for advertising all types of property for sale and rent.

Blue Homes (🖳 www.bluehomes.de/blue-en). Network of estate agents, working in five languages.

Coast-Country (🖳 www.coast-country.com). Thousands of properties; nine multilingual agents throughout France.

Domus Abroad (🖳 www.domusabroad.com). UK-based agency.

Find Your Property (🖳 www.findyourproperty.com). Global property finder.

Francophiles (🖳 www.francophiles.co.uk). UK-based property company specialising in all areas of France.

French Connections (🖳 www.frenchconnections.co.uk). Advertising portal for property owners and agents selling or renting in France.

French Property News (🖳 www.french-property-news.com). Site containing advertisements from estate agents, solicitors, financial advisers, builders, removal companies, surveyors, etc..

Gites in France (🖳 www.gites-in-france.co.uk). Gîte businesses for sale.

Green Acre (🖳 www.green-acre.com). Private sales, no agents, contact vendors directly. Well arranged site, easy to search. The French version is 🖳 www.immofrance.com.

Internet French Property (🖳 www.french-property.com). Property website with advertisements of properties for sale, rental and ancillary services.

Outbound Publishing (💻 www.outboundpublishing.com). Information on emigration, jobs and property.

Properties in France (💻 www.propertiesinfrance.com). Properties include *gîte* complexes, vineyards and stud farms.

Renovation-EU (💻 www.renovation.eu.com). Excellent site with properties for sale and extensive information on renovation and links to UK press articles on all aspects of living in France.

La Résidence (💻 www.laresidence.co.uk). *Gîte* complexes and B&Bs for sale in the north, west and south-west.

Salut-France (💻 http://salut-france.com). Property search agency providing an English-language service in Brittany and Loire-Atlantique.

Property Websites in French

Estate Agents' Sites

123 Immo (💻 www.123immo.fr). Displays over 4,000 estate agencies' advertisements.

3d Immo (💻 www.3d-immo.com). Portal displaying advertisements from individuals and estate agents.

Abimmo (💻 www.abimmo.com). Many properties for sale – new and old, houses and apartments.

Abonim (💻 www.abonim.com). Displays advertisements from individuals and estate agents.

Century 21 (💻 www.century21.fr). Estate agent with offices throughout France.

FNAIM (💻 www.fnaim.fr). French national estate agents' organisation with advice on buying property and property advertisements.

Guy Hoquet (🖳 www.guy-hoquet.com). Property company for buying or renting private or business premises.

Logic-immo (🖳 www.logic-immo.com). Monthly magazine listing houses for sale and rent.

Nota (🖳 www.nota.fr). *Notaires'* website covering Calvados and Manche.

Orpi (🖳 www.orpi.com). Displays over 1,000 estate agencies' advertisements.

Panorimmo (🖳 www.panorimmo.com). Links to property websites.

Le Partenaire Européen (🖳 www.partenaire-europeen.fr). Property search agency helping buyers and sellers of property throughout France.

Propriétés de France (🖳 www.proprietesdefrance.com). Website providing advice and listing estate agencies for top-of-the-range properties.

Le Site Immobilier (🖳 www.lesiteimmobilier.com). Website containing many estate agents' advertisements.

SNPI (🖳 www.snpi.fr). Website of the estate agents' organisation, containing advertisements and advice.

Le Tuc (🖳 www.letuc.com). Estate agent with offices throughout France.

UNPI (🖳 www.unpi.org). Website of the estate agents' organisation.

Private Advertisement Sites

L'Annonce (🖳 www.lannonce.com/immobilier/index.html). Property for sale and to rent.

Appel Immo (🖳 www.appelimmo.fr). Property for sale.

Entreparticuliers (🖳 www.entreparticuliers.com). Property for sale and to rent.

Explorimmo (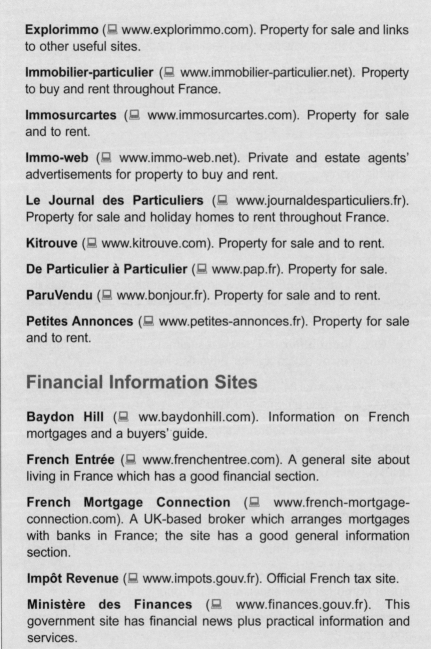 www.explorimmo.com). Property for sale and links to other useful sites.

Immobilier-particulier (www.immobilier-particulier.net). Property to buy and rent throughout France.

Immosurcartes (www.immosurcartes.com). Property for sale and to rent.

Immo-web (www.immo-web.net). Private and estate agents' advertisements for property to buy and rent.

Le Journal des Particuliers (www.journaldesparticuliers.fr). Property for sale and holiday homes to rent throughout France.

Kitrouve (www.kitrouve.com). Property for sale and to rent.

De Particulier à Particulier (www.pap.fr). Property for sale.

ParuVendu (www.bonjour.fr). Property for sale and to rent.

Petites Annonces (www.petites-annonces.fr). Property for sale and to rent.

Financial Information Sites

Baydon Hill (ww.baydonhill.com). Information on French mortgages and a buyers' guide.

French Entrée (www.frenchentree.com). A general site about living in France which has a good financial section.

French Mortgage Connection (www.french-mortgage-connection.com). A UK-based broker which arranges mortgages with banks in France; the site has a good general information section.

Impôt Revenue (www.impots.gouv.fr). Official French tax site.

Ministère des Finances (www.finances.gouv.fr). This government site has financial news plus practical information and services.

HM Revenue and Customs (⌨www.hmrc.gov.uk) UK inland revenue (tax) site; add /cnr for the centre for non-residents.

Business and Information Sites

All sites are in French unless otherwise stated.

Agence Nationale pour l'Information sur le Logement (⌨ www. anil.org). Information on letting, with rules and regulations and guidance for both owners and tenants.

Agence Pour la Création d'Entreprises (⌨ www.apce.com). Official government site with information on starting a business. Some information in English.

Assemblée des Chambres Françaises de Commerce et d'Industrie/ACFCI (⌨ www.acfci.cci.fr). Association of French chambers of commerce.

Conseil Géneral (⌨ www.cg00.fr). To find the *conseil général* site for your department, substitute your department number for the '00' (e.g. for Dordogne enter ⌨ www.cg24.fr).

European Union (⌨ www.europa.eu.int). General information about working in France (and other EU countries) and details of the economic situation and employment situation in each region (in English).

FEEF (⌨ www.feef.org). Site of the Fédération des Entreprises et Entrepreneurs de France, providing general information about starting a business.

Fiducial (⌨ www.fiducial.fr). Information for small businesses.

France Initiative Réseau (⌨ www.fir.asso.fr). Information about loans and other assistance for entrepreneurs.

Government Portal (⌨ www.premier-ministre.gouv.fr). French official government site (in English).

Info Travail (💻 www.infotravail.com). Government site with information on the legal aspects of employment.

Inforeg (Chambre de Commerce de Paris) (💻 www.inforeg.ccip.fr). Paris-based site containing legal information with a good section on holiday letting.

Institut National de la Statistique et des Études Économiques (💻 www.insee.fr). Official French site for national statistics, census results and surveys.

Internet French Property Co. (💻 www.french-property.com). This property site also has a good community section with news, finance, legal, and travel information and a discussion forum (in English).

Kifaikoi (💻 www.kifaikoi.com). Information for holiday accommodation businesses (in English), with a very good forum (in French).

Logement.org (💻 www.logement.org). General information on renting or letting a property, including legalities.

Ministry of Employment (💻 www.travail.gouv.fr). Site of the Ministère de l'Emploi, du Travail et de la Cohésion Sociale.

Ministère de l'Équipement, Transport et Logement (💻 www.logement.equipement.gouv.fr and 💻 www.equipement.gouv.fr). Government site with rules and regulations for letting and housing.

Ministère des Petites et Moyennes Entreprises (💻 www.pme.gouv.fr). Official French site for information on small and medium-size businesses.

Notaires (💻 www.notaires.fr). Explains the role of *notaires* and their services and lists properties for sale (click on '*Rechercher un bien*'). English version available – click the tiny Union Jack at the top.

Monter une Entreprise (💻 www.montermonentreprise.com). Online magazine with information about starting a business.

Panoranet (🖥 www.panoranet.com). Mortgage and insurance information.

Paris Entreprises (🖥 www.paris-entreprises.com). Official site for information about setting up a business in the Paris area, but offers clear information relevant to all areas of France.

Perval (🖥 www.immoprix.com). General land and property prices.

Total France (🖥 www.totalfrance.com). Properties to buy or rent, plus fact sheets, news, events, advertising, and a useful forum (in English).

URSSAF (🖥 www.urssaf.fr). Official site of the main social security agency, with details of social security contributions.

Other Useful Sites

Anglo Info (🖥 www.angloinfo.com). General information site with a useful forum,.

Gîte Courses (🖥 www.gitecomplexes.co.uk). Chloe and Tim Williams.

Lay My Hat (🖥 www.laymyhat.com). Advice for rental owners, from rental owners, with a good discussion forum.

Living France (🖥 www.livingfrance.com). General information site with a lively forum.

Maison de la France (🖥 www.franceguide.com). Official French tourism website, available in many languages. Lots of information, holidays, guide, festivals, heritage & culture.

This French Life (🖥 www.thisfrenchlife.com). Includes articles about setting up a variety of necessary services, from bank accounts to internet connections.

Appendix D: Maps

The map opposite shows the 22 regions and 96 departments of France (excluding overseas territories), which are listed below. Departments 91 to 95 come under the Ile-de-France region, which also includes Ville de Paris (75), Seine-et-Marne (77) and Yvelines (78), shown in detail opposite. The island of Corsica consists of two departments, 2A and 2B. The maps on the following pages show major airports and ports with cross-Channel ferry services, high-speed train (*TGV*) routes, and motorways and other major roads.

01 Ain	32 Gers	64 Pyrénées-Atlantiques
02 Aisne	33 Gironde	65 Hautes-Pyrénées
2A Corse-du-Sud	34 Hérault	66 Pyrénées-Orientales
2B Haute Corse	35 Ille-et-Vilaine	67 Bas-Rhin
03 Allier	36 Indre	68 Haut-Rhin
04 Alpes-de-Hte-Provence	37 Indre-et-Loire	69 Rhône
05 Hautes-Alpes	38 Isère	70 Haute-Saône
06 Alpes-Maritimes	39 Jura	71 Saône-et-Loire
07 Ardèche	40 Landes	72 Sarthe
08 Ardennes	41 Loir-et-Cher	73 Savoie
09 Ariège	42 Loire	74 Haute-Savoie
10 Aube	43 Haute-Loire	75 Paris
11 Aude	44 Loire-Atlantique	76 Seine-Maritime
12 Aveyron	45 Loiret	77 Seine-et-Marne
13 Bouches-du-Rhône	46 Lot	78 Yvelines
14 Calvados	47 Lot-et-Garonne	79 Deux-Sèvres
15 Cantal	48 Lozère	80 Somme
16 Charente	49 Maine-et-Loire	81 Tarn
17 Charente-Maritime	50 Manche	82 Tarn-et-Garonne
18 Cher	51 Marne	83 Var
19 Corrèze	52 Haute-Marne	84 Vaucluse
21 Côte-d'Or	53 Mayenne	85 Vendée
22 Côte-d'Armor	54 Meurthe-et-Moselle	86 Vienne
23 Creuse	55 Meuse	87 Haute-Vienne
24 Dordogne	56 Morbihan	88 Vosges
25 Doubs	57 Moselle	89 Yonne
26 Drôme	58 Nièvre	90 Territoire de Belfort
27 Eure	59 Nord	91 Essonne
28 Eure-et-Loir	60 Oise	92 Hauts-de-Seine
29 Finistère	61 Orne	93 Seine-Saint-Denis
30 Gard	62 Pas-de-Calais	94 Val-de-Marne
31 Haute-Garonne	63 Puy-de-Dôme	95 Val-d'Oise

REGIONS & DEPARTMENTS

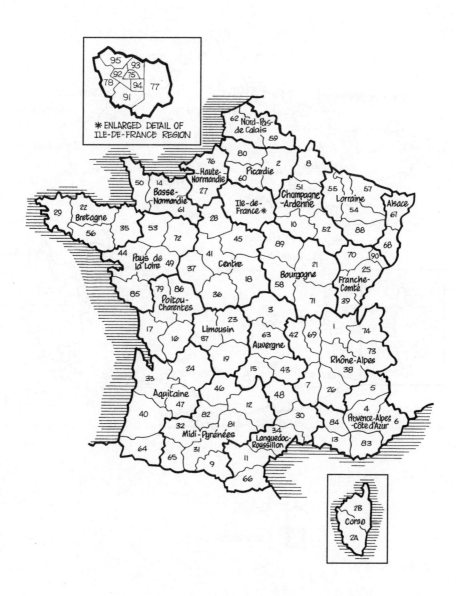

* ENLARGED DETAIL OF
ILE-DE-FRANCE REGION

Airports & Ports

✈ Airports

⚓ Ferry ports

TGV Network

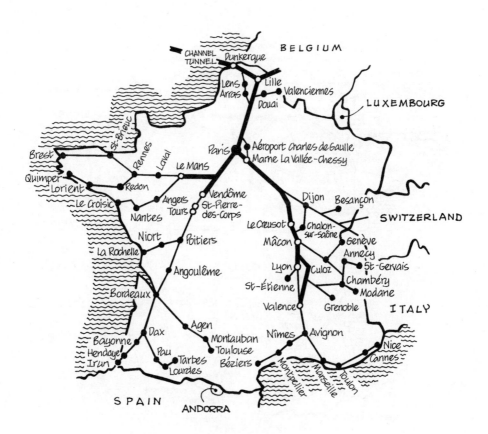

━━━━━━━ Special track, on which trains can run at up to 300kph (187mph).

───────── Ordinary track, on which trains are restricted to around 200kph (122mph).

Motorways & Major Roads

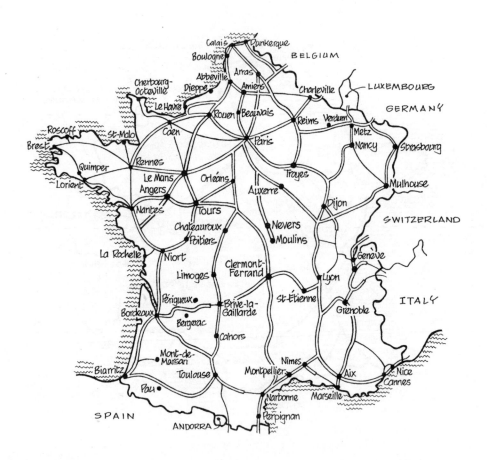

APPENDIX E: ORGANISATIONS & STANDARDS

There are several official organisations with which a *chambres d'hôtes* or *gîte* business may register. Although they're all national organisations, they operate at departmental level. Whereas some of their criteria might apply to all properties, and most are broadly similar, there are many variations between departments. The requirements listed below should therefore be taken as typical, but you should contact the relevant office in your own department (those of Gîtes de France are listed below) for a definitive list.

Accueil Paysan

Accueil Paysan Féderation Nationale (9 rue de la Poste, 38000 Grenoble, ☎ 04 76 43 44 83, 🖳 www.accueil-paysan.com) works in conjunction with farmers, marketing holidays whereby the guests experience the countryside, animals, plants and 'the rhythm of the seasons'. The organisation includes *chambres d'hôtes*, *gîtes* and campsites. There are currently 545 farms in the scheme.

Bienvenue à la Ferme

5,500 farmers are members of the Bienvenue à la Ferme network, at various levels from simply opening their farms for visits and the sale of regional products to running *gîtes* and *chambres d'hôtes* businesses. For details, contact the Assemblée Permanente des Chambres d'Agriculture (APCA), 9 avenue Georges V, 75008 Paris (☎ 01 53 57 11 44, ✉ bienvenue-a-la-ferme@apca.chambagri.fr, 🖳 www.bienvenue-a-la-ferme.com).

Clévacances

Clévacances has two main categories of accommodation: *La Location Clévacances* for self-catering accommodation, and *La*

Chambre Clévacances for B&B. There are around 24,000 Clévacances *gîtes* registered in 80 departments. Unlike Gîtes de France, Clévacances handles urban as well as rural properties, including houses, flats and maisonettes. Clévacances classifies self-catering properties with one to five *clés* (keys), as detailed below. Reasons for non-acceptance, apart from non-compliance with the requirements listed below, include the following:

- dampness;

- little or no natural light;

- insufficient ventilation in any room;

- unsatisfactory arrangement of rooms – e.g. access to the bathroom or lavatory from the kitchen (except studio flats);

- outside lavatory;

- difficult vehicle access;

- environmental problems (e.g. noise, smells, right of way across land);

- rooms too small (see **Dimensions** below).

The usual criteria for each classification are listed below; for further details contact the head office, Fédération Nationale des Locations de France Clévacances, 54 boulevard de l'Embouchure/BP52166, 31022 Toulouse Cedex 2 (☎ 05 61 13 55 66, 🖳 www.cle vacances.com). You should, however, check local variations by contacting the Clévacances representative at the Comité Départemental de Tourisme.

1 Clé

Individual apartment or house for the exclusive use of the clients; no access allowed by the owner or others.

Bathroom(s): Must be independent, inside the building, with a door or partition, and equipped with a ventilation system (window, *ventilation méchanique contrôlée/VMC*, or ventilation grilles). For more than six people there must be two bathrooms, one of which must be separate. Each bathroom must contain a shower or bath, a basin with mixer tap, fixed soap holder (with a shower), wall-mounted towel rail, mirror, shelf, bathroom waste bin, coat peg or hook, razor socket and light over the basin.

Bedding: Bedding (mattress and divan base) must be clean, in perfect condition and fitted with a mattress protector. Mattresses must be good quality and in perfect condition. Metal bases and horsehair aren't allowed. One bedspread and two blankets or one duvet minimum per bed (in the south, except in the mountains, one blanket may be allowed in summer), one bolster and/or one pillow per person, one bedside table per occupant or one between twin beds, clothes rail with hangers. Any other bedding must be of good quality and in good condition. In overseas departments, a mosquito net for each bed is advised.

Bedrooms: Single beds must be 90cm wide and 190cm long (80cm bunk beds might be allowed). Double beds must be 140cm wide and 190cm long. Excepting studio flats, bedrooms must be separated from day rooms by a door or partition (for alcoves by a curtain, for cabins by a door). All bedrooms must have natural ventilation (window or roof opening). Shutters, blinds or curtains must obscure all light.

Cupboards: For two people 2.5m^2; for each extra person 1m^2.

Curtains & blinds: Exterior shutters must be fitted to windows in rooms occupied at night unless the curtains ensure obscurity. When rooms are overlooked, net curtains must be fitted.

Electricity: The electrical system must conform to current electrical standards. Electricity must be available in all rooms. There must be at least one socket per room and one or two lights totalling at least 15W per m^2 or equivalent. There must be free access to the fuse box.

Entrance hall: Must have a doormat!

Exterior: Roofs must be covered with traditional regional materials, which must be in good condition. The facade must conform to the architecture of the site, and approaches to the house must be in good condition and unobstructed. If the accommodation allows, there must be a set of garden furniture with a parasol (unless there's natural shade), and a light for eating outside in the evening. Parking for visitors must be near the accommodation.

Floors: Must be in good condition and easily cleaned, soundproof and waterproof (e.g. parquet, tiles, paving, plastic flooring, carpets). No bitumen or cement floors.

Furniture: Must be in good condition, clean and suitable for its purpose: hanging cupboards, chests of drawers, wardrobes, chairs, sideboards, armchairs, sofas, divans, cupboards, table lamps, side tables and bedside tables according to the capacity of the accommodation.

Heating: The heating in each room must ensure a minimum temperature of 19C during the letting period. For overseas territories, air-conditioning or ventilators are obligatory.

Kitchen or kitchen area: Ventilation or air-conditioning must be installed (an extractor hood in studio apartments), and there must be enough room for the maximum number of people accommodated. There must be a double or triple burner and mini-oven, sink with mixer tap, wooden or plastic draining rack (unless there's a dishwasher), pressure cooker, electric coffee maker, salad spinner and refrigerator (e.g. 140 litres for five people). The cooking utensils and dishes (two for each person) must be in perfect condition, not chipped or unmatched. Matching cutlery must be of sufficient quantity and quality (no aluminium or plastic).

Lavatory: Must be indoors, separate or in the bathroom, with ventilation and everything necessary for its use (e.g. brush, cover and paper holder).

Living/Dining room: There must be an eating area adjacent to and independent of the kitchen with a table and chairs in perfect condition and sufficient for the capacity of the accommodation. If there's a fireplace, it must be well restored and in good working order, possibly with an insert (not a wood stove).

Walls & ceilings: Walls and ceilings must be covered with materials such as painted plaster, paint, wallpaper, tiles or fabrics. They must be waterproof and in good condition, with good acoustic qualities. Wood is allowed where it guarantees comfort and insulation. Ceilings must be a minimum height of 2.2m (1.80m in attic spaces).

Water: Hot and cold water must be available at all times in all facilities. There must be a minimum of 40 litres of hot water per person per day.

Windows, etc.: Sufficient ventilation and lighting for all rooms. One opening window for each living room.

Other facilities & equipment: There must be an iron and ironing cloth, vacuum cleaner (if there's carpet), indoor clothes line, waste bin (not a bucket), broom, bucket, shovel and floor cloth. Cleaning products advisable. Bathroom and kitchen towel hire must be available, as well as a folder with emergency numbers and practical information, and tourist leaflets. If an apartment is higher than the third floor, there must be a lift. No shared landings.

2 Clés

As for 1 *clé* with the following limitations or additions:

Bathroom(s): Shower with curtain or bath with a shower system. Ventilation must be by *VMC*.

Bedrooms: Apart from studio flats, the main bedroom must be independent, with a double bed (140 x 190cm) or two single beds (90 x 190cm). Studio flats and apartments may have 80cm single beds. Hanging space and shelves with a door – for two people 3m^2; for each extra person 1m^2. The main light must have switches at the entrance and next to the bed. Sheet hire must be available. In overseas departments there must be a mosquito net for each bed.

Entrance hall: Must have a coat rack.

Exterior: Apartments must have a balcony or terrace with exterior lighting. A portable barbecue (unless forbidden by bylaws).

Kitchen or kitchen area: Must have an extractor hood, a *maxi-four* oven (for more than two people) and a washing machine (which may be shared with the owner and other tenants).

Living room: Must have a television socket, armchairs or sofas sufficient for the number of people, and a coffee table.

Windows, etc.: Rooms must be well ventilated and have sufficient natural light.

Other: Ironing board.

3 Clés

As for 2 *clés* with the following limitations or additions:

Bathroom(s): Must have a shower with plastic or glass doors, ceiling light and fan heater.

Bedrooms: There must be a chair or armchair and net curtains or double curtains in each bedroom.

Exterior: Houses must have a private yard or outside area (minimum 50m²) with grass and flowers, and one reserved parking space for clients.

Kitchen: Must have *VMC*, a four-burner hob (gas or electric), oven, microwave oven, double sink, food processor, refrigerator with freezer compartment, washing machine, toaster, electric knife and *raclette* set. For more than four people, there must be a dishwasher large enough for eight place settings. There must be three times the number of dishes as people.

Lavatory: For more than six people, there must be two lavatories, one of which must be separate.

Other: Cleaning products, colour television (TV), telephone with *service restreint*, which blocks all usage except local, emergency and incoming calls. A cleaning service must be available at a moderate cost. The accommodation must be furnished 'in good taste', with matching furniture co-ordinating with the decor.

4 Clés

As for 3 *clés* with the following limitations or additions:

Bathroom: For more than six people, there must be two bathrooms, one of which must be independent. Both must have a bath with a shower screen in excellent condition, a mixer tap with a single swivel control (*mitigeur*), and good quality lighting (low wattage or halogen).

Bedrooms: There must be a TV socket in the main bedroom and not more than one double bed or two single beds per room. Double beds must be 160 x 190cm. Each bedroom must have a wardrobe with hangers.

Exterior: Apartments must have a loggia or terrace (minimum 9m²). Houses must have a well kept garden with shade. There must be a paved area or terrace, good quality garden furniture (e.g. teak or cast iron) including sun-loungers, a swimming pool (which may be shared with the owner or other tenants), and a good view. There must be private parking, indoor or covered.

Kitchen: Must have a window, tumble dryer, freezer or fridge/freezer. For more than six people, there must be a dishwasher large enough for 12 sets of crockery.

Lavatory: Must have a window.

Living room: There must be a sitting room separate from the main room.

Other: Vacuum cleaner, folder with tourist information, hi-fi system and board games. All rooms must have direct fresh-air ventilation. Main rooms must have good natural light. Decoration must be to a high standard.

5 Clés

As for 4 *clés* with the following limitations or additions:

Bathroom(s): Heated towel rail.

Bedrooms: Colour TV in the main bedroom. Linen must be included in the rental price. At least one bedroom must have an ensuite bathroom.

Exterior: The house must be surrounded by enclosed grounds and have a private swimming pool.

Kitchen: Must be separate from the living room.

Other: Video/DVD player. Sheets and towels must be provided. Cleaning at the end of the stay must be included in the rental price.

Dimensions

Generally, the living space must be in proportion to the capacity of the accommodation. The following criteria may vary according to the accommodation as well as the department:

- The minimum total area including kitchen or kitchen area, but excluding bathroom and lavatory for accommodation for two people (over five years old), must be as follow:

- 1 *clé*: 12m^2
- 2 *clés*: 14m^2
- 3 *clés*: 16m^2
- 4 *clés*: 18m^2
- 5 *clés*: 24m^2

Add 3m^2 for each additional person.

● The minimum area of extra bedrooms must usually be as shown below:

- 1 *clé*: 7m^2
- 2 *clés*: 8m^2
- 3 *clés*: 9m^2
- 4 *clés*: 10m^2
- 5 *clés*: 12m^2

Fleurs de Soleil

The 'Fleurs de Soleil' label is awarded by the organisation Les Maisons d'Amis en France to *chambres d'hôtes* businesses. Members must conform to the conditions in its 'quality charter', the main requirements of which are listed below. Further details and addresses of departmental offices can be obtained from the head office: Fleurs de Soleil, 52 avenue Thermale, 03200 Vichy (☎ 08 26 62 03 22, ⌨ www.fleursdesoleil.fr). The label also applies to upmarket self-catering accommodation, but only around 400 properties are labelled, so details aren't included here; for information, contact Fleurs de Soleil.

General

Detached properties with character, whether old or modern, are preferred, and they should be set in pleasant, well maintained gardens with climbing plants, trees, shrubs and flowers. There must be no hotel or restaurant business on the site. If in a town, a property must be away from noise such as busy roads or a railway, or any noisy commercial activities. When activities such as swimming or tennis are mentioned in the description of the accommodation, these may not be subject to any supplementary charge.

Accommodation

There must be one to five bedrooms, with bathrooms, catering for up to 12 guests; breakfast must be included in the rental price. The guest rooms must be situated in the hosts' house or in an annexed building. Guests must have rooms, shared by the hosts or by other guests, where they can eat breakfast, socialise, read, and maybe listen to music or watch television.

Bathroom: Each bedroom must normally have its own bathroom and WC. When a bathroom is shared by two rooms, these must be described as a suite and the bathroom cannot be shared without the assent of their occupants. In all cases, a basin and a shower or bath must be available, with a bathroom waste bin, all clean and in perfect working order, fresh soap and paper tissues. Towels and flannels must be renewed at least every three days. Cleaning and emptying of waste bins must be done every day.

Bedrooms: Bedrooms must have an area of at least 12m^2 (excluding areas under eaves, for example) and a height of 1.8m. Ventilation and heating must be provided, with at least one window or roof opening offering a view of the surrounding countryside. Double beds must be at least 140cm wide (160cm is recommended); single beds must be at least 80cm wide (90cm recommended). Twin beds must be identical. Beds must be not less than 40cm high and have a divan base and mattress in perfect condition. There must be a bedside rug, table and light for each person, a writing table, shelving or wardrobe, hanging space and clothes hangers. Blankets or duvets must be of good quality, as must bedspreads and pillows. Sheets and pillowcases are to be changed at least every five days. A cold drink (bottle or carafe with glasses) must be provided in each room. Facilities for preparing hot drinks (kettle, cups and sachets) are appreciated. Eating in bedrooms isn't allowed.

Stairs: If the layout of the accommodation means that guests have to use a staircase, this must be solid and not too steep. Stairs with treads higher than 18cm or narrower than 25cm must be mentioned in the description of the accommodation.

Meals

Breakfast: Breakfast must be included in the rental price. It must be plentiful and prepared with care from fresh ingredients: fresh tea, coffee or chocolate, a variety of breads, butter and jams (often home-made), regional and seasonal products. The host must be able to respond to any reasonable request, e.g. cereals, yoghurts or eggs. Breakfast should be taken at a reasonable time for all involved according to their schedules.

Evening meal: Evening meals are extra, as described in the details of accommodation, with an all-inclusive set price, and booked according to how long the host needs to prepare the meal. The service need be available only to those without special dietary requirements. Two things are imperative: cleanliness and freshness.

Welcome

Emphasis is put on the welcome given to guests, and the hosts' sharing of their lifestyle and culture. The family opens its house to visitors, helping them to discover the region's cultural and natural attractions. After booking, the visitor must be sent a map and directions, making the house easy to find. Arrival time is between 5 and 7pm, unless otherwise agreed. Guests must be welcomed with a drink while their plans are discussed, then shown to their room(s), which must have been carefully prepared, with personal touches such as flowers, snacks and fruit. Hosts must be attentive and available to assist their guests with the language and local customs, supply maps and tourist information and materials for everyday needs such as sewing, writing and shoe polishing.

Gîtes de France

Gîtes de France (GdF) properties are classified by *épis* (wheatears), 1 being the lowest and 5 the highest. The requirements for the different types of *gîte* (see **Chapter 2**) are given below. Departmental addresses are listed below; for general information, contact the head office, La Maison des Gîtes de France et du Tourisme Vert, 59 rue Saint-Lazare, Paris 75439 CEDEX 09 (☎ 01 49 70 75 75, 💻 www.gites-de-france.fr).

Departmental Offices

Ain: 21 place Bernard/BP198, 01005 Bourg-en-Bresse Cedex (☎ 04 74 23 82 66, ✉ gites-de-france-ain@wanadoo.fr, 💻 www.gites-de-france-ain.com).

Aisne: Comité Départemental du Tourisme, 24–28 avenue Charles de Gaulle, 02007 Laon Cedex (☎ 03 23 27 76 76, ✉ s.chamaux@cdt-aisne.com, 💻 www.gites-de-france-aisne.com).

Allier: Pavillon des Marronniers, Parc de Bellevue, 6 rue Jean Vidal/BP65, 03402 Yzeure Cedex (☎ 04 70 46 81 56, ✉ gitesdefrance@pays-allier.com, 💻 www.gites-de-france-allier.com).

Alpes-de-Haute-Provence: Maison du Tourisme, Rond Point du 11 Novembre/BP201, 04001 Digne-les-Bains Cedex (☎ 04 92 31 30 40, 💻 www.gites-de-france-04.fr).

Alpes-Maritimes: 57 promenade des Anglais/BP21614, 06011 Nice Cedex 01 (☎ 04 92 15 21 30, 💻 www.gites-de-france-alpes-maritimes.com).

Ardèche: 4 cours du Palais/BP402, 07004 Privas Cedex (☎ 04 75 64 70 70, 💻 www.gites-de-france-ardeche.com).

Ardennes: 29 rue du Petit Bois/BP370, 08106 Charleville-Mezières Cedex (☎ 03 24 56 89 65, 💻 www@gitardennes.com).

Ariège: 31bis avenue du Général de Gaulle/BP143, 09004 Foix Cedex (☎ 05 61 02 30 89, ✉ gites-de-france.ariege@wanadoo.fr, 💻 www.gites-de-france-ariege.com).

Aube: Chambre d'Agriculture, 2bis rue Jeanne d'Arc/BP4080, 10014 Troyes Cedex (☎ 03 25 73 00 11, ✉ aube@champagne-ardenne-reservation.com, 💻 www.gites-de-zfrance-aube.com).

Aude: Maison du Tourisme Vert, 78ter rue Barbacane, 11000 Carcassonne (☎ 04 68 11 40 70, ✉ contact@gites11.com, 💻 www.gites-de-france-aude.com).

Aveyron: APATAR Maison Départementale du Tourisme, 17 rue Aristide Briand/BP 831, 12008 Rodez Cedex 9 (☎ 05 65 75 55 55, ✉ gites.de.france.aveyron@wanadoo.fr, 💻 www.gites-de-france-aveyron.com).

Bas-Rhin: 7 place des Meuniers, 67000 Strasbourg (☎ 03 88 75 56 50, ✉ alsace@gites67.com, 💻 www.alsace-gites-de-france.com).

Bouches-du-Rhône: Domaine du Vergon, 13370 Mallemort (☎ 04 90 59 49 39, ✉ gitesdefrance@visitprovence.com, 💻 www.gdf13.com).

Calvados: 6 promenade de Madame de Sévigné, 14050 Caen Cedex 4 (☎ 02 31 82 71 65, 💻 www.gites-de-france-calvados.fr).

Cantal: 34 avenue des Pupilles de la Nation/BP631, 15006 Aurillac Cedex (☎ 04 71 48 64 20, 💻 www.gites-de-france-cantal.fr).

Charente: 23 avenue des Maréchaux, 16000 Angoulème (☎ 05 45 69 48 62, 💻 www.gitescharente.com).

Charente-Maritime: 18, Rue Emile Picard Résidence l'Amirauté Les Minimes/BP32, 17002 La Rochelle Cedex 01 (☎ 05 46 50 63 63, ✉ GITES.17@wanadoo.fr, 💻 www.itea.fr/GDF/17).

Cher: 5 rue de Séraucourt, 18000 Bourges (☎ 02 48 48 00 13, ✉ tourisme.berry@cdt18.tv, 💻 www.gites-du-cher.com).

Corrèze: Immeuble Consulaire Tulle Est Puy Pinçon 19001 Tulle Cedex (☎ 05 55 21 55 61, ✉ gites-de-france@correze.chambagri.fr, 💻 www.gites-de-france-limousin.com).

Corse: 77 cours Napoléon/BP10, 20181 Ajaccio Cedex 01 (☎ 04 95 10 06 14, 💻 www.gites-corsica.com).

Côte-d'Or: 5, rue René Char/BP 17011, 21070 Dijon Cedex (☎ 03 80 45 97 15, ✉ gites.de.france21@wanadoo.fr, 💻 www.gites-de-france-cotedor.com).

Côtes-d'Armor: 7 rue St Benoit/BP 4536, 22045 Saint-Brieuc Cedex 2 (☎ 02 96 62 21 73, ✉ contact@gitesdarmor.com, 💻 www.gitesdarmor.com).

Creuse: Maison de l'Agriculture 1, rue Martinet/BP89, 23011 Gueret Cedex (☎ 05 55 52 87 50, ✉ gites.de.france.creuse@wanadoo.fr, 💻 www.gites-de-france-limousin.com).

Deux-Sèvres: 15 rue Thiers/BP8524, 79025 Niort Cedex 9 (☎ 05 49 77 87 79, ✉ gites-de-France-deux-sevres@wanadoo.fr, 💻 www.itea.fr/GDF/79/F).

Dordogne: 25 rue Wilson/BP2063, 24002 Périgueux Cedex (☎ 05 53 35 50 24, ✉ dordogne.perigord.tourisme@wanadoo.fr, 💻 www.dordogne-perigord-tourisme.fr).

Doubs: 4ter Faubourg Rivotte, 25000 Besançon (☎ 03 81 82 80 48, ✉ loisirs.accueil.doubs@wanadoo.fr, 💻 www.gites-de-france-doubs.fr).

Drôme: Plateau de Lautagne, 42 avenue des Langories Bât. C/BP169, 26906 Valence Cedex 09 (☎ 04 75 83 16 42, 💻 www.gites-de-france-drome.com).

Essonne: Maison du Tourisme, 19 rue des Mazières, 91000 Evry (☎ 01 64 97 23 81, 💻 www.gites-de-france-essonne.com).

Eure: 9 rue de la Petite Cité, 27008 Evreux Cedex (☎ 02 32 39 53 38, 💻 www.gites-de-france-eure.com).

Eure-et-Loir: Maison de l'Agriculture 10, rue Dieudonné Costes, 28024 Chartres (☎ 02 37 84 01 02, ✉ reservation@tourisme28.com, 💻 www.gites-de-france-eure-et-loir.com).

Finistère: Accueil Rural Finistère, 5 allée Sully, 29322 Quimper Cedex (☎ 02 98 64 20 20, 💻 www.gites-finistere.com).

Gard: Gîtes de France Gard, 3 rue Cité Foulc/BP59, 30007 Nîmes Cedex 4 (☎ 04 66 27 94 94, 💻 www.gites-de-france-gard.fr).

Gers: Maison de l'Agriculture, Route de Tarbes/BP161, 32003 Auch Cedex (☎ 05 62 61 79 00, ✉ contact@gers-tourisme.com, 💻 www.gers-gites-france.com).

Gironde: Chambre d'Agriculture de la Gironde, 17, cours Xavier Arnozan, 33000 Bordeaux (☎ 05 56 81 54 23, ✉ gites33@wanadoo.fr, 💻 www.gites-de-france-gironde.com).

Haut-Rhin: Maison du Tourisme, 1 rue Schlumberger/BP371, 68007 Colmar Cedex (☎ 03 89 20 10 68, ✉ gitesdefrance 68@tourisme68.com, 💻 www.itea.fr/GDF/68).

Haute-Garonne: 14 rue Bayárd/BP845, 31015 Toulouse Cedex 06 (☎ 05 61 99 70 60, 💻 www.gites-de-france-31.com).

Haute-Loire: Hôtel du Département/BP332, 43012 Le Puy-en-Velay Cedex (☎ 04 71 07 41 56, ✉ gitesdefrance43@free.fr, 💻 www.gites-de-france-haute-loire.com).

Haute-Marne: Cours Marcel Baron/BP2048, 52902 Chaumont Cedex 2 (☎ 03 25 30 39 03, ✉ haute-marne@gites-champagne-ardenne.com, 💻 www.gites-de-france-hautemarne.com).

Haute-Saône: Relais des Gîtes de France, Vesoul Technologia, rue Max Devaux/BP50077, 70002 Vesoul Cedex (☎ 03 84 97 10 75, ✉ info@gites-de-france70.com, 💻 www.itea.fr/GDF/70).

Haute-Savoie: Maison du Tourisme Vert, 16 rue Guillaume Fichet, 74000 Annecy (☎ 04 50 10 10 11, 💻 www.gites-de-france-haute-savoie.com).

Haute-Vienne: Maison de l'Agriculture, 32 avenue du Général Leclerc, 87065 Limoges Cedex (☎ 05 55 77 09 57, ✉ gites.de.france.87@wanadoo.fr, 💻 www.gites-de-france-limousin.com).

Hautes-Alpes: 1 place du Champsaur/BP55, 05002 Gap Cedex (☎ 04 92 52 52 92, ✉ gdf05@wanadoo.fr, 💻 www.gites-de-france-hautes-alpes.com).

Hautes-Pyrénées: Maison de l'Agriculture, 22 place du Foirail, 65000 Tarbes (☎ 05 62 34 31 50, ✉ contact@gites-france-65.com, 💻 www.gites-de-france-65.com).

Hérault: Maison du Tourisme, Avenue des Moulins, 34184 Montpellier Cedex 4 (☎ 04 67 67 71 62, ✉ contact@gdf34.com, 🖥 www.gites-de-france-herault.asso.fr).

Ille-et-Vilaine: 107 avenue Henri Fréville/ BP70336, 35203 Rennes Cedex 2 (☎ 02 99 22 68 68, ✉ gitesdefrance35@wanadoo.fr, 🖥 www.gitesdefrance35.com).

Indre: 7bis rue Bourdillon, 36000 Châteauroux (☎ 02 54 22 91 20, ✉ gites36@wanadoo.fr, 🖥 www.itea.fr/GDF/36).

Indre-et-Loire: 38 rue Augustin Fresnel/BP139, 37171 Chambray-les-Tours (☎ 02 47 27 56 10, 🖥 www.gites-touraine.com).

Isère: 40 avenue Marcelin Berthelot/BP2641, 38036 Grenoble Cedex 2 (☎ 04 76 40 79 40, ✉ sirt38@wanadoo.fr, 🖥 www.gites-de-france-isere.com).

Jura: 8 rue Louis Rousseau, 39000 Lons-le-Saunier (☎ 03 84 87 08 88, 🖥 www.jura-tourism.com).

Landes: Chambre d'Agriculture, Cité Galliane/BP279, 40005 Mont-de-Marsan Cedex (☎ 05 58 85 44 44, ✉ gites-de-france@landes.chambagri.fr, 🖥 www.gites-de-france-landes.com).

Loir-et-Cher: 5 rue de la Voûte du Château/BP249, 41001 Blois Cedex (☎ 02 54 58 81 64, ✉ GITES41@wanadoo.fr, 🖥 www.gites-de-france-blois.com).

Loire: 43 avenue Albert Raimond/BP20048, 42272 St-Priest-en-Jarez Cedex (☎ 04 77 79 18 49, ✉ contact@gites42.com, 🖥 www.gites-de-france-loire.com).

Loire-Atlantique: 3-5 rue Félibien/ BP93218, 44032 Nantes Cedex 1 (☎ 02 51 72 95 65, 🖥 www.gites-de-france-44.fr).

Loiret: 8 rue d'Escures, 45000 Orleans (☎ 02 38 62 04 88, ✉ gitesdefrance@loiret.chambagri.fr, 🖥 www.gites-de-france-loiret.com).

Lot: Maison du Tourisme, Place François Mitterand, 4600 Cahors (☎ 05 65 53 20 75, ✉ loisirs.accueil.lot@wanadoo.fr, 🖥 www. gites-de-france-lot.com).

Lot-et-Garonne: 11 rue des Droits de l'Homme, 47000 Agen (☎ 05 53 47 80 87, ✉ gites-de-france.47@wanadoo.fr, 🖥 www.gites-de-france-47.com).

Lozère: 14 boulevard Henri Bourillon, 48001 Mende Cedex (☎ 04 66 65 60 00, 🖥 www.lozere-tourisme.com).

Maine-et-Loire: Gîtes de France Anjou/BP52425, 49024 Angers Cedex 02 (☎ 02 41 88 00 00, ✉ gites-de-france-anjou@ wanadoo.fr, 🖥 www.gites-de-france-anjou.com).

Manche: 98 route de Candol, Maison du Département, 50008 Saint-Lô Cedex (☎ 02 33 56 28 80, ✉ manchetourisme@cg50.fr, 🖥 www.manche-locationvacances.com).

Marne: Complexe Agricole du Mont Bernard, Route de Suippes/BP525, 51000 Chalons-en-Champagne (☎ 03 26 64 95 05, 🖥 www.gites-de-france-marne.com).

Mayenne: 84 avenue Robert Buron/BP0325, 53009 Laval Cedex (☎ 02 43 53 58 78, ✉ gites-de-france-53@wanadoo.fr, 🖥 www. gites-de-france-mayenne.com).

Meurthe-et-Moselle: Square Herzog, ZAC Ban la Dame, 54390 Frouard (☎ 03 83 23 49 50, ✉ gites-de-france54@wanadoo.fr, 🖥 www.gites54.com).

Meuse: Relais des Gîtes Ruraux de la Meuse, Hôtel du Département, 55012 Bar-le-Duc Cedex (☎ 03 29 45 79 76, 🖥 www.gites-de-meuse.fr).

Morbihan: 42 avenue Wilson/BP30318, 56403 Auray Cedex (☎ 02 97 56 48 12, ✉ gites-de-france.morbihan@wanadoo.fr, 🖥 www.gites-de-france-morbihan.com).

Moselle: Gîtes de Moselle, 6 rue de l'Abattoir, 57630 Vic-sur-Seille (☎ 03 87 01 18 50, ✉ gitesdefrance.moselle@wanadoo.fr, 🖥 www.gites57.com).

Nièvre: 2 avenue Saint-Just/BP 10728, 58007 Nevers Cedex (☎ 03 86 36 42 39 ✉ gites-de-france-nievre@wanadoo.fr, 🖥 www. gites-de-france-nievre.com).

Nord: 359 Bd du Président Hoover/BP1210, 59013 Lille Cedex (☎ 03 20 14 93 93, ✉ gites.de.france.nord@wanadoo.fr, 🖥 www. itea.fr/GDF/59).

Oise: 8 rue Auguste Delaherche/BP80822, 60008 Beauvais Cedex (☎ 03 44 06 25 85, ✉ gites@oisetourisme.com, 🖥 www.itea.fr /GDF/60/F).

Orne: CDT/BP50, 61002 Alençon Cedex (☎ 02 33 28 07 00, ✉ info@ornetourisme.com, 🖥 www.itea.fr/GDF/61).

Pas-de-Calais: La trésorerie, Wimille/BP79, 62930 Wimereux (☎ 03 21 10 34 40, ✉ gitesdefrance@pas-de-calais.com, 🖥 www. gitesdefrance-pas-de-calais.com).

Puy-de-Dôme: Relais des Gîtes du Puy-de-Dôme, Place de la Bourse, 63038 Clermont-Ferrand Cedex 1 (☎ 04 73 42 22 61, 🖥 www.gites-de-france-puydedome.com).

Pyrénées-Atlantiques: 20 rue Gassion/BP537, 64010 Pau Cedex (☎ 05 59 11 20 64, 🖥 www.gites64.com).

Pyrénees-Orientales: 3 boulevard de Clairfont, Bât. D, Naturopôle, 66350 Toulouges (☎ 04 68 68 42 88, 🖥 www.gites-de-france-66.com).

Rhône: 1 rue Général Plessier, 69287 Lyon Cedex 2 (☎ 04 72 77 17 50, 🖥 www.gites-de-france-rhone.com).

Saône-et-Loire: Esplanade du Breuil/BP522, 71010 Mâcon Cedex (☎ 03 85 29 55 60, ✉ gites71@sl.chambagri.fr, 🖥 www.itea.fr/ GDF/71).

Sarthe: 78 avenue du Général Leclerc, 72000 Le Mans (☎ 02 43 23 84 61, ✉ gites-de-France-72@wanadoo.fr, 🖥 www.gites-de-france-sarthe.com).

Savoie: Maison du Tourisme, 16 rue Guillaume Fichet, 74000 Annecy (☎ 50 10 10 11, 🖥 www.gites-de-france-savoie.com).

Seine-et-Marne: 9-11 rue Royale, 77300 Fontainebleau (☎ 01 60 39 60 53, ✉ mdt@tourisme77.net, 🖥 www.itea.fr/GDF/77/F).

Seine-Maritime: Seine-Maritime Tourisme Réservation (SMTR), Chambre d'Agriculture, Chemin de la Bretèque/BP59, 76232 Bois-Guillaume Cedex (☎ 02 35 60 73 34, ✉ info@gitesdefrance76.com, 🖥 www.gites-normandie-76.com).

Somme: 21 rue Ernest Cauvin, 80000 Amiens (☎ 03 22 71 22 70, ✉ accueil@somme-tourisme.com, 🖥 www.itea.fr/GDF/80/F).

Tarn: Maison des Agriculteurs, 96 rue des Agriculteurs/BP80332, 81027 Albi Cedex (☎ 05 63 48 83 01, ✉ resa81@free.fr, 🖥 www.gites-tarn.com).

Tarn-et-Garonne: 64, rue de la Résistance, 82000 Montauban (☎ 05 63 03 84 06, ✉ gitesdefrance@cg82.fr, 🖥 www.gitesdefrance82.com).

Territoire-de-Belfort: 2bis rue Clémenceau, 90000 Belfort (☎ 03 84 21 27 95, ✉ gitesdefrance@ot-belfort.fr, 🖥 www.itea.fr/GDF/90).

Val d'Oise: BP06, 95270 Viarmes (☎ 01 34 09 81 73, ✉ gites@val-doise-tourisme.fr, 🖥 www.gites-val-doise.com).

Var: Conseil Général du Var, 37 avenue Lazare Carnot, 83300 Draguignan Cedex (☎ 08 20 82 28 28, 🖥 www.gites-de-france-var.fr).

Vaucluse: BP164, 84008 Avignon Cedex 1 (☎ 04 90 85 45 00, ✉ gites.vaucluse@wanadoo.fr, 🖥 www.gites-de-france-vaucluse.com).

Vendée: Relais des Gîtes de France et du Tourisme Vert, 124 boulevard Aristide Briand/BP735, 85018 La Roche-sur-Yon (☎ 02 51 37 87 87, ✉ gites-de-France-vendee@wanadoo.fr, 🖥 www.gites-de-france-vendee.com).

Vienne: 33 place Charles de Gaulle /BP287, 86007 Poitiers Cedex(☎ 05 49 37 19 77, 🖥 www.gitesdefrance-vienne.com).

Vosges: 31 rue François de Neufchâteau/BP236, 88006 Epinal (☎ 03 29 35 50 34, ✉ gites-88@wanadoo.fr, 💻 www.vosges-gites.com).

Yonne: Chambre d'Agriculture, 14bis rue Guynemer, 89015 Auxerre Cedex (☎ 03 86 72 92 15, ✉ gitesdefrance@yonne.chambagri.fr, 💻 www.itea.fr/GDF/89).

Yvelines: Hôtel du Département, 2 place André Mignot, 78012 Versailles Cedex (☎ 01 30 21 36 73 ✉ gitesdefrance@cg78.fr, 💻 www.gites-de-france-yvelines.com).

Gîte Rural Standards

1 *épi*: Outside area, garden furniture, one shower room with WC for up to six people, second shower room for more than six people, rotisserie or mini-oven, hob unit, pressure cooker, fridge, cooking utensils and basic household cleaning products, iron. High chair to be provided on request.

2 *épis*: In addition to the above: barbecue (where bylaws permit), washing machine (for six or more guests), mixer, electric coffee maker, television socket. Sheets, table and bath linen on request.

3 *épis*: In addition to the above: separate entrance and private garden, two WCs (for seven or more guests), washing machine, dishwasher (for five or more guests), oven, colour television, telephone. Cleaning service on request.

4 *épis*: In addition to the above: house with character, high-quality setting and interior decoration, log fireplace or stove (where bylaws permit), microwave, refrigerator with freezer compartment, clothes dryer (for six or more guests).

5 *épis*: In addition to the above: private landscaped garden or grounds, use of leisure facilities (e.g. tennis court, swimming pool, sauna and Jacuzzi), stereo, video recorder, garage or shelter, dishwasher and clothes dryer (for three or more guests).

Gîte d'Étape Standards

Living room, dining area, kitchen or equipped kitchen area for guests' use, telephone, clothes drying area, storeroom. Relaxation area or activity room, dishwasher, clothes dryer, sheets and towels on request. Up to 50 per cent of sleeping facilities may be 'board beds'.

Gîte de Séjour Standards

Living room, dining area, relaxation area or activity room, telephone, clothes drying area, storeroom, adjacent laid-out or equipped grounds, library, board games or musical instruments, dishwasher, washing machine and dryer, sheets and towels on request. No 'board beds'.

Chambres d'Hôtes Standards

The forms on the following pages are those used by Gîtes de France for grading *chambres d'hôtes*.

Tourist Board

Each department has a tourist board (Comité Départemental du Tourisme – look in the local yellow pages under *Offices de tourisme, syndicats d'initiative*) which grades accommodation by *étoiles* (stars), as follows:

1 Etoile

Accommodation must have the following:

* floors, walls, ceilings in good condition and watertight;
* fixed partitions between rooms;

- light and air sufficient for all rented rooms (interior rooms with no outside doors aren't counted in the number of rooms rented);
- exterior blinds, interior curtains/blinds;

- floor covering (e.g. carpet, tiles or parquet);

- soundproofing according to housing regulations;

- an electric socket in each room and one or more lamps (minimum 15W per m^2);

- central or electric heating sufficient for a minimum temperature of 19C in each room;

- enough furniture for the number of occupants, in good condition;

- clean mattresses, in good condition, with protectors, and bases in good condition;

- one bolster or pillow per bed;

- a bedside lamp for each person;

- two blankets (one wool) or one duvet per bed;

- a mixer tap (*mélangeur*) in the bathroom;

- in a property for up to six people, an indoor bathroom with ventilation and a basin and shower or a bath with shower attachment;

- in a property for more than six people, two bathrooms, one with independent access;

- an indoor lavatory;

- a hob (with two rings for up to five people, four rings for more than five people);

- an oven or rotisserie;

- a refrigerator large enough for the number of people;

- utensils and matching dishes for the number of people;

- pressure cooker;

- cleaning equipment appropriate for the accommodation;
- a washing line or tumble dryer;
- an iron and ironing cloth;
- a high-chair (on request);
- a telephone within 500m;
- a lift to reach the fourth floor (if applicable);
- parking nearby;
- brochures and leaflets (with practical and tourist information).

2 Etoiles

As above, with the following limitations and additions:

- a TV socket in the living room;
- sheets available on request (may be at extra charge);
- towels on request (at extra charge);
- a mixer tap in the kitchen;
- matching dishes;
- three sets of cutlery, dishes and glasses per person;
- table linen on request (at extra charge).

3 Etoiles

As above, with the following limitations and additions:

- a TV socket in the living room and a TV set;
- one bolster and pillow per bed;
- an extra lavatory (separate or in one of the bathrooms);

- a hob with four rings;

- an oven;

- a cooker hood or controllable ventilation;

- an electric mixer and coffee maker;

- a dishwasher for more than four people;

- an ironing board;

- a telephone in the building, billed for the period of the let;

- a colour TV;

- a lift to reach the third floor (if applicable);

- private parking;

- a well kept balcony, terrace, loggia or garden of at least 4m^2;

- a cleaning service on request (at extra charge).

4 Etoiles

As above, with the following limitations and additions:

- matching furniture;

- high-quality furniture and decoration;

- an electric hairdryer;

- in a property for up to six people, an indoor bathroom with ventilation, basin and bath with shower above;

- in a property for more than six people, two bathrooms with a bath with a shower above;

- a microwave oven;

- a refrigerator with a freezer compartment;

- a washing machine for more than five people;

- a tumble dryer for more than five people.

5 Etoiles

As above, with the following limitations and additions:

- a portable TV set and sockets in each main room;
- a mixer tap with a single swivel control (*mitigeur*) in bathroom;
- a dishwasher for more than two people;
- a washing machine for more than two people;
- a tumble dryer for more than two people;
- a cordless telephone;
- a hi-fi system;
- a video/DVD player;
- a well kept balcony, terrace, loggia or garden of at least 9m^2;
- leisure equipment (e.g. tennis court, pool, sauna, Jacuzzi).

Dimensions

Area: The minimum total area of the accommodation (excluding bathroom and WC, but including kitchen) is as follows:

- One-room accommodation for two people:
    - 1 *étoile*: 12m^2
    - 2 *étoiles*: 14m^2
    - 3 *étoiles*: 16m^2
    - 4 *étoiles*: 18m^2
    - 5 *étoiles*: 24m^2

- Add 3m² for each extra person.

- Add the following for each extra bedroom:

  - 1 *étoile*: 7m²

  - 2 *étoiles*: 8m²

  - 3 *étoiles*: 9m²

  - 4 *étoiles*: 10m²

  - 5 *étoiles*: 12m²

Beds: The following restrictions apply:

- Single beds must be at least 80cm wide (1 to 3 *étoiles*) or 90cm wide (4 to 5 *étoiles*).

- Double beds must be at least 140cm wide (1 to 4 *étoiles*) or 160cm wide (5 *étoiles*).

- Single and double beds must be at least 190cm long (1 to 4 *étoiles*) or 200cm long (5 *étoiles*).

Cupboards: There must be at least the following cupboard or shelf space in two-person accommodation:

  - 1 *étoile*: 2.5m²

  - 2 to 4 *étoiles*: 3m²

  - 5 *étoiles*: 4m²

Add 1m² for each extra person.

Inventory

The following is a typical kitchen inventory for a property accommodating four to six people:

- 12 each of the following: glasses, dinner plates, soup plates, dessert plates, forks, knives, dessert spoons, soup spoons;

- 1 cutlery tray;

- 6 coffee bowls;

- 6 cups;

- 1 serving plate;

- 1 serving bowl;

- 2 salad bowls;

- 2 ovenproof dishes;

- 1 cake or flan tin;

- 4 saucepans;

- 2 saucepan lids;

- 1 or 2 casserole dishes;

- 2 frying pans (1 non-stick);

- 1 each of the following: sieve, egg timer, measuring jug, vegetable mincer, lemon squeezer, salad spinner, grater, chopping board, bread knife, carving knife, scissors, vegetable peeler, spatula, wooden spoon, set of salad servers, ladle, corkscrew, tin opener, sardine tin key.

INDEX

SURVIVAL BOOKS

Survival Books was established in 1987 and by the mid-'90s was the leading publisher of books for people planning to live, work, buy property or retire abroad.

From the outset, our philosophy has been to provide the most comprehensive and up-to-date information available. Our titles routinely contain up to twice as much information as rival books and are updated frequently. All our books contain colour photographs and some are printed in two colours or full colour throughout. They also contain original cartoons, illustrations and maps.

Survival Books are written by people with first-hand experience of the countries and the people they describe, and therefore provide invaluable insights that cannot be obtained from official publications or websites, and information that is more reliable and objective than that provided by the majority of unofficial sites.

Survival Books are designed to be easy – and interesting – to read. They contain a comprehensive list of contents and index and extensive appendices, including useful addresses, further reading, useful websites and glossaries to help you obtain additional information as well as metric conversion tables and other useful reference material.

Our primary goal is to provide you with the essential information necessary for a trouble-free life or property purchase and to save you time, trouble and money.

We believe our books are the best – they are certainly the best-selling. But don't take our word for it – read what reviewers and readers have said about Survival Books at the front of this book.

To see our current list of titles, visit our website: **www.survivalbooks.net**

CULTURE WISE SERIES
The Essential Guides to Culture, Customs & Business Etiquette

Our **Culture Wise** series of guides is essential reading for anyone who want to understand how a country really 'works'. Whether you're planning to stay for a few days or a lifetime, these guides will help you quickly find you feet and settle into your new surroundings.

Culture Wise guides reduce the anxiety factor in adapting to a foreign culture; explain how to behave in everyday situations in order to avoid cultural and social gaffes; help you get along with your neighbours, make friends and establish lasting business relationships; and enhance your understanding of a country and its people.

People often underestimate the extent of the cultural isolation they can face abroad, particularly in a country with a different language. At first glance, many countries seem an 'easy' option, often with millions of visitors from all corners of the globe and well-established expatriate communities. But, sooner or later, newcomers find that most countries are indeed 'foreign' and many come unstuck as a result.

Culture Wise guides will enable you to quickly adapt to the local way of life and feel at home, and – just as importantly – avoid the worst effects of culture shock.

Culture Wise – the wise way to travel

To see our current list of titles, visit our website: **www.survivalbooks.net**

LIVING AND WORKING SERIES

Our **Living and Working** guides are essential reading for anyone planning to spend a period abroad, whether it's an extended holiday or permanent migration, and are packed with priceless information designed to help you avoid costly mistakes and save you both time and money.

Living and Working guides are the most comprehensive and up-to-date source of practical information available about everyday life abroad. They aren't, however, simply a catalogue of dry facts and figures, but are written in a highly readable style - entertaining, practical and occasionally humorous.

Our aim is to provide you with the comprehensive practical information necessary for a trouble free life. You may have visited a country as a tourist, but living and working there is a different matter altogether; adjusting to a different environment and culture and making a home in any foreign country can be a traumatic and stressful experience. You need to adapt to new customs and traditions, discover the local way of doing things (such as finding a home, paying bills and obtaining insurance) and learn all over again how to overcome the everyday obstacles of life.

All these subjects and many, many more are covered in depth in our **Living and Working** guides - don't leave home without them!

To see our current list of titles, visit our website: **www.survivalbooks.net**

BUYING A HOME SERIES

Buying a home abroad is not only a major financial transaction but also a potentially life-changing experience; it's therefore essential to get it right. Our *Buying a Home* guides are required reading for anyone planning to purchase property abroad and are packed with vital information to guide you through the property jungle and help you avoid disasters that can turn a dream home into a nightmare.

The purpose of our *Buying a Home* guides is to enable you to choose the most favourable location and the most appropriate property for your requirements, and to reduce your risk of making an expensive mistake by making informed decisions and calculated judgements rather than uneducated and hopeful guesses. Most importantly, they will help you save money and will repay your investment many times over.

Buying a Home guides are the most comprehensive and up-to-date source of information available about buying property abroad – whether you're seeking a detached house or an apartment, a holiday or a permanent home (or an investment property), these books will prove invaluable.

To see our current list of titles, visit our website: **www.survivalbooks.net**

OTHER SURVIVAL BOOKS

A New Life Abroad: The most comprehensive book available for anyone planning to live, work or retire abroad, containing surveys of over 50 countries.

The Best Places to Buy a Home in France/Spain: Unique guides to where to buy property in France and Spain, containing regional profiles and market reports.

Buying, Selling and Letting Property: The best source of information about buying, selling and letting property in the UK.

Earning Money From Your Home: Essential guides to earning income from property in France and Spain, including short- and long-term letting.

Foreigners in France/Spain: Triumphs & Disasters: Real-life experiences of people who have emigrated to France and Spain, recounted in their own words.

Investing in Property Abroad: Essential reading for anyone planning to buy property abroad, containing surveys of over 30 countries.

Making a Living: Comprehensive guides to self-employment and starting a business in France and Spain.

Renovating & Maintaining Your French Home: The ultimate guide to renovating and maintaining your dream home in France.

Retiring in France/Spain: Everything a prospective retiree needs to know about the two most popular international retirement destinations.

Running Gîtes and B&Bs in France: An essential book for anyone planning to invest in a gîte or bed & breakfast business in France.

Rural Living in France: An invaluable book for anyone seeking the 'good life' in France, containing a wealth of practical information about all aspects of country life.

Shooting Caterpillars in Spain: The hilarious and compelling story of two innocents abroad in the depths of Andalusia in the late '80s.

Wild Thyme in Ibiza: A fragrant account of how a three-month visit to the enchanted island of Ibiza in the mid-'60s turned into a 20-year sojourn.

To see our current list of titles, visit our website: **www.survivalbooks.net**